P9-EEE-091

REGENCY EDITION

prNpls
v spdri̱
srlhN

Regency Edition

prNpls v spdrị srthN*

JOE M. PULLIS, Ed.D.
Professor, Department of Office Administration
and Business Communication
College of Administration and Business
Louisiana Tech University

Glencoe Publishing Company
Encino, California

*PRINCIPLES OF SPEEDWRITING SHORTHAND

Linda Bippen
Lesson/Exercise Writer

Graphic Arts Coordination: Bob Reed
Calligraphy: Juana Silcox
Cover and interior design: Harkavy Publishing Services/ Levavi & Levavi
System editor: Karl C. Illg, Jr.
Typesetter: Compolith Graphics
Printer: R. R. Donnelley and Sons Company

Copyright © 1984, 1977 by Bobbs-Merrill Educational Publishing Company, Inc.
Copyright © 1975, 1973, 1966, 1965, 1964, 1954, 1951, 1950, 1925 by Speedwriting Publishing Company, Inc.
Copyrights transferred to Glencoe Publishing Company, a division of Macmillan, Inc.

All rights reserved. No part of this book shall be reproduced or transmitted in any form or by any means, electronic or mechanical, including photocopying, recording, or by any information or retrieval system, without written permission from the Publisher.

Send all inquiries to:
Glencoe Publishing Company
17337 Ventura Boulevard
Encino, California 91316

Library of Congress Cataloging in Publication Data
Pullis, Joe M. Principles of speedwriting shorthand.

On t.p.: Prnpls v spdri srthn.
1. Shorthand—speedwriting. I. Title. II. Title:
Prnpls v spdri srthn.
Z56.2.S6P84 1984 653'.2 83-21373

Printed in the United States of America
ISBN 0-02-679810-7

3 4 5 6 7 90 89 88 87 86

CONTENTS

Appendix

TEXT

Organization of Principles Text

The seven chapters of the principles text for *Speedwriting Shorthand, Regency Edition*, are organized into 50 lessons which contain principles, words illustrating each new principle, lists of brief forms and abbreviations, and Reading and Writing Exercises containing new vocabulary and reinforcement of vocabulary previously studied. The Reading and Writing Exercises contain thousands of words of shorthand practice material presented in shorthand notebook format. The key following each Reading and Writing Exercise is marked in 20-word intervals for ease in timing reading or giving dictation.

Order of Principles Presentation

The order of presentation of the principles is arranged to distribute the learning load equitably and to allow the introduction of realistic, business-related connected matter in the very early lessons.

Every seventh lesson is a review of the previous six lessons, with extensive word development activities providing reinforcement.

Lessons 43-50 are primarily for speed building and serve as a review of the brief forms and abbreviations of the system.

The English language consists of sounds which may be pronounced differently in various parts of our country. In order to have one standard pronunciation, the *New College Edition* of *The American Heritage Dictionary of the English Language* was used.

Transcription Skills

Because the transcription of mailable letters is the primary objective of shorthand instruction, pre-transcription skills are introduced early in the *Speedwriting Shorthand* principles text. In each lesson beginning with Lesson 8, one or more business vocabulary words are defined. These words are then used in context in the Reading and Writing Exercises for that lesson.

Spelling and Punctuation

Beginning with Lesson 16, commonly misspelled words are presented.

Punctuation rules begin with Lesson 22. Research has indicated that relatively few rules of punctuation account for the overwhelming majority of usage in typical business correspondence. The eight comma rules taught in the

Speedwriting Shorthand principles text account for the majority of all commas used in business correspondence.

After a comma rule has been introduced, examples of that rule are highlighted in the Reading and Writing Exercises and reinforced with notations. The highlighting gives the instructor a valuable resource for expanding the classroom emphasis on punctuation.

Appendix Materials

The appendix of the text contains a summary of brief forms, abbreviations, and phrases; abbreviations of the states, U. S. possessions, and Canadian provinces; abbreviations of metric terms; and the principles by order of presentation and system category.

WORKBOOK

Organization of Workbook

A workbook, correlated by lesson, is available to accompany the *Speedwriting Shorthand* principles text. The primary purpose of the workbook is the reinforcement of theory and principles, brief forms, and abbreviations. The workbook is structured with drills designed to help the student:

1. Review *Speedwriting Shorthand* principles by writing shorthand outlines for words that have been studied.
2. Develop the ability to form new shorthand outlines from outlines that have already been learned.
3. Increase business and shorthand vocabulary.
4. Improve the ability to read from shorthand notes and to transcribe them accurately.
5. Review nonshorthand elements needed in transcription.

The last eight lessons of the workbook are designed specifically to review previously covered material as follows:

Lesson 43 reviews Lessons 1-7
Lesson 44 reviews Lessons 8-14
Lesson 45 reviews Lessons 15-21
Lesson 46 reviews Lessons 22-28
Lesson 47 reviews Lessons 29-35
Lesson 48 reviews Lessons 36-42
Lesson 49 reviews word beginnings
Lesson 50 reviews word endings

Utilization of Workbook

The workbook may be used as a homework device, as a daily classroom activity, or as a remedial exercise. Keys to the worksheets are printed at the end of each lesson so that students may check their mastery of the material presented in that lesson.

TAPES

Cassette Tape Contents

A set of 50 principles tapes is available for the *Speedwriting Shorthand* principles text. Each tape corresponds to a lesson in the principles text.

The format for the tapes follows this general outline:

1. A presentation of new theory and principles from the corresponding lesson.
2. A presentation of brief forms and/or abbreviations from the corresponding lesson.
3. Warm-up dictation, beginning with Tape 2, usually related to previously studied business letters in the text.
4. A review of the theory and principles from the *preceding* lesson.
5. A review of brief forms and/or abbreviations from the preceding lesson.
6. Dictation of letters from the preceding lesson, in speed-building format.

Tapes are 30 minutes per lesson. Approximately the last 15 minutes of each tape is dictation for speed development. Dictation speeds begin at 40 words per minute and progress to 90 words per minute.

Utilization of Tapes

Tapes may be used for review of previously introduced lessons or for review of principles from the previous lesson. In addition, the tape lessons strongly reinforce the brief forms and abbreviations introduced in the correspondingly numbered text and workbook lessons. Another primary use of the tapes is to provide practice dictation to increase dictation speeds. One other benefit is that if students miss a lesson, the tapes may be used to introduce the theory, principles, brief forms, and abbreviations that were missed.

DICTIONARY

Dictionary Contents and Utilization

The *Speedwriting Shorthand Abridged Dictionary, Regency Edition,* contains over 6,000 of the most frequently used words in business communications, as well as a list of the rules utilized for word division. All places where these words can be correctly divided in typewriting/transcription applications are also shown.

The appendix of the dictionary contains a summary of brief forms, abbreviations, and phrases; abbreviations of the states, U. S. possessions, and Canadian provinces; abbreviations of metric terms; and the principles by order of presentation.

RESOURCE MANUAL

Resource Manual Contents and Usage

The Resource Manual provides shorthand methodology, with specific suggestions for classroom procedures, sound-spelling, testing, and grading. Lesson Notes for the 50 lessons in the principles text are included in Part Two of the manual.

Included in the manual are 25-word shorthand vocabulary tests correlated to Chapters 1-6. Two 50-word brief form tests are provided, one to follow Lesson 21 and the other to follow Lesson 42. A 50-word abbreviation test is provided to follow Lesson 42. Keys are provided for all of the tests.

Lesson Indexes

Computer-controlled lesson indexes for every lesson in the textbook are provided in Part Three of the Resource Manual.

* SECTION ONE
PRINCIPLES AND
APPLICATIONS

You are about to study a shorthand system which is based primarily on what you already know—the alphabet—to represent the sounds that make up our language. As a result, taking notes, building speed, and transcribing are accelerated in *Speedwriting Shorthand*.

The *Speedwriting Shorthand* system covers all words in the English language. Words used in business, law, medicine, science, and the arts all fall under a shorthand principle you will study in this course. You will learn to apply these principles as easily and naturally as you now write longhand.

As you study the *Speedwriting Shorthand* system, you will also learn techniques for practicing and writing your shorthand quickly and successfully. Begin today to develop good writing and study habits.

***Chapter One**

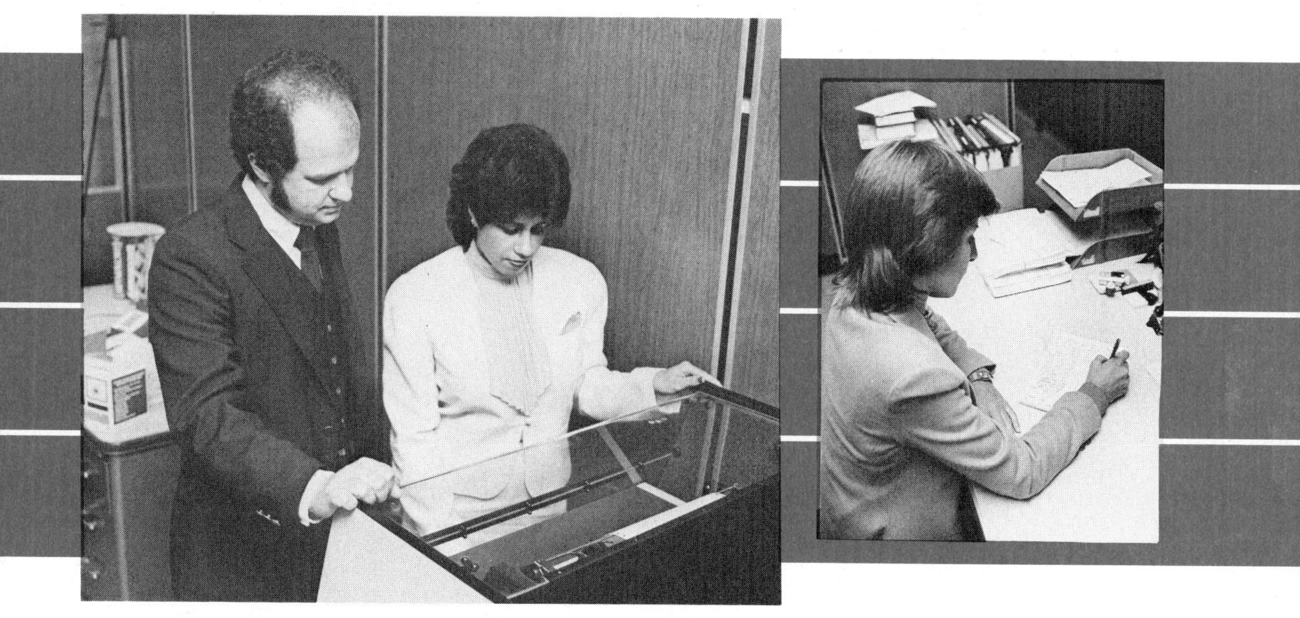

Before You Begin

Choose your pens carefully. Use a good ball-point pen that glides easily across the paper. If the pen glides easily, you'll save time and energy with each stroke. And always have more than one pen ready—just in case the first one stops during dictation.

Use a spiral bound pad. Use a shorthand notebook that is spiral bound at the top so that pages will flip easily and the book will lie flat while you are writing.

A line down the center divides the page in half. Write on only one side of the page until that side is filled. Then move to the top of the other side of the same page. When you have filled the entire page, flip the paper and continue writing on the completely new page that follows.

When you've reached the last page, turn the pad over and begin writing from back to front using the same procedure.

LESSON 1

Streamline letters as you write. Every time you lift your pen to cross a *t* or dot an *i*, you lose valuable time and reduce your speed. *Speedwriting Shorthand* eliminates extra strokes by avoiding loops, dots, and crosses whenever possible. As you practice, you will become comfortable with this technique, and you will find that streamlining letters makes writing faster, easier, and just as easy to read. Look at these examples:

t   b
f   i
j   y
g   p
h   z

1. Write what you hear. The English language contains many silent letters. In longhand, we write h-i-g-h even when we hear only the sound *hi* and k-n-o-w when we hear only *no*. In shorthand we write what we hear: hi and no.

fee, f-e fe   tie, t-i ti
free, f-r-e fre   tray, t-r-a tra
view, v-u vu   ate, a-t at
knew, n-u nu   sigh, s-i si

Using this principle, then, how would you write the outlines for the words *see, pay, low,* and *fly*?

see, s-e se   pay, p-a pa
low, l-o lo   fly, f-l-i fli

2. Drop medial vowels. Omit vowels that fall in the middle of the word.

build, b-l-d	bld	save, s-v	sv
*legal, l-gay-l	lgl	*glass, gay-l-s	gls
did, d-d	dd	bulletin, b-l-t-n	bltn
budget, b-j-t	bjt	*grade, gay-r-d	grd

*The shorthand letter for g is pronounced *gay*; gay-l-s for glass; gay-r-d for grade; l-gay-l for legal.

Using Principle 2, then, how would you write the outlines for the words *given*, *said*, *visit*, and *paper*?

given, gay-v-n	gvn	said, s-d	sd
visit, v-z-t	vzt	paper, p-p-r	ppr

3. Write initial and final vowels. Write the vowels you hear at the beginning and end of the word.

office, o-f-s	ofs	easy, e-z-e	eze
ahead, a-h-d	ahd	ready, r-d-e	rde
*do, d-u	du	often, o-f-n	ofn
follow, f-l-o	flo	*few, f-u	fu

*Note that *u* is used for the long vowel sounds of $\overline{oo}$ and ū.

Using Principle 3, how would you write the outlines for *value*, *enough*, *open*, and *happy*?

value, v-l-u	vlu	enough, e-n-f	enf
open, o-p-n	opn	happy, h-p-e	hpe

The three principles you have just learned will allow you to write many words you will encounter on your job. In the remaining lessons, you will learn additional principles which will enable you to write other sounds quickly and easily. Before going on, practice these additional words. First, read the word aloud and spell it according to its sound: grow, gay-r-o. Then sound-spell the outline as you write it: grow, gay-r-o *gro* .

deposit, d-p-z-t	*dpzt*	type, t-p	*tp*
news, n-z	*nz*	*review, re-v-u	*rvu*
sell, s-l	*sl*	knowledge, n-l-j	*nlj*
written, r-t-n	*rtn*	apply, a-p-l-i	*apli*
lease, l-s	*ls*	*reason, re-z-n	*rzn*
benefit, b-n-f-t	*bnft*	unit, u-n-t	*unt*

*Since medial vowels are omitted, the word beginning *re* is represented by an *r*.

Punctuation Symbols. Use quick, distinct symbols to show punctuation in shorthand notes. To show capitalization, draw a small curved line under the last letter of the outline: Bill, *bl* .

Sue, s-u	*su*	Ed, e-d	*ed*
Dallas, d-l-s	*dls*	Debbie, d-b-e	*dbe*
Ted, t-d	*td*	New Haven, n-u h-v-n	*nu hvn*

To indicate a period at the end of a sentence, write \ .

Let Bill know. *lt bl no* \

To indicate a question mark, write x .

Does Bill know? *dz bl no* x

To indicate the end of a paragraph, write > .

Bill does know. *bl dz no* >

Brief Forms. You will use some words so often that you will find it helpful to write shortened outlines for them. We call these shortened outlines **brief forms.** Since brief forms are not written in full, you should commit them to memory. Study and practice the brief forms until you can write them as quickly, easily, and accurately as you write your own name—without hesitation.

More than one word can be represented by the same brief form. When read in context, however, only one meaning will make sense.

a, an

we

will, well

the

it, at

is, his

to, too

in, not

PRINCIPLES SUMMARY

1. Write what you hear: know, n-o no.
2. Drop medial vowels: build, b-l-d bld.
3. Write initial and final vowels: office, o-f-s ofs; ready, r-d-e rde.

Reading and Writing Exercises

You will find that reading and writing *Speedwriting Shorthand* is easy as well as fun, and fluency in reading and writing shorthand will develop with practice.

The following steps should assist you in studying each of the *Speedwriting Shorthand* lessons:

1. Study the principles and the words illustrating each principle at the beginning of each lesson.
2. Sound-spell (aloud if possible) as you write and pronounce each word. Write each word (while sound-spelling) two or three times, or until you feel comfortable writing the word.
3. Read the Reading and Writing Exercises, using the key as necessary until the material can be read fluently. Beginning with Lesson 3, each letter and memorandum is marked in groups of 20 standard shorthand words (28 syllables). Small, consecutive numbers are placed in the key after each group of 20 shorthand words; therefore, if while reading you are able to reach the number 4 in one minute, you would be reading at the rate of 80 words per minute (20 x 4); if you reach the number 5, you would be reading at the rate of 100 words per minute, etc. As a general rule, you should be able to read about twice as fast as you expect to write from dictation.
4. Write the Reading and Writing Exercises from the key while self-dictating.
   (a) Read several words from the key.
   (b) Write the words while sound-spelling and saying each word aloud. Normally, it is not necessary to sound-spell the brief forms.
   (c) Repeat this procedure until a letter or memorandum has been written, remembering to check the shorthand notes in the textbook for any outlines you may not know how to write.
   (d) Read back the letter or memorandum from your own shorthand notes.

You now know enough shorthand to read and write complete sentences. Read the sentences on page 9 aloud. When you encounter an unfamiliar outline, sound-spell the word. If the correct word still does not come to mind, read on to the end of the sentence. The context, or meaning, of the sentence will help you identify the unfamiliar outline. If you are still unable to read the outline, look in the printed key which follows the Reading and Writing Exercises.

SERIES A

1. e hp l se u sn \
2. l u pa . fe x
3. / , . nu fl unl \
4. , (unl l ll x
5. su l n fle l dls \

SERIES B

1. ed , n , ofs \
2. dd u rsv . bl x
3. ll dbe l pa / \
4. u l du l n . ofs jb \
5. e l gv u . rz n pa \

SERIES C

1. , bl / (ofs x
2. (rvu , eze l lp \
3. su l grd / \
4. , (nu byl rde l rvu x
5. e dd n rsv / \

Key

SERIES A

1. We hope to see you soon.
2. Will you pay a fee?
3. It is a new file unit.
4. Is the unit too tall?
5. Sue will not fly to Dallas.

SERIES B

1. Ed is in his office.
2. Did you receive a bill?
3. Tell Debbie to pay it.
4. You will do well in an office job.
5. We will give you a raise in pay.

SERIES C

1. Is Bill at the office?
2. The review is easy to type.
3. Sue will grade it.
4. Is the new budget ready to review?
5. We did not receive it.

Four Steps to Follow in Learning Shorthand

As you work through each lesson, use these steps as a study plan:

1. *Read the principle and think about it.* How does it apply to each of the words listed under it?

2. *Practice each word listed under the principle.* First, say the word aloud: *glass.* Then sound-spell the word aloud as you would write it in shorthand: gay-l-s. Then sound-spell and write the shorthand outline for the word: gay-l-s *gls* .

3. *Read the shorthand exercises aloud.* If the correct word for an outline does not immediately come to mind, sound-spell the outline. If the translation is not readily apparent, read on to the end of the sentence. The context, or meaning, of the sentence will help you identify the unfamiliar outlines. Consult the key if you cannot determine the correct word with the help of sound-spelling and context.

4. *Write the shorthand exercises.* After you have read the exercises, write them. Writing the outlines will help you develop reading skill as well as an accurate writing style.

LESSON 2

1. Write c for the sound of *k*.

copy, k-p-e cpe

like, l-k lc

package, p-k-j pcj

school, s-k-l scl

clerk, k-l-r-k clrc

desk, d-s-k dsc

2. Write a capital C for the sound of *ch, cha* (pronounced *chay*).

change, chay-n-j Cnj

such, s-chay sC

chosen, chay-z-n Czn

teach, t-chay tC

check, chay-k Cc

church, chay-r-chay CrC

More about writing. To write *m* and *w* with ease and speed, streamline the outlines.

3. Write for the sound of *m*.

may, m-a

name, n-m

mail, m-l

much, m-chay

my, m-i

same, s-m

4. Write for the sound of *w* and *wh*.

way, w-a

when, w-n

what, w-t

winner, w-n-r

week, w-k

wage, w-j

where, w-r

which, w-chay

5. To add *ing* or *thing* as a word ending, underscore the last letter of the outline.

billing, b-l-ing

*paying, p-a-ing

something, s-m-thing

attaching, a-t-chay-ing

watching, w-chay-ing

*saying, s-a-ing

*Note: Always write long vowels before marks of punctuation.

6. To form the plural of any outline ending in a mark of punctuation, double the last mark of punctuation.

billings, b-l-ings

savings, s-v-ings

7. *Adding s.* Write to form the plural of any outline ending in a letter: books, b-k-s . Write to form possessives: girl's, gay-r-l-s . Write to add *s* to a verb: runs, r-n-s . Add even though the final sound of such words may be *z*.

checks, chay-k-s

hopes, h-p-s

helps, h-l-p-s

jobs, j-b-s

Bill's, b-l-s

gives, gay-v-s

An is also used in the writing of proper nouns ending in *s*, even though the final sound may be *z*.

James, j-m-s

Ames, a-m-s

Burns, b-r-n-s

Charles, chay-r-l-s

Practice writing these additional words:

care, k-r cr

games, gay-m-s gms

room, r-m rm

truck, t-r-k trc

buildings, b-l-d-ings bld

training, t-r-n-ing trn

claim, k-l-m clm

course, k-r-s crs

units, u-n-t-s unts

match, m-chay mC

each, e-chay eC

coverings, k-v-r-ings cvr

Abbreviations. Many abbreviations are so common that they come to mind automatically. *Speedwriting Shorthand* makes use of these abbreviations. Since you already know many of these abbreviations, you will be able to write them quickly from the beginning.

company co

information inf

vice president VP

catalog cal

president P

and +

return ret

Brief Forms

are, our r

for, full f

of, have, very v

can c

us s

PRINCIPLES SUMMARY

1. Write c for the sound of *k*: copy, k-p-e cpe .
2. Write a capital C for the sound of *ch, cha*: check, chay-k Cc .
3. Write ⌒ for the sound of *m*: may, m-a ⌒a .
4. Write ◡ for the sound of *w* and *wh*: way, w-a ◡a ; when, w-n ◡n .
5. To add *ing* or *thing* as a word ending, underscore the last letter of the outline: billing, b-l-ing bl̲ ; something, s-m-thing s⌒̲ .
6. To form the plural of any outline ending in a mark of punctuation, double the last mark of punctuation: billings, b-l-ings bl̳ .
7. Write s to form the plural of any outline ending in a letter, to form possessives, to add *s* to a verb: jobs, j-b-s jbs ; Bill's, b-l-s bls ; gives, gay-v-s gvs ; or to write the final *s* of a proper noun: James, j-m-s jms .

Reading and Writing Exercises

SERIES A

1. r u rde l du rln, s⌒ lp̲ x

2. e l hlp u ufe c, (, r jb,

3. (P + VP v r co l se s n . ◡c,

4. du u v (nu blln x (, v l

5. ◡C ◡c r u pln̲ l vzl (ofs x

SERIES B

1. ll ⌒e no ◡n (inf arvs,

2. i l ⌒l . f dpzl,

3. u l rsv . fre gfl
f eC sv͇ dpzl.

4. i l rel , Cc l
, co.

5. hr , . Cc l
cvr , fe n f.

SERIES C

1. e r ~c̲ Cnys
n r co cal.

2. e l ~l u . cpe
v sn.

3. e r alC̲ . cpe
v , bl. ~n c
u ~l s . Cc x

4. bb̆ nds l no
s̲ v sn.

5. i l lv , inf
, , dsc.

Key

SERIES A

1. Are you ready to do some typing?
2. We will help you if we can. It is our job.
3. The president and vice president of our company will see us in a week.
4. Do you have the new bulletin? It is very well written.
5. Which week are you planning to visit the office?

SERIES B

1. Let me know when the information arrives.
2. I will mail a full deposit.
3. You will receive a free gift for each savings deposit.
4. I will return the check to the company.
5. Here is a check to cover the fee in full.

SERIES C

1. We are making changes in our company catalog.
2. We will mail you a copy very soon.
3. We are attaching a copy of the bill. When can you mail us a check?
4. Bob needs to know something very soon.
5. I will leave the information at his desk.

LESSON 3

1. Write *m* for the sounds of *mem* and *mum.*

memo, mem-o *mo*

memory, mem-r-e *mre*

members, mem-b-r-s *mbrs*

mumps, mum-p-s *mps*

Write *m* for the sounds of *men, mon,* and *mun.*

menu, men-u *mu*

monetary, mon-t-r-e *mtre*

minutes, min-t-s *mts*

money, mun-e *me*

2. Write *m* for the word endings *mand, mend, mind,* and *ment.*

demand, d-mand *dm*

replacement, re-p-l-s-ment *rplsm*

amend, a-mend *am*

judgment, j-j-ment *jjm*

remind, re-mind *rm*

*payment, p-a-ment *pam*

settlement, s-t-l-ment *stlm*

*agreement, a-gay-r-e-ment *agrem*

*Always write the final root-word vowel when adding word endings.

3. Write a capital *N* for the sound of *ent, nt* (pronounced *ent*).

sent, s-nt *sN*

entry, nt-r-e *Nre*

wants, w-nt-s *wNs*

renting, r-nt-ing *rN̲*

center, s-nt-r *sNr*

current, k-r-nt *crN*

Use *N* to form contractions.

don't, d-nt *dN*

couldn't, k-d-nt *cdN*

can't, k-nt *cN*

doesn't, d-z-nt *dzN*

Practice these additional words:

minimum, min-mum *mm*	front, f-r-nt *frN*
mineral, min-r-l *mrl*	apparent, a-p-r-nt *aprN*
memorize, mem-r-z *mrz*	agent, a-j-nt *ajN*
mental, men-t-l *mtl*	didn't, d-d-nt *ddN*
recent, re-s-nt *rsN*	won't, w-nt *wN*

PRINCIPLES SUMMARY

1. Write *m* for the sound of *mem* and *mum*: members, mem-b-r-s *mbrs* ; mumps, mum-p-s *mps* .
   Write *m* for the sounds of *men, mon,* and *mun*: menu, men-u *mu* ; monetary, mon-t-r-e *mtre* ; money, mun-e *me* .
2. Write *m* for the word endings *mand, mend, mind,* and *ment*: demand, d-mand *dm* ; amend, a-mend *am* ; remind, re-mind *rm* ; settlement, s-t-l-ment *stlm*.
3. Write a capital *N* for the sound of *ent, nt*: sent, s-nt *sN* ; and for contractions: don't, d-nt *dN* .

Reading and Writing Exercises

SERIES A

1. du u v plns f rtrm. e v . nu plse ⌒C pas v l.

2. ⌐ ajN sN s . mo rm̲ s l ⌒l r pam.

3. e r pa̲ l ⌒C me f ⌐ plse. ⌒a e lc f . nu ajN.

4. e cd fl . nu cl⌒. e l lt u no if e rC . sltm.

5. e r se̲ . hi dm f ⌐ nu plse.

SERIES B

1. e rcm uz̲ r nu Ccs.

2. e l prN nu Ccs f u. du u ⌒N s l ⌒l ⌐ Ccs l u ⌐ h⌒.

3. u l v l pa . mm fe + ⌒c . dpzl if u ⌒N l uz r nu Ccs.

4. ⌐ P ⌒Ns . cpe sN l eC v ⌐ brd mbrs.

5. ⌐ dsc clrc l rel ⌐ dpzl l u.

-1-

mo t lvn crlr
i c gv u r inf u
nd t c r Cnys
n r sls pln. i
v . cpe v r nu
pln C gvs f
dlls, / r crN
L r ofs, cp
. v bze scjl. e
r c plns f
s bq evNs f
r cs ahd.
n cs u lri t
rC e / u
ofs i l lv r
cpes u nd / r
frN dsc, fl fre
t cl e f hlp n
r fCr f u nd
/ .

-2-

mo t jde jcsn u
mo, t rm u v r
plns t hld bjt hr
n r nr fCr, r
rzn f r hr, t rvu
nu bjt ls + r
me e l nd t pa
f sC Nres. e r
c . scjl f eC
ofs. u l rsv .
nls asn u . dfnl
L, f u v nu
ls or rplsms
pln t gv . brf
sre v eC / r
hr.

Key

SERIES A

1. Do you have plans for retirement? We have a new policy which pays very well.
2. The agent sent us a memo reminding us to mail our payment.
3. We are paying too much money for the policy. May we look for a new agent?
4. We could file a new claim. We will let you know if we reach a settlement.
5. We are seeing a high demand for the new policy.

SERIES B

1. We recommend using our new checks.
2. We will print new checks for you. Do you want us to mail the checks to you at home?
3. You will have to pay a minimum fee and make a deposit if you want to use our new checks.
4. The president wants a copy sent to each of the board members.
5. The desk clerk will return the deposit to you.

1

MEMO TO: Melvin Carter

I can give you the information you need to make the changes in our sales plan. I[1] have a copy of the new plan which gives full details.

At the current time, our office is keeping a very busy[2] schedule. We are making plans for some big events for the weeks ahead. In case you try to reach me at my office,[3] I will leave the copies you need at the front desk.

Feel free to call me for help in the future if you need it.[4] (80)

2

MEMO TO: Judy Jackson

My memo is to remind you of our plans to hold budget hearings in the near future.[1]

The reason for the hearings is to review new budget items and the money we will need to pay for such[2] entries. We are making a schedule for each office. You will receive a notice assigning you a definite[3] time.

If you have new items or replacements, plan to give a brief summary of each at the hearing. (78)

LESSON 4

1. Write for the sound of *ish* or *sh*.

finish, f-n-ish

show, ish-o

machine, m-ish-n

wish, w-ish

should, ish-d

issuing, i-ish-u-ing

2. Write a capital for the word beginnings *ad* and *al* (pronounced *add*, *al*, or *all*).

advise, ad-v-z

also, al-s-o

admit, ad-m-t

advice, ad-v-s

album, al-b-m

admire, ad-m-r

If a word begins with the letters a-d or a-l but does not incorporate the blended sounds of *ad* or *al* in the same syllable, write the word according to the sound.

adopt, a-d-p-t

align, a-l-n

3. Write for the initial sound of *en* or *in* (pronounced *n*).

anything, en-e-thing

engine, en-j-n

indent, in-d-nt

engineers, en-j-n-r-s

involve, in-v-l-v

intent, in-t-nt

Brief Forms

from

letter

manage

would

firm

perhaps

on, own

market

part, port

your

Brief Form Development. Use brief forms and abbreviations to build related words. For instance:

Brief Form: *for*

form, for-m

inform, in-for-m

formal, for-m-l

formula, for-m-l-a

fortune, for-chay-n

Brief Forms: *can* and *not*

cancel, can-s-l

cannot, can-not

Abbreviation: *company*

accompanying, a-company-ing

accompaniment, a-company-ment

Write some outlines according to the rule to avoid possible reading and transcribing problems.

William, w-l-y-m

mechanical, m-k-n-k-l

New Brief Form Development

management

manager

managing

marketing

letters

yours

wouldn't

report

depart

letterhead

Abbreviations

Mr.

Mrs.

Ms.

Miss

Salutations

Dear Mr. Gray

Dear Mrs. Chase

Dear Ed

Dear Ms. Miller

Dear Miss Temple

Dear Sue

Complimentary Closes

Sincerely yours

Cordially yours

Sincerely

Cordially

Very truly yours

Yours truly

Yours very truly

Respectfully yours

PRINCIPLES SUMMARY

1. Write for the sound of *ish*, *sh*: show, ish-o .
2. Write a capital for the word beginnings *ad* and *al*: advice, ad-v-s ; also, al-s-o .
3. Write for the initial sound of *en* or *in*: entire, en-t-r .

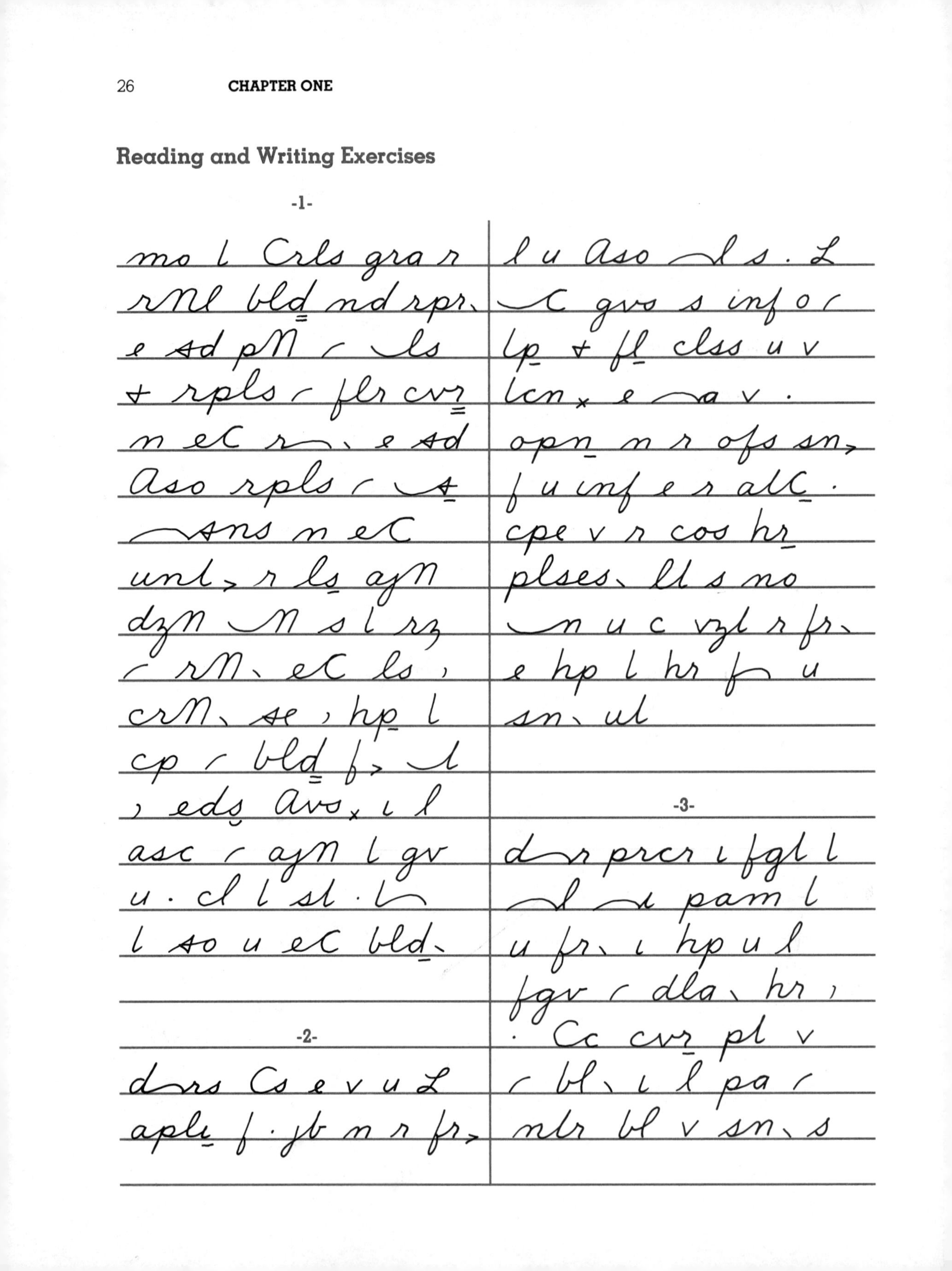

Reading and Writing Exercises

-1-

-2-

-3-

-4-

mo l M su grn
i sN . nfl L
l c P v c fr asc
l se . cpe v c
nu r rpl, l
i nlj e du n
yl v . rpli, du
Aso rm c P e
dv C lc l
no , plns f opn
r nu ofss. / ,
l dsd o C
frnt e l nd, e d
lc l v u Avs l,
ll e no n
u c c c lrp
l r nu plN, i
sl lri l se u /
c ofs n u
arv,

-5-

d s hrpr Ph u
v n sn r nu
cal, f n l u
lc . fu mls l rd
c f e r alC.
u l se e r so
me nu ls, f
u d lc l rsv .
cpe v c cal sn
c f + rel c l
r ofs, e l rs c
cal l u, me ppl
lc l uz r cal l
sp c h, Nu
Cz c eze al
sp l . cu

-6-

mo l bl dvdsn
e du n v . pln f

lrn r ppl l rn
r nu ⁀ns, Ph
c plN ⁀yr + r
Cf nynr c hlp
dzn . pln e cd
uz f c ntr co,
ll s no ⁀l u
pln l du, Aso

l u ⁀l s . cpe
v u nu byl x e
nd l rvu / /
⁀ym pln l,
Ph e c sv me n
c fCr uf e lc
l l lc / eC
pl v r byl,

Key

1

MEMO TO: Charles Gray

Our rental buildings need repair. We should paint the walls and replace the floor coverings in each[1] room. We should also replace the washing machines in each unit.

Our leasing agent doesn't want us to raise the[2] rent. Each lease is current. She is hoping to keep the buildings full.

What is Ed's advice? I will ask the agent to[3] give you a call to set a time to show you each building. (70)

2

Dear Mrs. Chase:

We have your letter applying for a job in our firm.

Will you also mail us a letter which[1] gives us information on the typing and filing classes you have taken? We may have an opening in our[2] office soon.

For your information, we are attaching a copy of our company's hiring policies. Let[3] us know when you can visit our firm. We hope to hear from you soon.

Yours truly, (74)

3

Dear Mr. Parker:

I forgot to mail my payment to your firm. I hope you will forgive the delay. Here is a[1] check covering part of the bill. I will pay the entire bill very soon.

Sincerely, (35)

4

MEMO TO: Miss Sue Green

I sent an informal letter to the president of the firm asking to see a copy[1] of the new marketing report. To my knowledge, we do not yet have a reply.

Would you also remind the[2] president we would very much like to know his plans for opening our new offices? It is time to decide[3] on which furnishings we will need. We would like to have your advice too.

Let me know when you can make the trip to our[4] new plant. I shall try to see you at the office when you arrive. (91)

5

Dear Ms. Harper:

Perhaps you have not seen our new catalog. If not, will you take a few minutes to read the form[1] we are attaching? You will see we are showing many new items.

If you would like to receive a copy of[2] the catalog, sign the form and return it to our office. We will rush the catalog to you.

Many people[3] like to use our catalog to shop at home. Won't you choose the easy way to shop too?

Cordially yours, (78)

6

MEMO TO: Bill Davidson

We do not have a plan for training our people to run our new machines. Perhaps the[1] plant manager and our chief engineer can help design a plan we could use for the entire company. Let us[2] know what you plan to do.

Also, will you mail us a copy of your new budget? We need to review it at[3] management planning time. Perhaps we can save money in the future if we take time to look at each part of our[4] budget. (81)

LESSON 5

You will not have to change your basic handwriting style for *Speedwriting Shorthand*. However, it is important to develop writing habits that clearly distinguish one outline from another.

Take a moment now to review your writing style. Do you omit unnecessary loops, crosses, dots, and initial and final strokes where appropriate? Compare the following examples with the outlines you have written so far.

Streamlining *m* and *w*:
Write *m* and *w* with a swift, smooth sweep of the pen.

m		me	
w		way	

Loops and Solid Lines:
Write *l* with a clearly defined loop; write *t* with a solid stem. Your stroke for *t* should be clearly taller (about twice the height) than your *i*. The same is true for *l* and *e*, *nt* and *n*, *chay* and *k*.

l	l	*t*	t
t	t	*i*	i
l	l	*e*	e
nt	n	*n*	n
chay	C	*k*	c

Closed Circles:
It is important to close the circles in *s*, *d*, *p*, *gay*, and *a*.

s	s	sell	sl
d	d	due	du
p	p	pay	pa
gay	g	get	gt
a	a	aim	a

Stems on Tall Letters:
Develop the habit of writing the stem long enough to distinguish *d* from *a*.

d	d	do	du
a	a	ache	ac

Writing *s, ish, and* (ampersand):
Develop a curve in the *s* to distinguish it clearly from the *ish*.

s	s	so	so
ish		show	
ampersand		and	

Streamline Letters:
Omit loops and upward strokes for *h, t, b, f, u,* and *i* when these letters occur at the beginning of an outline. Omit tails at the end of an outline.

h	h	hope	hp
t	l	take	lc
b	b	big	bq
f	f	fine	fn
u	u	unit	unl
i	l	item	

Writing *v* and *u*:
The outline for the letter *v* ends with a brief tail at the top; *u* ends in a swift downward stroke. Write *v* with a sharp point to distinguish it from *u*.

v	v	save	sv
u	u	view	vu

Final *gay* and *j*:
These end in a swift, solid downward stroke.

gay	q	dog	dq
j		judge	

Final *o*:
This ends at the top of the circle; *a* ends in a downward stroke.

o	o	low	lo
a	a	say	sa

1. Write o for the sound of *ow* (ou). The sound of *ow* is a special vowel called a *diphthong*. Always write this sound in an outline.

allow, a-l-ow alo	doubt, d-ow-t dol
now, n-ow no	out, ow-t ol
proud, p-r-ow-d prod	town, t-ow-n lon

2. Write a printed capital S (joined) for the word beginnings *cer, cir, ser, sur* (pronounced *sir*).

certain, cer-t-n Sln

survey, sur-v-a Sva

service, ser-v-s Svs

circle, cir-k-l Scl

serve, ser-v Sv

certificate, cer-t-f-k-t Slfcl

sermon, ser-mun Sm

surprise, sur-p-r-z Sprz

Salutations

Gentlemen /

Ladies l

Ladies and Gentlemen lj

Dear Sir dS

Dear Sir or Madam dS

Punctuation Symbols

Write ! to indicate an exclamation mark:

What happy news we have for you! d hpe nz e v f u !

Write = to indicate a hyphen:

Will you recommend a well-known book? l u rcm . l = nnbc x

Write ═ to indicate a dash:

We do not know the reason—do you? e du n no r rzn = du u x

To indicate solid capitalization, double the curved line underneath the last letter of the outline.

MONEY MANAGEMENT, mun-e manage-ment me ym

To indicate an underlined title, draw a solid line under the outline.

<u>Newsweek</u>, n-z-w-k nz c

PRINCIPLES SUMMARY

1. Write o for the sound of *ow* (ou): allow, a-l-ow alo.
2. Write a printed capital S (joined) for the word beginnings *cer, cir, ser, sur (sir)*: certain, cer-t-n Sln.

Reading and Writing Exercises

-1-

d su c u ll e
n u l fnt u
rpl o sv Sfcls.
bl bron lld e
u r c. Sva, if
e c e d lc l uz
, inf n u Sva
n r o rpl, vlu

ho me ppl l u
r s hld. Aso
l , u mm
rNl fe. ho c
l du u alo
f rzrv , r .
e hp l c r fnl
plns v sn, su

-2-

1 e r hp l hld.
co lnCn n u hll
sn, c u gv s inf
o u plse f rN
lnCn r s. l
Svss du u ofr +

-3-

d jo l v rln. L
l gl bron ll hr
e r csl hr plse,
e r Sln l hr f
hr , ml se rsvs
, L, Ph e c rcm

. nu ajN f hr, ll
e no if u v.
n l gv hr, ul

-4-

dS r u pa hr rN
+ yl v v lll l so
f / x Ph u d lc l
o u o h yl cn
s l sv enf
me f / don pam,
if so e c hlp u,
e r no ofr. nu
h pam pln
C l alo u l
pls . lo don pam
o u nu h , e
Aso v . byl pln
f hos pams, if
u lc ol . ln f
s no u c scyl

u pams ne a
u s> gv s.
ml v u l +
e l so u . eze
pam pln f u
hoshld, cu

-5-

1 e r rel / cpe
sn e bl f u
fr, s d s /
sn l n prN,
n / dz prN /
cpes r n clr, e
v d me cls n
SC v . ajN hu
Svss u sns,
nn c gl / pls
e nd f rprs,
e hp u c ofr s
. sn C gvs

blr Svs, l u ll
s no l u pln
l du, su

-6-

dS no , (l
vzl r sp, e v
. nu lrcld v
h frns C

e r ofr / bq bq
sv l u, dN
dla! vzl s no
+ Cz f me fn
s sn o eC
flr, dN fgl=
vzl r sp no +
sv, uvl

Key

1

Dear Sue:

Can you tell me when you will finish your report on savings certificates? Bill Brown told me you are[1] making a survey. If we can, we would like to use the information in your survey in our own report.

Very[2] truly yours, (42)

2

Gentlemen:

We are hoping to hold a company luncheon in your hotel soon. Can you give us information[1] on your policy for renting luncheon rooms? What services do you offer, and how many people will your rooms[2] hold? Also, what is your minimum rental fee? How much time do you allow for reserving the room?

We hope to[3] make our final plans very soon.

Sincerely yours, (69)

3

Dear Joe:

I have written a letter to Gail Brown telling her we are canceling her policy. We are certain[1] to hear from her the minute she receives the letter. Perhaps we can recommend a new agent for her. Let me[2] know if you have a name to give her.

Yours truly, (49)

4

Dear Sir or Madam:

Are you paying high rent and yet have very little to show for it? Perhaps you would like to[1] own your own home, yet cannot seem to save enough money for the down payment.

If so, we can help you. We are now[2] offering a new home payment plan which will allow you to place a low down payment on your new home. We also[3] have a budget plan for house payments. If you take out a loan from us now, you can schedule your payments any way[4] you wish.

Give us a minute of your time, and we will show you an easy payment plan for your household.

Cordially[5] yours, (101)

5

Gentlemen:

We are returning the copying machine we bought from your firm. Sometimes the machine will not print. When[1] it does print, the copies are not clear.

We have made many calls in search of an agent who services your machines.[2] None can get the parts we need for repairs.

We hope you can offer us a machine which gives better service. Will you[3] let us know what you plan to do?

Sincerely yours, (69)

6

Dear Sir:

Now is the time to visit our shop. We have a new truckload of home furnishings which we are offering[1] at big, big savings to you.

Don't delay! Visit us now and choose from many fine items shown on each floor. Don't forget[2] —visit our shop now and save.

Yours very truly, (50)

LESSON 6

1. To form the past tense of any regular verb, write a hyphen after the outline (pronounced *duh* or *ed*).

used, u-z-duh	uz-	received, re-s-v-duh	rsv-
limited, l-m-t-ed	lmt-	finished, f-n-ish-duh	fns-
helped, h-l-p-duh	hlp-	copied, k-p-e-duh	cpe-

Writing Numbers. Write figures to indicate cardinal numbers.

someone	s 1	12 pairs	12 prs
anyone	ne 1	two girls	2 grls

Abbreviations

north	N	west	W
south	S	corporation	corp
east	E	enclose, enclosure	enc

Abbreviated Word Development

northern	Nrn	eastern	Ern
*southern	Srn	western	Wrn

*Note: Word beginnings and endings may be added to brief forms and abbreviations to form derivatives, even though the pronunciation of the derivative may differ from the root word.

Brief Forms

be, but, been, buy, by	b	accept	ac
during	du	after	af
necessary	nes	appropriate	apo
why	y	determine	dt

PRINCIPLES SUMMARY

1. To form the past tense of any regular verb, write a hyphen after the outline: used, u-z-duh uz- .

Reading and Writing Exercises

-1-

d dvd of u r l l
~v bc E + ac ,
fb v plN ~yr ,
l b nes f u l sn
, enc- agrem .
af u rel , agrem
e c dl ~n u
dles l bgn, , hp
u l dsd l b · mbr
v r corp . s

-2-

dS f . l l- l~
e l ofr , ~cs
fre vzl l r clys
b , se . f u ac ,
l n b nes f u l
pa ne f u r~ +
~ls, du u vzl
e l so u nu +
uz- ~dl clys
C u ~a b o r
eze pam pln b

dN dla, y n cl
no + dl. [illegible] f u
fre [illegible] c., e d lc
l so u ho hpe lf
c b / dys b / se,
su

-3-

dS e cs Ccs f
rydNs v r lon,
af u v fl-ol /
apo f[illegible]s u l
rsv. Cc=cs crd
[illegible]C alos u l cs
Ccs hr / ne [illegible],
e hp l Sv u sn,
vlu

-4-

d ed enc-, . cpe
v / L u [illegible]N-l
se, / L Us y /
l b nes l ncrs
r [illegible]l fes + Aso
ho e dl- / ncrss,
af u v rd / L rel
/ l / apo fl, s

-5-

dS v rd u arlcl
o sl hoss i d
lc l asc u f.
fvr, d u alo s
l rprN u arlcl
n r co blln.,
e r Sln [illegible]l u
sa, bru=/ [illegible]r
l gl blr [illegible]n e
se. ncrs n ln
me, e r U r
ayNs l b psN +
u arlcl l hlp, l

u ll s no uf e
c uz / x ru

-6-

dS i d lc l b . cpe
v u nu bc ho l
ncrs rll sls . af
rd . rsN rvu v
/ bc i blv / l
hlp n . cly crs
n — C i v nrl- .

bcz clss v bgn i
nd / bc no . cd
u rt . cpe l — i
h— adrs gvn n
/ abv Lhd x > i
v alC- . Cc l
cvr / prs v / bc
+ —l fes . i l b
egr l v u rpli .
su

Key

1

Dear David:

If you are willing to move back East and accept the job of plant manager, it will be necessary[1] for you to sign the enclosed agreement. After you return the agreement, we can determine when your duties[2] will begin.

I hope you will decide to be a member of our corporation.

Sincerely, (57)

2

Dear Sir:

For a limited time, we will offer one week's free visit to our Cottages by the Sea. If you[1] accept, it will not be necessary for you to pay anything for your room and meals.

During your visit we will[2] show you new and used model cottages which you may buy on our easy payment plan, but don't delay. Why not call[3] now and determine a time for your free week?

We would like to show you how happy life can be at Cottages by[4] the Sea.

Sincerely yours, (84)

3

Dear Sir:

We cash checks for residents of our town. After you have filled out the appropriate forms, you will receive[1] a check-cashing card which allows you to cash checks here at any time. We hope to serve you soon.

Very truly yours,[2] (40)

4

Dear Ed:

Enclosed is a copy of the letter you wanted to see. The letter tells why it will be necessary[1] to increase our mailing fees and also how we determined the increases. After you have read the letter,[2] return it to the appropriate file.

Sincerely, (49)

5

Dear Sir:

Having read your article on selling houses, I would like to ask you for a favor. Would you allow[1] us to reprint your article in our company bulletin?

We are certain what you say is true—the market[2] will get better when we see an increase in loan money. We are telling our agents to be patient, and your[3] article will help.

Will you let us know if we can use it?

Respectfully yours, (74)

6

Dear Sir:

I would like to buy a copy of your new book, *How to Increase Retail Sales.* After reading a recent[1] review of the book, I believe it will help in a college course in which I have enrolled. Because classes have begun,[2] I need the book now. Could you rush a copy to my home address given in the above letterhead?

I have[3] attached a check to cover the price of the book and mailing fees. I will be eager to have your reply.

Sincerely[4] yours, (81)

LESSON 7

RECAP AND REVIEW

You now know enough shorthand to write most of the words used in business correspondence. Before going on, let's review the principles you've studied so far. No new principles will be introduced in this lesson. Instead, use this opportunity to check your progress.

1. The following words illustrate principles you studied in Lessons 1-6:

view, v-u
build, b-l-d
easy, e-z-e

billing, b-l-ing
billings, b-l-ings
something, s-m-thing

member, mem-b-r
money, mun-e
remind, re-mind
settlement, s-t-l-ment

patient, p-ish-nt
engineers, en-j-n-r-s
house, h-ow-s

package, p-k-j
much, m-chay
while, w-l

jobs, j-b-s
Ted's, t-d-s
helps, h-l-p-s

she, ish-e
wish, w-ish
advice, ad-v-s
also, al-s-o

certain, cer-t-n
surplus, sur-p-l-s
copied, k-p-e-duh

2. Following are the brief forms you have studied. How quickly can you write the outlines for each?

are	of	is
at	very	for
a	too	in
the	not	us
will	his	full
can	it	have
our	well	to
an	we	from
during	firm	your
part	perhaps	own
letter	port	on
market	would	manage
be	after	buy
why	but	determine
by	appropriate	been
accept	necessary	

3. Can you write the outlines for these words which are developed from some of the above brief forms?

haven't	yours	cancel
welfare	manager	formal
report	forgotten	cannot
forgive	informing	letters

4. The following outlines represent the abbreviations you have studied. How quickly can you read them?

co	corp	p
enc	+	vp
inf	rel	E
W	N	S
mr	mrs	m
ms	cal	

Reading and Writing Exercises

-1-

q e r hpe u v
dsd-l b u nu co
crs f s, y dN
u vzl s s
du r c + dl
C dls u
l b, e v
me crs C d
b apo f u corp,
r Svs ppl r v
l lrn- + l cp u
crs n lp sp. /
r fr e lc prd n
r Svs + e N
u l b hpe. e r
rde l hlp n
ne a e c . s

pam , du. d u
lc . ml l ls
. Cc, e v b psN
b e du n no f u
v rsv- r Ls rm
u l c u pam o
l . N u cl s.
/ , n nes l pa
u bl n f. f u cn
y l pa r nlr
bl e l ac pl v /,
f r crN pln , l
C f u bjl y n
vzl r ln ofs. r
ajN a b v hlp
l u . uvl

-2-

dS Ph u v fgln u

-3-

d ed enc-, r inf
u N- . / , . rpl

bs- o . old ⌒r
Sva ⌒d b r VP.
i hp u l fgv r
dla n gl r inf
l u. e cd n gl
/ b r ⌐ u ⌣N-
/ bcz v r cpe
⌒sn. r P v r fr
sN r ⌒sn ol
f rprs r s⌒
⌣c e rsv- u L.
e v . co plse
⌣C dz n alo s
l lc fl ⌣s ol
v r ofs. cu

-4-

d jl e r gld l
rpl u v b ac-f
clss bgn n r fl.
e rcm u pln

no ⌣l crss u
⌣s l lc. r enc-
cal sd b v hlp,
u ⌒a b Sln r
scls u lrn hr l
b apo f ne ofs.
if u Cz r ⌒dcl
or njnr flds u
lrn l Sv u l,
du fl fre l asc
s f avs / ne
⌐. e r hpe l
b . pl v u fCr.
su

-5-

d r Crd no , r
⌐ l pln r
s⌒r sl. me
rll ⌒yrs hld
lry sls du dfrN

Ls v r yr, y
dN e lri s
nu + dl. L f
l bq s r evN.
e c lrn r nlr
sp sNr nl.
yr sd c sl,
i d lc l se r
sl rn f. f c.
Ph e cd cp r sps
opn af rglr clz.
Ls, f u agre
i l lc l r
rCNs + ll u
no l, dsd-.
ul

cpe v . nu pln
ofr- b . sv + ln
co n lon, af rd
r brsr i fll Sln
u d N l se r.
Ph e cd uz r
pam pln ofr-,
v crs i no e l
nd C inf l
dl f r pln, apo
f r co. l u ll
e no f u lc
r pln. i l b
gld l sl. L f
r yr + s l lc.
vlu

-6-

d hord alC-, .

Key

Brief Forms

r	v	)
/	v	b
.	l	n
(	n	s
l	)	b
c	/	v
r	l	l
.	e	f
du	fr	u
pl	Ph	o
L	pl	o
r	d	1
b	af	b
y	b	dl
b	apo	b
ac	nes	

Brief Form Development

vN	us	csl
lfr	-yr	fl
rpl	fgln	cn
fgv	nf-	Ls

Abbreviations

company	corporation	president
enclose, enclosure	and	vice president
information	return	east
west	north	south
Mr.	Mrs.	Miss
Ms.	catalog	

1

Gentlemen:

We are happy you have decided to buy your new company cars from us.

Why don't you visit us[1] sometime during the week and determine which models you wish to buy? We have many cars which would be appropriate[2] for your corporation.

Our service people are very well trained and will keep your cars in top shape. At our firm,[3] we take pride in our service, and we want you to be happy. We are ready to help in any way we can.[4]

Sincerely, (81)

2

Dear Sir:

Perhaps you have forgotten your payment is due. Would you take a minute to mail us a check?

We have been[1] patient, but we do not know if you have received our letters reminding you to make your payment on time. Won't you[2] call us? It is not necessary to pay your bill in full. If you cannot manage to pay the entire bill, we[3] will accept part of it.

If the current plan is too much for your budget, why not visit our loan office? Our agent[4] may be of help to you.

Yours very truly, (89)

3

Dear Ed:

Enclosed is the information you wanted. It is a report based on an old market survey made by[1] our vice president. I hope you will forgive the delay in getting the information to you. We could not get[2] it by the time you wanted it because of our copy machine. The president of our firm sent the machine out[3] for repairs the same week we received your letter. We have a company policy which does not allow us to[4] take file items out of the office.

Cordially yours, (89)

4

Dear Jill:

We are glad to report you have been accepted for classes beginning in the fall. We recommend you[1] plan now what courses you wish to take. The enclosed catalog should be of help.

You may be certain the skills you learn[2] here will be appropriate for any office. If you choose the medical or engineering fields, your training[3] will serve you well.

Do feel free to ask us for advice at any time. We are happy to be a part of your[4] future.

Sincerely yours, (84)

5

Dear Richard:

Now is the time to plan our summer sale. Many retail managers hold large sales during different[1] times of the year. Why don't we try something new and determine a time for one big summer event? We can turn the[2] entire shopping center into a major sidewalk sale.

I would like to see the sale run for a full week. Perhaps[3] we could keep the shops open after regular closing times.

If you agree, I will talk to the merchants and let[4] you know what is decided.

Yours truly, (87)

6

Dear Howard:

Attached is a copy of a new plan offered by a savings and loan company in town. After[1] reading the brochure, I felt certain you would want to see it. Perhaps we could use the payment plan offered.

Of course,[2] I know we will need much information to determine if the plan is appropriate for our company. Will[3] you let me know if you like the plan? I will be glad to set a time for the manager and us to talk.

Very[4] truly yours, (82)

WHAT WILL SHORTHAND DO FOR ME?

Now that you are studying shorthand, you are developing a skill you can be proud of. Your new skill will do much toward bringing you success in your career.

Shorthand will give you an advantage in the marketplace. Why? *Shorthand gives you an added skill and makes you a more versatile employee.* Your employer will also know that you had the ambition and ability to learn this skill.

Here are some facts about shorthand and what it can do for you:

Shorthand enables you to begin at higher levels in the business world, which in turn leads to advancement in other areas. The future of office work is rapidly changing to adjust to the needs and ambitions of today's workers. You will find that shorthand is helpful at any level—either for taking dictation or giving dic-

*Chapter Two

tation. Your shorthand can help you get a good job. Advancement from there will depend on your ambition, career goals, and performance.

You can use shorthand in many ways at any job level. Reporters find shorthand helpful in taking notes for a news story. Executives may make notes in shorthand while listening to a presentation, talking on the phone, or sitting in a meeting. Anyone who does research—administrative assistant, student, teacher, or writer—will find shorthand invaluable in recording notes. Using shorthand saves time and reduces fatigue.

*You can learn **Speedwriting Shorthand** quickly.* ***Speedwriting Shorthand*** is an alphabetic system of shorthand which can be learned quickly and easily. With more experience on the job, your speed and accuracy will continue to improve.

LESSON 8

1. Write for the sound of *ith* or *th*.

them, ith-m

then, ith-n

growth, gay-r-ith

health, h-l-ith

methods, m-ith-d-s

although, al-ith-o

2. Write for the word ending *ly* or *ily* (pronounced *lee* or *uh-lee*).

family, f-m-ly

yearly, y-r-ly

certainly, cer-t-n-ly

easily, e-z-ly

recently, re-s-nt-ly

rapidly, r-p-d-ly

3. Write a capital for the word beginning *dis*.

discuss, dis-k-s

display, dis-p-l-a

dismay, dis-m-a

disturb, dis-t-r-b

dislike, dis-i̇-k

distant, dis-t-nt

4. Write a capital for the word beginning *mis*.

mistake, mis-t-k

mislead, mis-l-d

misplaced, mis-p-l-s-duh

mislay, mis-l-a

misfit, mis-f-t

misgivings, mis-gay-v-ings

Word beginnings, word endings, and sound blends which can also be individual words may be used to express those words.

add

all

missing

*men

*Remember that man is written .

Read and practice these additional words. Each word will be used in the reading and writing exercises at the end of this lesson.

discover, dis-k-v-r

evidently, e-v-d-nt-ly

really, r-l-ly

nearly, n-r-ly

gladly, gay-l-d-ly

either, e-ith-r

these, ith-z

this, ith-s

there, their, ith-r

misprint, mis-p-r-nt

Brief Form Development. Use the principles you've learned in this lesson to develop new outlines from brief forms.

necessarily

appropriately

partly

reportedly

willingly

firmly

Your Business Vocabulary

When you begin your office career, you will learn many words that are commonly used in business offices. Some you may already know. Others will become familiar as you use them. The following words will appear in the reading and writing exercises at the end of this lesson. Make these words part of your business vocabulary.

marketing — Those activities involved in getting a product from the producer to the consumer, such as advertising, promoting, and selling.

yearly report — A summation of the activities of a department, division, or entire corporation over a 12-month period.

PRINCIPLES SUMMARY

1. Write l for the sound of *ith* or *th*: them, ith-m lm ; growth, gay-r-ith grl .
2. Write l for the word ending *ly* (lee) or *ily* (uh-lee): family, f-m-ly fml .
3. Write a capital D for the word beginning *dis*: discuss, dis-k-s Dcs .
4. Write a capital M for the word beginning *mis*: mistake, mis-t-k Mtc .
5. Word beginnings, word endings, and sound blends which can also be individual words may be used to express those words.

Reading and Writing Exercises

-1-

mo l bb sd , ,
nsl lm f r fml
cmp l bgn, e v
n hrd fm a c
fmls, l u cl +
rm lm l fl ol
lr hll fms. c
fms c b —l- l
s, e rll nd c
fms bf cmp opns,

alC- r c ns v
M fls, aprMl c
fls v b Mpls-, d
eC v u lc lru u
pprs l se f c M
fls cd v b Mla-
o u dsc. me v r
fldrs r old + v
Mld Uls, ls Mlcs
c ezl b —d,

-2-

mo l a co —yrs

-3-

d —rs —lsn ,

n l U u ho
C i lc nu
hll fd Dplas u
v n u fr se . , ,
ncry l se grl
n hll fds n ls
sle . i U u d lc
l se enc-
artcl C Dcss
s rzns e r
se sC . rpd Cny
n hll fd r .
Ph / l ncry u l
cp A l u Dpla .
s

Dpla nlr so-
ne dy / h .
n Crs arv-
/ u h i fll
v Dlrb- . l u
Da i Dcvr- .
nlr lry rp n
fbrc . elr i dd
n se rp n
i bl Crs or /
hpn- du lrp l
u hos . n elr
cs Crs l v l
b rel- . s

-4-

dS rsNl i bl 2
lvl Crs f u
co . alo Crs
v b uz- f . flr

-5-

mo l A r hds
n u yrl rpl l u
Dcs s nu
lds v r r
nu nyns x e r

-6-

pln̲ l sl hu gls
f sls ls yr +
nd ⌣as l hlp
s aCv l⌒. Ph
u cd gv s ⌐ rzlts
v u rsN ⌒r
rSC n ⌣C u
asc- dlrs f lr
vus o fCr sls.
/ ⌒a b nes l
dl . nu plse l
b uz- n r co. if
so u rpl d Stnl
b v hlp.

d⌒r bron e r hpe
l sa e r enc̲ .
Cc f ⌐ me e o u.
e dd ndd Dcvr
. Mlc n u hll bl
+ r gld l rel u
me. e d lc u
l ac ⌐ enc- gfl
Stfcl f . fre vzl
l r hll. e hp
l hr f⌒ u sn.
⌣n ⌒c̲ u trvl
plns b Stn l
gv s . cl. su

Key

1

MEMO TO: Bob Smith

It is nearly time for our family camp to begin. We have not heard from all the families.[1] Will you call and remind them to fill out their health forms? The forms can be mailed to us. We really need the forms before[2] camp opens. (43)

2

MEMO TO: All Company Managers

Attached are the names of missing files. Apparently the files have been[1] misplaced. Would each of you look through your papers to see if the missing files could have been mislaid on your desk?

Many of[2] our folders are old and have misleading titles. Thus, mistakes can easily be made. (55)

3

Dear Mrs. Wilson:

I want to tell you how much I like the new health food displays you have in your pharmacy. It[1] is encouraging to see the growth in health foods in this city. I thought you would like to see the enclosed article[2] which discusses some reasons we are seeing such a rapid change in the health food market. Perhaps it will[3] encourage you to keep adding to your display.

Sincerely, (70)

4

Dear Sir:

Recently I bought two lovely chairs from your company. Although the chairs have been used for a floor display,[1] neither showed any damage at the time. When the chairs arrived at my home, I felt very disturbed. To my dismay,[2] I discovered a rather large rip in the fabric. Either I did not see the rip when I bought the chairs, or it[3] happened during the trip to my house. In either case, the chairs will have to be returned.

Sincerely, (77)

5

MEMO TO: All Marketing Heads

In your yearly report, will you discuss some new methods of marketing our new[1] engines? We are planning to set high goals for sales this year and need ways to help us achieve them. Perhaps you could give[2] us the results of your recent market research in which you asked dealers for their views on future sales. It may be[3] necessary to determine a new policy to be used in our company. If so, your report would[4] certainly be of help. (84)

6

Dear Mr. Brown:

We are happy to say we are enclosing a check for the money we owe you. We did indeed[1] discover a mistake in your hotel bill and are glad to return your money. We would like you to accept the[2] enclosed gift certificate for a free visit to our hotel. We hope to hear from you soon. When making your[3] travel plans, be certain to give us a call.

Sincerely yours, (70)

LESSON 9

1. Retain beginning or ending vowels when building compound words. When you combine two words to make one word, you are building a compound word. If one of these words begins or ends in a vowel, keep the vowel in the outline: payroll = pay + roll *parl* .

headache, hd + ak *hdac*	teenage, tn + aj *tnaj*
seaside, se + sd *sesd*	highway, hi + wa *h-a*

2. Retain the initial and final root-word vowel when adding prefixes and suffixes. When a prefix contains a long vowel followed by a root-word vowel, omit the prefix vowel.

disappear, dis-a-p-r *Dapr*	misuse, mis-u-z *Muz*
payment, p-a-ment *pam*	disallow, dis-a-l-ow *Dalo*
reapply, re-a-p-l-i *rapli*	readmit, re-ad-m-t *rA-t*

3. Write ordinal numbers as follows:

42nd *42 d*	53rd *53 d*
85th *85 t*	

Abbreviations

credit *cr*	number *No*
total *tot*	percent *%*
amount *a-t*	attention *att*

Brief Forms

as, was	3	great, grate	gr
hospital	hsp	were, with	◡
general	jn	that	la
arrange	ar		

Brief Form Development. Use your new brief forms to develop other outlines.

within	◡n	generally	jnl
greatly	grl	without	◡ol
arrangements	arms		

Your Business Vocabulary

reassess rass	To re-evaluate, or to determine a new value of property as a basis for taxation.
minimum payment mm pam	The minimum amount of money required at specific dates on a credit purchase.

PRINCIPLES SUMMARY

1. Retain beginning and ending vowels when building compound words: payroll = pay + roll parl .
2. Retain the initial and final root-word vowel when adding prefixes and suffixes: reopen, re-o-p-n ropn ; payment, p-a-ment pam .
3. Write ordinal numbers as follows: 42nd, 42d 53rd, 53d 85th, 85l .

Reading and Writing Exercises

SERIES A

1. e l ad u l c hsp z sn z e c ar / .

2. e r ncrs c ad v u cr. c nu lol v u ln , sn blo.

3. e r ofr ls Cr / 20% ls ln c rglr prs.

4. dd u no la . gr No v lnaj drvrs r nsr- ⌣ r fr ×

5. n jn c lrn cls ⌣N l evn lo lr z . gr dl v Dagrem.

SERIES B

1. c lol ad z du b c 12l . u all l ls ⌣dr d b . gr hlp.

2. lr ⌣ z me m z lr ⌣ ⌣m n c lol No v ppl o c parl.

3. u l rsv u nu cr crd ⌣ol dla.

4. z sn z c ⌣dr z brl l ⌣u all i asc- la nu arms b ⌣d.

5. e ⌣ hpe l lrn la sls r jnl du v l n c E.

SERIES C

1. alo e v no jbs
opn , ls ⌣ e
avz u l rapli
⌣n c nu hsp
opns. e l ⌢c
arms l Dcs
u L , la ⌣.

f ls jbs e rasn
⌣ l nu dles. i
blv la e l rasn
. gs No ls yr.

2. e l A . lol v 20
nu m l c parl.
e l nd la me l
hlp bld c nu
hla.

3. z . rl r co dz n
la of ppl. rlr
ln rls m + ⌣m

4. n jn r co ofrs
blr bnfls ln ne
lrj fr n lon. i
v b ⌣ ls corp
f 11 yrs no + i
no la ls , lru.

5. e l b hpe l
rAl u n r
clss. u l rsv
f cr f c crss u
lc erlr.

-1-

mo l A cl⌒s
⌒yrs z hd v ls
corp l z v hpe
l lrn ⌣l . gr jb
u r A du . No v
ppl v rln l sa
la lr cl⌒s ⌣ gvn
v fn all ⌣ol .
dol A v u dzrv
cr f u pl n gv ls
co . gr n⌒ .

-2-

dS pa bls c ⌒n
hdac af hdac .
la , y e r ofr .
nu cr pln . ⌣
ls pln u pa , lol
a⌣l . ln e uz la
a⌣l l pa A v (
bls u o , if u bls
r lc l ⌒C cs
f⌒ u bjl ll s
ar . eze pln f u .
⌣n . yr u bls l
b pd + u hdac
l b gn . su

-3-

1 e rsv- u L nf⌒
s la r sesd cly l
b rass- o (14l .
(L ⌣N o l sa
la (vlu v ls
hos ncrs- grl=
b 25%= ⌣n (nu
hia z bll , e r
sre b u v⌒d .
Mlc . (hia
⌣C rns nr r
bC hos , n nu .
if ne (, old +

bdl n nd v rpr.
c hea z bll . fu
yrs af e bl r
bC hos. l r nly
c rd z nvr rpr-
af c z bll, e hp
la u ofs l lc . blr
lc c la hea. if r
hos, rass-e d
lc l se apo rprs
d o c rd. vlu

-4-

dr lr e dd Cc
l se if u l rsv
u crs o scyl. e
cl- c lrc fr l dl
n c crs d arv
n nu hvn + c
yr sd c crs
lfl erl ls rn.

alo s v c lrcs
r b dla- us sd
arv o b ls c.
c yr asr- s u l
gl . cl if ls, ne
nu l rpl. e r
hpe l v b v hlp.
vlu

-5-

d lu c rsv- . L f
c bron + as lrc
fr asc f . cpe v
r yrl agrem. c
v lc- n a v c fl
cbnls b c v n
sn c agrem.
cd c v b Mpls- x
lr r 2 fls C sd
v . cpe v c agrem.
eC cpe s s l

b M̲ , i hp u
c Avz ⌒e o ho
l gl . cpe , ul

-6-

d M hnre alC- r
(cpes u nd ,
bcz r fls v grn
so lrj + r uz-
b so me ppl /
, nes l uz . dfrN
fl̲ ⌒ld , crNl a

lgl dcms r b̲
cpl n r lgl ofs ,
⌒n u nd . ⌒
. fl̲ clrc l b gld
l gl / f u , ls
⌒ld +d rds
fl̲ Mlcs + aso
alo u l gl inf
rpdl , e hp /
Svs u l f⌒ no
o , c

Key

SERIES A

1. We will admit you to the hospital as soon as we can arrange it.
2. We are increasing the amount of your credit. The new total of your loan is shown below.
3. We are offering this chair at 20 percent less than the regular price.
4. Did you know that a great number of teenage drivers are insured with our firm?
5. In general, the training class went well even though there was a great deal of disagreement.

SERIES B

1. The total amount was due by the 12th. Your attention to this matter would be a great help.
2. There were as many men as there were women in the total number of people on the payroll.
3. You will receive your new credit card without delay.
4. As soon as the matter was brought to my attention, I asked that new arrangements be made.
5. We were happy to learn that sales are generally doing very well in the East.

SERIES C

1. Although we have no jobs open at this time, we advise you to reapply when the new hospital opens. We will make arrangements to discuss your letter at that time.
2. We will add a total of 20 new men to the payroll. We will need that many to help build the new highway.
3. As a rule, our company does not lay off people. Rather than release men and women from their jobs, we reassign them to new duties. I believe that we will reassign a great number this year.
4. In general, our company offers better benefits than any large firm in town. I have been with this corporation for 11 years now, and I know that this is true.
5. We will be happy to readmit you in our classes. You will receive full credit for the courses you took earlier.

1

MEMO TO: All Claims Managers

As head of this corporation, I was very happy to learn what a great job[1] you are all doing. A number of people have written to say that their claims were given very fine attention.[2] Without a doubt, all of you deserve credit for your part in giving this company a great name. (57)

2

Dear Sir:

Paying bills can mean headache after headache. That is why we are offering a new credit plan. With this[1] plan, you pay one total amount. Then we use that amount to pay all of the bills you owe.

If your bills are taking[2] too much cash from your budget, let us arrange an easy plan for you. Within a year, your bills will be paid and your[3] headache will be gone.

Sincerely yours, (66)

3

Gentlemen:

We received your letter informing us that our seaside cottage will be reassessed on the 14th.[1] The letter went on to say that the value of this house increased greatly—by 25 percent—when the[2] new highway was built.

We are sorry, but you have made a mistake. The highway which runs near our beach house is not new.[3] If anything, it is old and badly in need of repair. The highway was built a few years after we bought our[4] beach house. To our knowledge, the road was never repaired after it was built.

We hope that your office will take a better[5] look at that highway. If our house is reassessed, we would like to see appropriate repairs made on the road.[6]

Very truly yours, (124)

4

Dear Mr. Miller:

We did check to see if you will receive your cars on schedule. We called the trucking firm to[1] determine when the cars would arrive in New Haven, and the manager said the cars left early this morning. Although[2] some of the trucks are being delayed, yours should arrive on time this week. The manager assured us you will get a[3] call if there is anything new to report. We are happy to have been of help.

Very truly yours, (78)

5

Dear Lou:

I received a letter from the Brown and Ames trucking firm asking for a copy of our yearly agreement.[1] I have looked in all of the file cabinets, but I have not seen the agreement. Could it have been misplaced? There are[2] two files which should have a copy of the agreement. Each copy seems to be missing. I hope you can advise[3] me on how to get a copy.

Yours truly, (68)

6

Dear Miss Henry:

Attached are the copies you need. Because our files have grown so large and are used by so many[1] people, it is necessary to use a different filing method. Currently, all legal documents are[2] being kept in our legal office. When you need an item, a filing clerk will be glad to get it for you. This[3] method should reduce filing mistakes and also allow you to get information rapidly. We hope it serves you[4] well from now on.

Cordially, (85)

LESSON 10

1. Write a capital P (disjoined from other letters) for the word beginnings *per* and *pur*.

person, per-s-n Psn

personnel, per-s-n-l Psnl

permit, per-m-t Pml

per P

purchase, pur-chay-s PCs

purpose, pur-p-s Pps

Write a capital P also for the word beginnings *pre, pro*, and *pro (prah)*.

prefer, pre-f-r Pfr

problem, prah-b-l-m Pblm

provide, pro-v-d Pvd

proper, prah-p-r Ppr

proposal, pro-p-z-l Ppzl

produce, pro-d-s Pds

2. Write q for the word ending *gram*.

program, pro-gram Pq

telegram, t-l-gram tlq

Your Business Vocabulary

proposal Ppzl	A plan of action, usually presented in writing.
out-patients ol=psNs	Patients receiving treatment at a hospital without being admitted for overnight stays.
building permit bld Pml	A legal document authorizing an organization or individual to begin construction of a building.

PRINCIPLES SUMMARY

1. Write a disjoined capital P for the word beginnings *per, pur, pre, pro,* and *pro (prah)*: person, per-s-n Psn; prepare, pre-p-r Ppr; produce, pro-d-s Pds; problem, prah-b-l-m Pbl.
2. Write q for the word ending *gram:* program, pro-gram Pq.

Reading and Writing Exercises

-1-

mo l yr v PCs
l , r crN
plse o PCs ofs
splis. C cos
v alo- s cr. du
e nd . cr crd
l c . PCs or c
e Pvd r ofs No.
aso l , / n
v / Psn hu
asns cr crds.
i hp u c Pvd
e ls inf.
/ l b . gr hlp l
lrn / Ppr PCs
lds.

-2-

mo l a Psnl enc-
, . cpe v / nu
Ppzl. z u c se
/ Pvds me nd-
Cnjs. ls pln
eC Psn l rsv dl
bnfls ol pa f
/ ncrs- cvrj.
Psnll i blv ls
pln , l e v
nd- f me yrs.
i se no Pbls

◡ / / a, e r
aso rvz r plse
f trn nu Psnl.
szn jns , Ppr.
mo ◡C l Pvd
a (dlls. i blv
la lz nu plses
l slv me Pbl◠s
n (co.

-3-

mo l ◠r rbrl
L◠pl n ◠i Ppzl
f (nu hsp i pln
l Pvd . dzn f (
bld z l z jn inf
nd- l gl . bld
P◠l. y dN u Ppr
. nz rls gv dlls
v (Ppzl, rzdNs
v ls sle sd no la

r hsp l ofr me
nu Pgs ◡C l
bnfl ol=psNs z
l z n=psNs,
e v rsv- ◠C
all f◠ (nzppr
rsNl du l ncrs-
hsp fes. ls d s◠
l b . apo L◠ l
ll ppl no r plns
l ncrs Svss.

-4-

mo l j◠s bron
◡l , u avs o (
alC- hll cr Pg,
◡ ls Pg (co d
Pvd . pls z l z .
L◠ f rn or s◠.
(z Ppz- la e uz
(S sd v (bld

f ls Pps, ls pln
z Ppz- b r P hu
blvs la ppl sd
b alo- l gl Ppr
hlt cr l o ls
jbs. du u se
ne Pbl s sC
. arm.

-5-

1 r Pps v ls L, l
dl y e v n rsv-
r crds e PCs- f
u co. n e dsd-
l b r crds u
Sln la e d v
ahd v . z l
rcl e asc- la r
crds b r4-. u
ajN asr- s la ls
d b no Pbl du

ls v r yr. e v
b psN b 3 cs v
gn b + e v n
rsv- r crds, e
hp la / l n b nes
l csl b af ls c
e l n ac r crds.
f no o d b apo
f u l nf s v
dlas b llg. ul

-6-

1 z r hd v ls hsp
l z hpe l hr la .
nu Cldrns unl
, b Ppz-. z pl v ls
Ppzl prNs l b alo-
l r n hr n r hsp
lr Cldrn. jnl
sC . arm Pvds .
gr bnft l r prNs

z l z (psNs, l
dl . nd f ls unt .
Sva z ⌒d ⌣ lcl
rzdNs. v (lol
Sva- 80% ⌣ n
fvr v ls unt. i
fl hpe + prod l

se ls ⌒dr fnll
rsv (all / nds.
z mbrs v (hsp
brd u l no dol ⌣s
l rsv . f rpl o
ls nu pln. vlu

Key

1

MEMO TO: Manager of Purchasing

What is our current policy on purchasing office supplies? Which[1] companies have allowed us credit? Do we need a credit card to make a purchase, or can we provide our office[2] number?

Also, what is the name of the person who assigns credit cards? I hope you can provide me with this[3] information. It will be a great help to learn the proper purchasing methods. (74)

2

MEMO TO: All Personnel

Enclosed is a copy of the new proposal. As you can see, it provides many[1] needed changes. With this plan, each person will receive death benefits without paying for the increased coverage.[2] Personally, I believe this plan is what we have needed for many years. I see no problems with it at all.[3]

We are also revising our policy for training new personnel. Susan Jones is preparing a memo[4] which will provide all the details. I believe that these new policies will solve many problems in the company.[5] (100)

3

MEMO TO: Mr. Robert Temple

In my proposal for the new hospital, I plan to provide a design[1] for the building as well as general information needed to get a building permit. Why don't you prepare[2] a news release giving details of the proposal? Residents of this city should know that our hospital will[3] offer many new programs which will benefit out-patients as well as in-patients.

We have received much attention[4] from the newspaper recently due to increased hospital fees. This would seem to be an appropriate time[5] to let people know our plans to increase services. (109)

4

MEMO TO: James Brown

What is your advice on the attached health care program? With this program, the company would[1] provide a place, as well as a time, for running or swimming. It was proposed that we use the south side of the building[2] for this purpose. This plan was proposed by the president, who believes that people should be allowed to get proper[3] health care while on their jobs. Do you see any problems with such an arrangement? (74)

5

Gentlemen:

The purpose of this letter is to determine why we have not received the cards we purchased from your[1] company. When we decided to buy the cards, you were certain that we would have them ahead of time. As I[2] recall, we asked that the cards be rushed. Your agent assured us that there would be no problem during this time of the[3] year. We have been patient, but three weeks have gone by and we have not received the cards.

We hope that it will not be[4] necessary to cancel, but after this week we will not accept the cards. From now on, it would be appropriate[5] for you to inform us of delays by telegram.

Yours truly, (110)

6

Gentlemen:

As the head of this hospital, I was happy to hear that a new children's unit is being proposed.[1] As part of this proposal, parents will be allowed to remain here in the hospital with their children.[2] Generally, such an arrangement provides a great benefit to the parents as well as the patients.

To determine[3] a need for this unit, a survey was made with local residents. Of the total surveyed, 80 percent were[4] in favor of this unit. I feel happy and proud to see this matter finally receiving the attention[5] it needs. As members of the hospital board, you will no doubt wish to receive a full report on this new plan.[6]

Very truly yours, (124)

LESSON 11

1. Write *y* for the sound of *oi* (oy).

boy, b-oi *by*

choice, chay-oi-s *Cys*

join, j-oi-n *jyn*

loyal, l-oi-l *lyl*

voice, v-oi-s *vys*

annoy, a-n-oi *any*

Write the months of the year this way:

January *Ja*

February *Fb*

March *Mr*

April *Ap*

May *Ma*

June *Jn*

July *Jl*

August *Ag*

September *Sp*

October *Oc*

November *Nv*

December *Dc*

Abbreviations

department *dpt*

envelope *env*

invoice *inv*

insurance *ins*

regard *re*

Brief Forms

between *bln*

ship *A*

situate *sil*

those *loz*

operate *op*

point *py*

participate *pp*

property *prp*

refer *rf*

respond, response *rsp*

suggest *sug*

Brief Form Development

leadership *ldrA*

operator *opr*

appointment *apym*

situated *sil-*

shipment *Am*

disappoint *Dapy*

PRINCIPLES SUMMARY

1. Write *y* for the sound of *oi* (oy): boy, b-oi *by* .

Reading and Writing Exercises

SERIES A

1. r nu ofss l b
sil- o r prp
bln r ⌒n plN
+ r old ofs bld.
v r plse , enc-n
r alC- env.

5. c u sug Cnys n
ls scjlx ⌒n ⌒a
l v u rsp l lz
plnsx

2. r plN l n op bln
Ja 28 + Fb 15. e l
uz loz ⌒cs l sil
frnt n r nu bld.
a v r ppl l pp n
r ⌒w.

3. du loz ⌒cs e
sug la a sms
b rf-l r ⌒n
plN. a invs sd
b rf-l r s dpl.

4. n re l u rsN
mo r ⌒w l b
cvr- b ins. . cpe

SERIES B

1. nsr lnaj drvrs
c b . gr hdac.
ndd s⌒ prNs
v cl- / hu a rbre.
f u r pa l ⌒C
l nsr u lnaj
drvrs ll jn lf
hlp. jn lf c nsr
u lnajs f 10% ls ln
ne lrj co n lon.

2. hr , gr nz f ‿ hd
v ‿ fd. r hlt
bnfts no pa z mC
z 90% v ‿ ttl hsp
bl. ⌣n c e ar l so
u ls plse?

3. all plsehldrs e r
no ofr ‿ nu dNl
cvrj u v b asc f.
u z l z u fl l
bnft grl f ls plse.

4. n rsp l ‿ ncrs-
nd e r opn .

sNrl clms dpl
l Sv ‿ ntr co.
bgn Ja 2 a clms
sd b rf- l ‿ sNrl
clms dpl. ls Cnj
l Pvd . efsN ms
v Pss a clms.

5. ‿ fls so la ‿ ,
no l l rvu u
hors ins plse.
‿a e gl lglr sn?
i l cl ls ‿c f.
apym.

-1-

d n u L v Ap 13 u
rf- l . dla n r Ja
sm v ofs splis.
e r sre f ne Pbls
cz- b c dla b r cpe
v c inv sos la u
splis ⌣ s- z sn
z pam z rsv-.
⌒a e sug ls ⌒d
f gl u sm v envs
o b. u c avyd
dla b ⌒l u Cc b
Ma 30. u envs l
b s- o Jn 7 or c
flo ⌣c. if u flo
ls pln f fCr PCss
e c Pvd u ⌣ blr
Svs. su

-2-

d ysn u rsN apym
z VP z gr nz. c co
Slnl ⌒d. ⌣z Cys.
z hd v c s dpl u
Pvd- me yrs v lyl
Svs. / , rasr l
se c co rsp b gv
u Ppr cr. ⌣ u ldrs
A dpls l no op
efsNl. i hp u l
cl o ⌒e l hlp n
ne ⌣a i c. z sn
z u v s⌒ fre b
y dN e gl lglr f
lnC. vlu

-3-

dS dd u no la u
⌒a b pa bln 15 +
20% l ⌒C f u ins.
dd u Aso no la
loz plses ⌒a n

cvr (crN vlu
v u h— + Psnl
prp. no , (L
l —c Sln la u
bnfls r a la u Ad
v, bln Mr 15 + Ap1
r ajN l cl o u, y
n —c / . py l v
u plses rde f rvu.
cu

-4-

mo l VP folr n
re l u mo v Sp 5
(prN —Ans l b
sil- n r plN b (
bgn v Dc, z u no
e —N- l v L rde
erl n Oc b cd n
ar l v L A- / la
L, e v asc- . lol
v 30 —An oprs l
pp n . lrn Pq du
Nv b e v n rsv-
rsps f— a v L.
Ph e Ad pln l hr
nu ppl l op (—Ans,
—l du u sug.

-5-

mo l frd gra i c
no gv u r nu plse
f nAr —Ans A- b
lrc, l u nf— a pp
dlrs la bgn Jl, e
l n rpls —Ans
dy- o (dlrs prp.
if (dlrs —A l Dcs
ls —lr rf L l (
cls dpl, e asc
la ne dy b An o
(inv / (py v

arvl, e d lc ⌐
dlrs l b Uld v ⌐
Cnys no. ⌣n. fu
⌣cs Ls l b ⌢l-
gv̲ f dlls v ⌐ nu
plse.

-6-

mo l ⌢yr v bys ⌣r
e l ofr sv̲ v bln
20 + 30 % o a bc=l=
scl nds = cll̲ z l z
splis. a cll̲ sd b
⌢rc- don 20%. a
scl splis l b Dpla-
bln ⌐ bys + grls dpls,
e l ac pam n ⌐f
v c4 cr crds + Psnl
Ccs. loz Psns ⌣4̲ l
c4 parl Ccs sd b
sN l ⌐ cr ofs. a
Psnl Ccs sd b sn
b ⌐ dpl ⌢yr, e
suq u clrcs rm a
sprs la cll̲ ⌣rs
⌢a b rel- ⌣n ,
⌣c flo̲ ⌐ PCs.

Key

SERIES A

1. Our new offices will be situated on the property between our main plant and the old office building.
2. Our plant will not operate between January 28 and February 15. We will use those weeks to situate furnishings in the new building. All of our people will participate in the move.
3. During those weeks, we suggest that all shipments be referred to our main plant. All invoices should be referred to our shipping department.
4. In regard to your recent memo, our move will be covered by insurance. A copy of our policy is enclosed in the attached envelope.
5. Can you suggest changes in this schedule? When may I have your response to these plans?

SERIES B

1. Insuring teenage drivers can be a great headache. Indeed, some parents have called it highway robbery. If you are paying too much to insure your teenage drivers, let GENERAL LIFE help. GENERAL LIFE can insure your teenager for 10 percent less than any large company in town.
2. Here is great news for the head of the family. Our health benefits now pay as much as 90 percent of the total hospital bill. When can we arrange to show you this policy?
3. Attention Policyholders: We are now offering the new dental coverage you have been asking for. You, as well as your family, will benefit greatly from this policy.
4. In response to the increased need, we are opening a central claims department to serve the entire company. Beginning January 2, all claims should be referred to the central claims department. This change will provide an efficient means of processing all claims.
5. My files show that it is now time to review your homeowner's insurance policy. May we get together soon? I will call this week for an appointment.

1

Gentlemen:

In your letter of April 13, you referred to a delay in our January shipment of[1] office supplies. We are sorry for any problems caused by the delay, but our copy of the invoice shows that[2] your supplies were shipped as soon as payment was received. May we suggest this method for getting your shipment of[3] envelopes on time? You can avoid delay by mailing your check by May 30. Your envelopes will be shipped on[4] June 7 or the following week.

If you follow this plan for future purchases, we can provide you with better[5] service.

Sincerely yours, (104)

2

Dear Jason:

Your recent appointment as vice president was great news. The company certainly made a wise choice.[1] As head of the shipping department, you provided many years of loyal service. It is reassuring to[2] see the company respond by giving you proper credit.

With your leadership, all departments will now operate[3] efficiently. I hope you will call on me to help in any way I can. As soon as you have some free time,[4] why don't we get together for lunch?

Very truly yours, (90)

3

Dear Sir:

Did you know that you may be paying between 15 and 20 percent too much for your insurance? Did[1] you also know that those policies may not cover the current value of your home and personal property?[2]

Now is the time to make certain that your benefits are all that you should have. Between March 15 and April 1,[3] our agent will call on you. Why not make it a point to have your policies ready for review?

Cordially yours,[4] (80)

4

MEMO TO: Vice President Fowler

In regard to your memo of September 5, the printing machines will be[1] situated in our plant by the beginning of December. As you know, we wanted to have them ready[2] early in October but could not arrange to have them shipped at that time. We have asked a total of 30 machine[3] operators to participate in a training program during November, but we have not received responses[4] from all of them.

Perhaps we should plan to hire new people to operate the machines. What do you suggest?[5] (100)

5

MEMO TO: Fred Gray

I can now give you our new policy for insuring machines shipped by truck. Will you inform[1] all participating dealers that beginning July 1 we will not replace machines damaged on the dealer's[2] property? If the dealers wish to discuss this matter, refer them to the claims department.

We ask that any[3] damage be shown on the invoice at the point of arrival.

We would like the dealers to be told of the changes[4] now. Within a few weeks, letters will be mailed giving full details of the new policy. (96)

6

MEMO TO: Manager of Boy's Wear

We will offer savings of between 20 and 30 percent on all[1] back-to-school needs—clothing, as well as supplies. All clothing should be marked down 20 percent. All school supplies will be[2] displayed between the boy's and girl's departments.

We will accept payment in the form of cash, credit cards, and personal[3] checks. Those persons wishing to cash payroll checks should be sent to the credit office. All personal checks should be[4] seen by the department manager.

We suggest your clerks remind all shoppers that clothing items may be returned[5] within one week following the purchase. (107)

LESSON 12

1. For words ending in a long vowel + *t* (*ate, ete, ite, ote, ute/oot*), omit the *t* and write the vowel.

rate, r-ate — right, write, r-ite
late, l-ate — might, m-ite

meet, m-ete — wrote, r-ote
beat, b-ete — boat, b-ote

cute, k-ute — suit, s-oot

Write these additional words which are used in the reading and writing exercises at the end of this lesson.

locate, l-k-ate — invite, in-v-ite
hesitate, h-z-t-ate — receipt, re-s-ete
defeated, d-f-ete-ed — promoted, pro-m-ote-ed
delighted, d-l-ite-ed — white, w-ite
vote, v-ote — fight, f-ite

Reviewing Proper Names. You have already learned how to write proper names. As a brief review exercise, read and write the following names. Each name is written according to the principles you have learned.

Janet, j-n-t — William, w-l-y-m
Pamela, p-m-l-a — David, d-v-d
Elizabeth, e-l-z-b-ith — Ronald, r-n-l-d
Claire, k-l-r — Martin, m-r-t-n
Shelley, ish-l-e — Jim, j-m
Barbara, b-r-b-r-a — Jeremy, j-r-m-e

PRINCIPLES SUMMARY

1. For words ending in a long vowel + *t*, omit the *t* and write the vowel: rate, r-ate *ra* .

Reading and Writing Exercises

-1-

d dvd i z dli- l hr
la u — P-o- l
dpl —yr. frd Slnl
Cz r ri Psn f r
jb, no la u r pl
v r —ym L i l
njy se u rglrl /
—e. i no la ls l
b. bze yr f u. f
u v Pbl—s lca
inf i hp u l cl
o —e. e a op z.
L hr. dN hzla l
asc f hlp. cu

Am v — i pN ,
du — —i lcl dlrs
b Fb 15. i —N v
—C l gl ls pN
+ bgn dcra —i
nu ofss, u L lls
—e la. rse f r pN
z enc-. r rse z n
n r L. l Al i
du, l i nd r rse
—n i gl r pN, f
so l u —l —e.
cpe ri a-a, cl
—e f lr, ne i
nd l du. uvl

-2-

1 i v. Pbl—.

-3-

d edlr brns e ⌣
dli- ⌣ ˏ gr cvry
u gv r fl crnvl,
e cd n v hp- f.
blr rsp ln e rsv-,
e r no nvr u l pp
n . evN e v b pln
f 2 yrs, ls evN l
b cl- ˏ vlj bo so,
ˏ bos l b Dpla-
n r vlj sp sMr,
ri no / lcs z lo
e ~a v s~ rlr
lry bos hr, if nes
loz bos l b lca-n
ˏ E prc ll, e r
pln l v bln 20 +
30 bos o Dpla f
1 ⌣c n Ap, l u
pln l ri . artcl l
rn du ˏ ⌣c v ˏ
so. e Aso sug rn
. artcl s~ la n
Mr, i fl Sln la i
cd ar . Pvu v ˏ
bos if la d hlp, y
dN e ~e f lnC l
Dcs ⌣as v P~ ˏ
so. s

-4-

dS enc- , u Jn bl,
if u pa ˏ tol a~l
b ˏ da sn o ˏ bl
u l sv me, flo la
da . 5% fe l b A-l
u bl, / d b ⌣z l
avyd la pams, if
u du da , . Pbl~ u
~u ⌣s l Dcs nu
bl das ⌣ r cr~yr,
if u cl f . apym ˏ

yr l b hpe l pln
. ve L. s

c, Ph / , n l la
l Cnj , m o ls dr.

-5-

mo l VP rbrls e
a Sprz- l lrn
la P i rzn- ,
ofs af / brd e.
z u no , Ppzl z
dfe- b . vo v 8 l 4.
evdNl / brds vo
z . dp Psnl Dapym,
e a fl sre la / P
fll / nes l rzn.
C v ls cos grl
z rla- l , ldrs. e
hp / P l dsd l
rn ls corp.
/ hlp yf u d
ri . L asc P i
l e / brd ls

-6-

d snlr rln z u
no s mbrs v r
grp v b nvlv- n .
fe l PvN ncrss n
yl + gsln ras. e
nvi u l hlp b vo l
dfe ls gsln bl, ls
bl d alo cos l dl
lr o ras. / d aso
Pvd nu plses f lca
yl o prps nr / se.
loz nu plses cd
b v dy l . gr No
v ppl n me as. e
hp la u l jyn r cz.
hlp s n ls fi. ul

Key

1

Dear David:

I was delighted to hear that you were promoted to department manager. Fred certainly chose[1] the right person for the job.

Now that you are part of the management team, I will enjoy seeing you regularly[2] at meetings. I know that this will be a busy year for you. If you have problems locating information,[3] I hope you will call on me. We all operate as a team here. Don't hesitate to ask for help.

Cordially yours,[4] (80)

2

Gentlemen:

I have a problem. A shipment of white paint is due at my local dealer's by February 15.[1] I want very much to get this paint and begin decorating my new offices.

Your letter tells me that[2] a receipt for the paint was enclosed. The receipt was not in the letter. What shall I do?

Will I need the receipt[3] when I get the paint? If so, will you mail me a copy right away?

Call me if there is anything I need to[4] do.

Yours very truly, (84)

3

Dear Editor Burns:

We were delighted with the great coverage you gave our fall carnival. We could not have hoped[1] for a better response than we received.

We are now inviting you to participate in an event we have[2] been planning for two years. This event will be called the Village Boat Show. The boats will be displayed in our village shopping[3] center. Right now it looks as though we may have some rather large boats here. If necessary, those boats will be located[4] in the east parking lot.

We are planning to have between 20 and 30 boats on display for one week[5] in April.

Will you plan to write an article to run during the week of the show? We also suggest running[6] an article sometime late in March. I feel certain that I could arrange a preview of the boats if that would help.[7]

Why don't we meet for lunch to discuss ways of promoting the show?

Sincerely, (154)

4

Dear Sir:

Enclosed is your June billing. If you pay the total amount by the date shown on the bill, you will save money.[1] Following that date, a 5 percent fee will be added to your bill.

It would be wise to avoid late payments.[2] If your due date is a problem, you might wish to discuss new billing dates with our credit manager. If you call[3] for an appointment, the manager will be happy to plan a meeting time.

Sincerely, (76)

5

MEMO TO: Vice President Roberts

We were all surprised to learn that President White resigned his office after[1] the board meeting. As you know, his proposal was defeated by a vote of 8 to 4. Evidently, the board's[2] vote was a deep personal disappointment.

We all feel sorry that the president felt it necessary to[3] resign. Much of this company's growth was related to his leadership. We hope the president will decide to[4] remain with this corporation. It might help if you would write a letter asking President White to meet with the[5] board this week. Perhaps it is not too late to change his mind on this matter. (113)

6

Dear Senator Martin:

As you know, some members of our group have been involved in a fight to prevent increases[1] in oil and gasoline rates. We invite you to help by voting to defeat this gasoline bill.

This bill would[2] allow companies to determine their own rates. It would also provide new policies for locating oil on[3] properties near the sea. Those new policies could be very damaging to a great number of people in many[4] ways. We hope that you will join our cause. Help us win this fight.

Yours truly, (92)

LESSON 13

1. Write for the word beginning *an*.

answer, an-s-r

anticipate, an-t-s-p-ate

antique, an-t-k

analyze, an-l-z

2. Write for the medial or final sound of any vowel + *nk* (*ank*, *enk*, *ink*, *onk*, *unk*).

bank, b-ank

length, l-enk-ith

blank, b-l-ank

rank, r-ank

thank, ith-ank

link, l-ink

Abbreviations

junior

second, secretary

senior

Brief Forms

am, more

go, good

charge

he, had, him

doctor, direct

they

Phrasing. We use some word combinations, such as *we are* and *to be*, so often that we usually say them and read them as a group. In shorthand, we take advantage of this natural association by joining words together in one outline. We call this practice *phrasing*.

we are

to be

The pronouns *I*, *we*, and *you* followed by a verb and the word *to* followed by a verb can be easily written and recognized as phrases.

I am	you are
I can	you can
we are	to be
we can	to go

With experience in taking dictation, phrases will occur to you naturally as you write. The context, or meaning, of the sentence will help you read the phrase correctly when you see it in your notes.

The following phrases will be used in the reading and writing exercises in this and following lessons.

I am	you are
I can	you can
I had	you have
I have	you know
I will	you will
I will be	you would
we are	to be
we can	to go
we have	to have
we hope	to have you
we would	to have your
we would be	to know
	to pay

Writing Contractions. When writing contractions that might be read back as a phrase, use an apostrophe to avoid confusion.

I will | I'll
you will | you'll
we are | we're

Words Omitted in High-Frequency Phrases. A few word combinations occur together so frequently that certain words within the combinations may be omitted from your shorthand notes. Three such high-frequency phrases are *thank you for, thank you for your,* and *thank you for your letter.*

*thank *you* for | thank *you* for *your*
thank *you* for *your* letter

*Italicized words have been omitted in the shorthand outlines.

PRINCIPLES SUMMARY

1. Write for the word beginning *an*: answer, an-s-r .
2. Write for the medial or final sound of any vowel + *nk*: bank, b-ank .

Reading and Writing Exercises

Watch for phrases beginning with the words *I*, *we*, *you*, and *to*.

SERIES A

1. (dr gv h . q rpl + sN h h⌒ ,

) cr + ar . ln f (f a‿d ×

2. h ‿Ns lq a‿a f . srl L ,

3. e h . dla n (dr fli f⌒ dnvz l sn frnssco ,

4. ⌒ pln l G ⌒ ln h Gs ,

5. h , no sr VP v (bq ,

SERIES B

1. alC- , . L f⌒ bl s‿d asc l rapli f . ln , c e rass

2. ls L , l nf⌒ u la u pam z du o (30l , f lr , s⌒ rzn y u cn pa (lol a‿d ll s no , e l dl . nu mm pam bs- o (a‿d u c pa ,

3. e jnl ‿d r bl o (15l , f u rel u pam ‿n , ‿c u l b cr- ‿ . sv u sv l a‿d l 2% v (lol bl ,

4. r bq l grN (sec

rgj la u apli-f,
e l Stnl lri l fnlz
ln + v me rde
f u bln das v
Aq 30 + Sp 6, n
nl s f r
fr l vzl prp l
c. assm v
crN vlu,

5. f ls py o u Cgs
l b Pss-b. nu
yr asn- l gv u
Psnl all la u
nd, f u l Dcs
. bl Psyr u a cl la
Psn drl, h or se l
rsp ol dla,

-1-

dr sd er v. gr
No v Pbls r
yc Ur bq ans.
evdNl ly n
Pq- l ac G crds
f ls sle. l ev
l rpls ans.
er hp la uc hlp
s avyd du la.
nu ans sl f.
hi prs l r uz-
ans r rl lll
ln jq> r r
yr, pln Ub n
sn frnssco v sn.
cd u e h. cu

ndd rq u lp
v u cls. edb gld
lvu apli. enc
. co blln C l
spli me v asrs
u nd> Alo jnl e
nd secs o . f=L
bss e s v . fu
pl=L opn f hi scl
jrs + srs> bl gra
, . sr hu, fn+,
sec yr r fr. l
suq la u lc h.
uc Aso gl inf
f r Psnl yr rc
lc. if u cn se h Psnll
, sec l gv u apo
fs l fl ol. vlu

-2-

dM adrsn lqf L
re jbs f hi scl
srs. u grds du

-3-

ds lr rel

- blq Cc u sN s
b Mlc. ehp la ul
—l s . sec Cc —ol
dla. bcz uv . q cr
rq ul n b G- . la fe,
ed lc l suq la u
uz r prN-envs f
—l u pams. loz
envs r adrs-l -
cr dpl + u pams
l b sN drl l - Ppr
ofs, lqf gv ls —lr
u all. ul

-4-

d bb lqf Avs o -
frq nlsn cs. frq
l b gld lno la . sr
mbr v - fr , l lq
l bl f h. frq + l v
h enf — l Dcs ,
Pbl— - lql. Alo h
dz n alspa rsv ,
old rq frq blvs la
. gr No v ppl l bnfl
uf h —ns ls cs. l
lq h , ri + ér hp -
jj lqs so l, íl Sml
ll uno uf uc hlp.
cu

-5-

ddr a—s l —N u
lno la — lc f
— alc frn f u
ofs. w lca- . dsc
+ Cr —C l lq ul
lc b — afrd la
- lql v - dsc ,
n ri f u ofs. —l
d b . q — f u l lc
/ / x> l Aso no v

. ns alc dsc f u
sec, u'l lv c li
oc fn4, l lq / d
b ⌒ apo f u ‿a
r⌒ ln f u ofs, e
⌒i v i Pbl⌒, c
4p ⌒yr, G . gr
dl ⌒ ln u ⌒a ‿4
lpa, Ph ec gl h l
lc ls, ll ⌒e no
‿n ic 4o u lz fn
alcs, su

-6-

d⌒s jcsn lgf asr
l ⌒i L, c bclls u

sN l grl hlp ⌒e
n du . rSC ppr
du ls lr⌒, l alspa
fn4 c ppr n 2 ‿cs,
c ol Pbl⌒ iv h,
obln dla f⌒ cos
lca- ol v lon, ol v
. lol v 7 iv hrd
f⌒ ol 4, ‿ no
‿a f rsps f⌒ c
r⌒n 3 bf alz c
fnl rzllts, ul Slnl
rsv . cpe v ⌒i
fn4- rpl, ul

Key

SERIES A

1. The doctor gave him a good report and sent him home.
2. He wants to go away for a short time.
3. We had a delay in the direct flight from Denver to San Francisco.
4. I am planning to charge more than he charges.
5. He is now senior vice president of the bank.

SERIES B

1. Attached is a letter from Bill Smith asking to reapply for a loan. Can we reassess his credit and arrange a loan for the full amount?
2. This letter is to inform you that your payment was due on the 30th. If there is some reason why you cannot pay the total amount, let us know. We will determine a new minimum payment based on the amount you can pay.
3. We generally mail our billings on the 15th. If you return your payment within one week, you will be credited with a savings. Your savings will amount to 2 percent of the total bill.
4. Our bank will grant the second mortgage that you applied for. We will certainly try to finalize the loan and have the money ready for you between the dates of August 30 and September 6. In the meantime, someone from our firm will visit the property to make an assessment of the current value.
5. From this point on, your charges will be processed by a new manager assigned to give you the personal attention that you need. If you wish to discuss a billing procedure, you may call that person directly. He or she will respond without delay.

1

Dear Mr. Smith:

We are having a great number of problems with our Magic Teller bank machines. Evidently[1] they were not programmed to accept charge cards from this city. Will we have to replace the machines? We are hoping that[2] you can help us avoid doing that. New machines sell for a high price, while our used machines are worth little more than junk.[3]

Our marketing manager is planning to be in San Francisco very soon. Could you meet with him?

Cordially[4] yours, (81)

2

Dear Miss Anderson:

Thank you for your letter regarding jobs for high school seniors. Your grades do indeed rank you at[1] the top of your class. We would be glad to have you apply. I am enclosing a company bulletin which will[2] supply many of the answers you need.

Although generally we need secretaries on a full-time basis,[3] we sometimes have a few part-time openings for high school juniors and seniors.

Bill Gray is a senior who is[4] finishing his second year with our firm. I suggest that you talk with him. You can also get more information from[5] our personnel manager, Mark Lee. If you cannot see him personally, his secretary will give you the[6] appropriate forms to fill out.

Very truly yours, (129)

3

Dear Ms. Miller:

I am returning the blank check you sent us by mistake. We hope that you will mail us a second[1] check without delay. Because you have a good credit rating, you will not be charged a late fee.

We would like to[2] suggest that you use our printed envelopes for mailing your payments. Those envelopes are addressed to the credit[3] department, and your payments will be sent directly to the proper office.

Thank you for giving this matter your[4] attention.

Yours truly, (84)

4

Dear Bob:

Thank you for your advice on the Frank Nelson case. Frank will be glad to know that a senior member of the[1] firm is willing to go to bat for him. Frank and I have had enough time to discuss his problem at length. Although[2] he does not anticipate receiving his old rank, Frank believes that a great number of people will benefit[3] if he wins this case. I think he is right, and we're hoping the judge thinks so too.

I'll certainly let you know if you[4] can help.

Cordially yours, (84)

5

Dear Dr. Ames:

I want you to know that I am looking for more antique furnishings for your office. I have[1] located a desk and chair which I think you will like, but I am afraid that the length of the desk is not right for your[2] office. What would be a good time for you to look at it?

I also know of a nice antique desk for your[3] secretary. You'll love the light oak finish. I think it would be more appropriate for your waiting room than for your[4] office. We might have one problem. The shop manager is charging a great deal more than you may wish to pay. Perhaps we[5] can get him to take less. Let me know when I can show you these fine antiques.

Sincerely yours, (116)

6

Dear Ms. Jackson:

Thank you for your answer to my letter. The booklets you sent will greatly help me in doing a[1] research paper due this term.

I anticipate finishing the paper in two weeks. The only problem I've had[2] is obtaining data from companies located out of town. Out of a total of seven, I have heard from[3] only four. I am now waiting for responses from the remaining three before analyzing the final[4] results.

You will certainly receive a copy of my finished report.

Yours truly, (94)

LESSON 14

RECAP AND REVIEW

You have earned another rest. No principles will be introduced in Lesson 14. Use this review to pinpoint any principles or outlines you need to practice.

1. Here are the word beginnings you studied in Lessons 8-13:

dis D

per, pur p

pre, pro, pro *(prah)* p

mis m

an a

2. The following word endings were also presented:

long vowel + t

*a*te a

*e*te e

*i*te i

*o*te o

*u*te/*oo*t u

ly l

gram g

3. The following words illustrate all of the principles you studied in Lessons 8-13:

dismay, dis-m-a

mistake, mis-t-k

recently, re-s-nt-ly

rate, r-ate

health, h-l-ith

reapply, re-a-p-l-i

answer, an-s-r

person, per-s-n

purpose, pur-p-s

prevent, pre-v-nt

program, pro-gram

loyal, l-oi-l

payroll, p-a-r-l

bank, b-ank

4. Months of the year are written this way:

January

February

March

April

May

June

July

August

September

October

November

December

5. Can you automatically write these brief forms? If you are unsure of any brief form, practice the outline until you can write it without hesitation.

that	arrange	were
participate	between	ship
response	great	as
was	with	hospital
those	situate	general
refer	property	operate
respond	suggest	am
more	direct	doctor
charge	go	he
good	had	they
him	point	

6. How do you write these brief form derivatives?

arrangement	generally	operators
within	without	wasn't
greatly	referred	shipping

7. How quickly can you read the following abbreviations?

cr	No	ins
re	all	a~l
%	env	dpl
inv	lol	jr
sr	sec	

Reading and Writing Exercises

-1-

d r bron , dlis
e l nf u la r
cr dpl agre- l c
lol a l v u ln.
ec Aso ar f. don
pam v bln 12 +
15 %, u ln z rf-
l c cr yr + /
rsv- cls all. z
u a no er v
Pbls gl prp lns
lru. / z . hlp la u
prp , lca- nr c nu
hsp. la As . gr dl l
c vlu v u prp, d
u rel c enc-
agrem n c env
Pvd-x e l nd u
rsp b Fb 10. su

-2-

mo l A Psnl hr ,
gr nz f loz v u hu
lc- r old hll pln.
ul lv r nu l, bgn
Ag 15 e l ofr . nu
plse C l Pvd me
v c bnfls uv b asc
f. / l pa z C z
80% v c lol hsp
bl. / Aso pas dcl
fes + Pvds dNl cvrj
z l, ls pln uc
ar f c ins co lpa u
dcl bls f u. lr l
b no nd f u l ri.
Cc v u o. ls Svs l
sv L + me f u,
loz v u l lrn
c dlls v ls pln l

b nvi-l Dcs / n
. ne / r ofs.

-3-

d szn e l sn b op
nu ldrs. rsNl
brd vo-l apy.
nu P. . No v ms
sug-. . ofr z d
ri a a b Psn
Czn dd n ac, / ls
ic sa la e nvi-
. v fn Psn l ac r
ofr + se rsp-l l
/ hr n l b gvn
/ brd e o Oc 4.
ehp la A brd mbrs
l b lr l pp. l u c
arms f s , Ub lr
f eC v r dpls. ul

-4-

d r evns ls, n
rsp l u L U s y
e dd n rsv Ja
sm. w Dcs-
Pbl ppl +
c no U u l hpn-
e dd v s , o dle /
sm arv-
b sm z n brl l
ri pls, n fCr
d u nf u lrc fr
la A sms sd arv
/ rsv dc o E
sd v r bld. e l
b Sln lv . Psn lr /
a l sn inv
+ ac sm. vlu

-5-

d bl ch . q e

dr jns. h lqs e
sd PCs r dl
S80 unl. / Pvds
. dr lq bln r opr
+ r sNrl mre
bq. ls , . nu Pq
Cc b ofr- / .
mm Cq, dr jns
fls la . sec unl
d alo s l op evn
efsNl. il b gld
lvu Avs, du u alspa
q l r e n ls vgs.
ilb lr if uc gl . dr
fli f dnvz. vlu

3d b z rsv- o r 9l.
r Jn + Jl sms arv-
nrl 2 cs la, ls
Pbl a v b cz- b
r rsN v. r L
v Ap 2 asc- u l
dla r Ma sm l
e gl sil- n r
nu bld. Ph e dd
n sa n l rz
4 / r rglr da.
uv r apljes f r
Mld sj, e no
4 l rel l r old
scjl. ul

-6-

d rs gbsn r sms
v b arv af r du da.
r Ma pcj z du o r

Key

Brief Forms

la	ar	⌣
pp	bln	ꞩ
rsp	gr	z
z	⌣	hsp
loz	sil	jn
rf	prp	op
rsp	sug	⌢
⌢	dr	dr
Cq	q	h
q	h	ly
h	py	

Brief Form Derivatives

arm	jnl	oprs
⌣n	⌣ol	zN
grl	rf-	ꞩ̲

Abbreviations

credit	number	insurance
regard	attention	amount
percent	envelope	department
invoice	total	junior
senior	second, secretary	

1

Dear Mr. Brown:

It delights me to inform you that our credit department agreed to the total amount of[1] your loan. We can also arrange for a down payment of between 12 and 15 percent.

Your loan was referred to[2] the credit manager, and it received close attention. As you may know, we are having problems getting property[3] loans through. It was a help that your property is located near the new hospital. That adds a great deal to[4] the value of your property.

Would you return the enclosed agreement in the envelope provided? We will[5] need your response by February 10.

Sincerely yours, (110)

2

MEMO TO: All Personnel

Here is great news for those of you who liked our old health plan. You will love our new one.[1]

Beginning August 15, we will offer a new policy which will provide many of the benefits you have[2] been asking for. It will pay as much as 80 percent of the total hospital bill. It also pays medical[3] fees and provides dental coverage as well.

With this plan, you can arrange for the insurance company to[4] pay your medical bills for you. There will be no need for you to write a check of your own. This service will save time[5] and money for you.

Those of you wishing to learn the details of this plan will be invited to discuss it in[6] a meeting at our office. (124)

3

Dear Susan:

We will soon be operating with new leadership. Recently the board voted to appoint a new[1] president. A number of names were suggested. An offer was made right away, but the person chosen did not[2] accept.

At this time I can say that we invited a very fine person to accept our offer, and she[3] responded well to it. Her name will be given at the board meeting on October 4. We hope that all board[4] members will be there to participate. Will you make arrangements for someone to be there from each of our departments?[5]

Yours truly, (102)

4

Dear Mr. Evans:

This is in response to your letter telling us why we did not receive the January[1] shipment. I have discussed the problem with my people and can now tell you what happened.

We did have someone on duty[2] at the time the shipment arrived, but the shipment was not brought to the right place.

In the future, would you inform[3] your trucking firm that all shipments should arrive at the receiving dock on the east side of our building? We will be[4] certain to have a person there at all times to sign the invoice and accept the shipment.

Very truly yours,[5] (100)

5

Dear Bill:

I had a good meeting with Dr. James. He thinks we should purchase the model S80 unit. It[1] provides a direct link between the operator and the central memory bank. This is a new program which can[2] be offered at a minimum charge.

Dr. James feels that a second unit would allow us to operate even[3] more efficiently. I'll be glad to have your advice.

Do you anticipate going to the meetings in Las[4] Vegas? I will be there if I can get a direct flight from Denver.

Very truly yours, (96)

6

Dear Mrs. Gibson:

Our shipments have been arriving after the due date. Our May package was due on the 3rd but[1] was received on the 9th. Our June and July shipments arrived nearly two weeks late.

This problem may have been caused by[2] our recent move. Our letter of April 2 asked you to delay the May shipment while we were getting situated[3] in the new building. Perhaps we did not say when to resume shipping at the regular date. You have our[4] apologies for the misleading message.

We now wish to return to the old schedule.

Yours truly, (98)

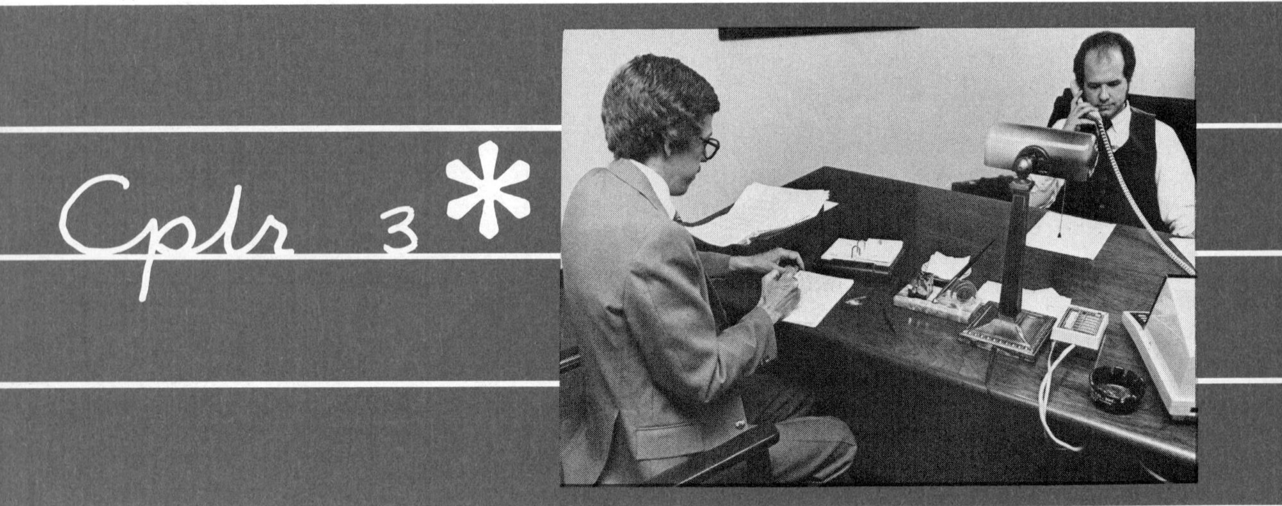

WHAT IS MEANT BY DICTATION AND TRANSCRIPTION?

Shorthand is a two-part process: **taking dictation** and **transcribing.** Since both are equally important to your success, let's take a look at the skills you'll need for each.

Taking Dictation. The ability to write shorthand continuously is a skill which comes with study and practice. As you move forward in this text, your speed and confidence will increase. Later, when you are on the job and taking dictation regularly, your writing efficiency will increase even more. You will become familiar with your supervisor's style of dictating and with the words used most often in your office. You will learn to write common phrases and terms as quickly as you hear them.

There are many techniques and habits that you should develop *now*—before on-the-job training begins. These techniques and habits, or dictation aids, will help you record dictation in a way that is efficient for you and your supervisor.

***Chapter Three**

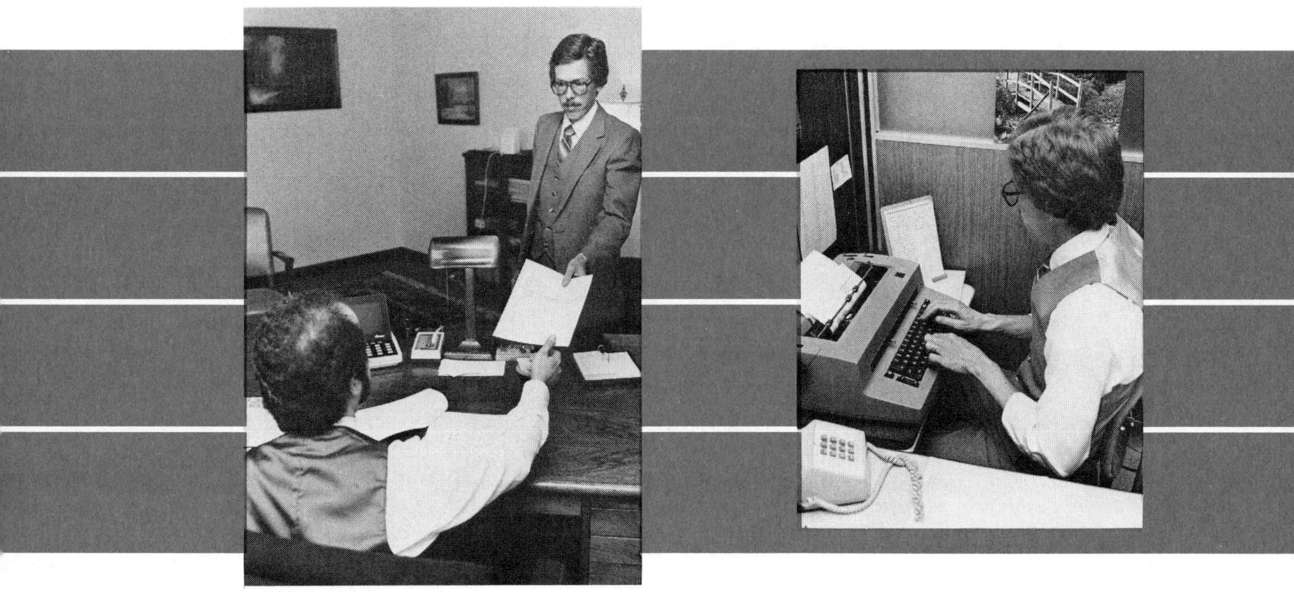

Transcribing Dictation. Transcription is the process of converting shorthand notes into mailable, printed form. The equipment you use may be as simple as a typewriter or as sophisticated as a word processor. Whatever the equipment, you'll need the ability to type (or keyboard) accurately; spell correctly (plan to keep a dictionary nearby); and punctuate as needed (no misplaced commas, please).

All transcribed documents have one thing in common—they should be absolutely free of errors.

Because transcription skills are so important, this text will present **Transcription Aids.** Beginning in Lesson 16, spelling words will be highlighted in each lesson. Those selected for practice are among the most commonly misspelled words in business correspondence.

Beginning in Lesson 22, basic rules for punctuation will be presented. The rules will be simple, but very important. They are the most commonly used punctuation rules in business correspondence.

If spelling and punctuation are not among your favorite subjects, don't despair. You are not alone! You will, however, need these skills to be successful in any office.

LESSON 15

1. Write a printed capital S (disjoined) for the word beginning *super.*

supervise, super-v-z Svz

superman, super-m-n Smn

supermarket, super-market Smr

supersonic, super-s-n-k Ssnc

superpower, super-p-ow-r Spor

supervisor, super-v-z-r Svzr

2. Write a printed capital S (disjoined) also for the word endings *scribe* and *script,* and for the sound of *scrip.*

describe, d-scribe dS

inscribe, in-scribe nS

described, d-scribe-duh dS-

script S

prescribe, pre-scribe PS

*manuscripts, m-n-script-s mnSs

*A disjoined word ending is disjoined from the letters which precede it, not from those which follow it.

3. Write el for the word beginning *electr.*

electric, electr-k elc

electrical, electr-k-l elcl

electronic, electr-n-k elnc

electronically, electr-n-k-ly elncl

More About Phrases. In Lesson 13, you learned to write phrases beginning with *I*, *we*, *you*, and *to*. You can also write other very common word groups as phrases. The following phrases are among those that appear in the reading and writing exercises in this and following lessons.

I could	icd	will be	lb	
I hope	ihp	would be	db	
to see	lse	it is	s	
for the	f	it's	's	(contraction)
of the	v	its	s	(possessive)
that you	lau	that your	lau	

Your Business Vocabulary

supermarket chain S-r Cn — A group of large grocery stores owned by the same individual or corporation.

programming Pg- — Providing a computer with programs, which are sets of coded instructions.

PRINCIPLES SUMMARY

1. Write a printed capital S (disjoined) for the word beginning *super*: supervise, super-v-z Svz.
2. Write a printed capital S (disjoined) for the sound of *scrip* and the word endings *scribe* and *script*: describe, d-scribe dS; manuscripts, m-n-script-s mSs.
3. Write el for the word beginning electr: electric, electr-k elc.

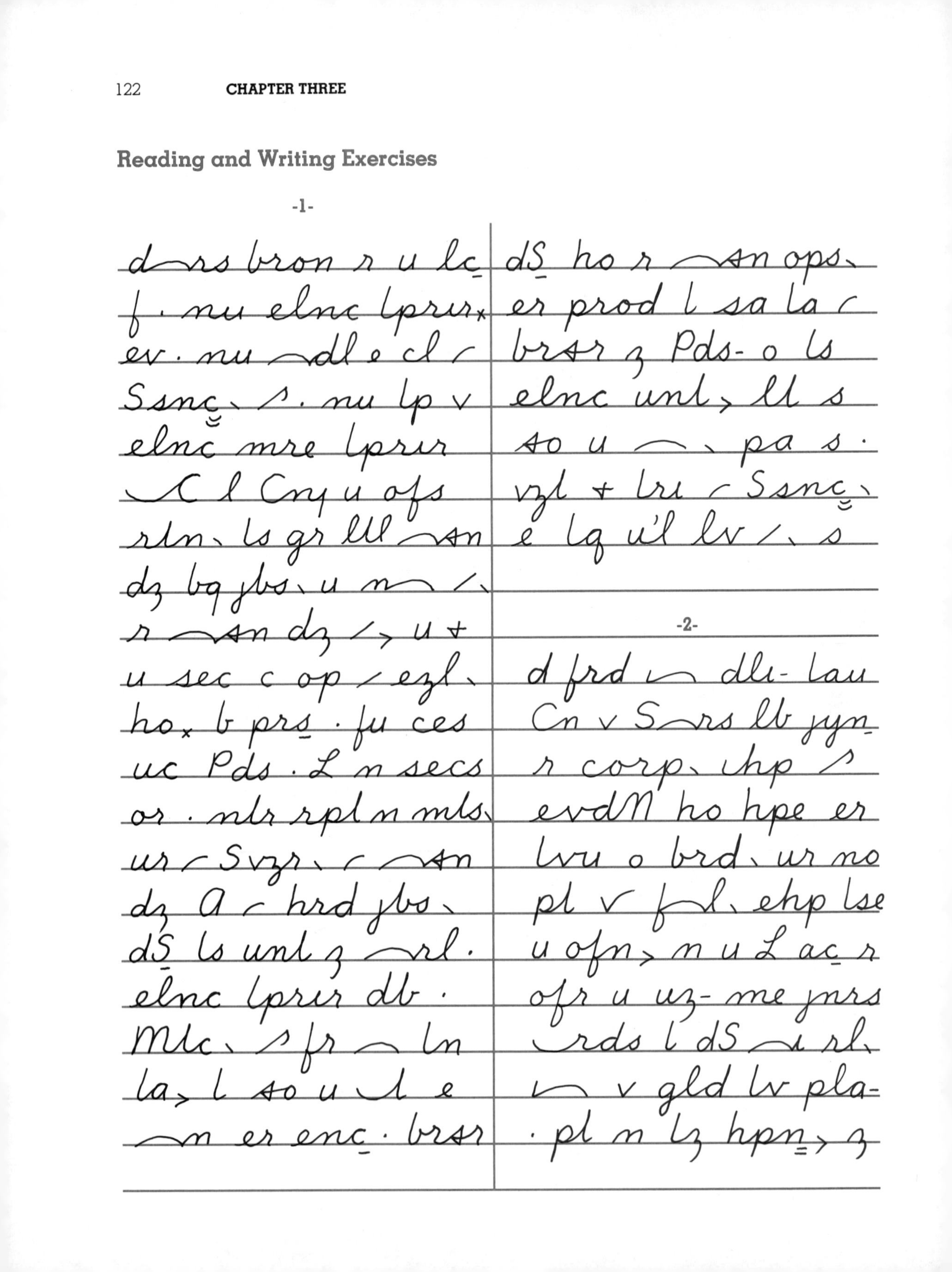

Reading and Writing Exercises

-1-

-2-

. er Sln l aCv
me Cnys n ls fr,
's q lno lau lb
Svz Cn, uvl

re . a dS , jb, i
suq la e pls / n
nynr jrnls +
se l hpns, ul

-3-

ddr evns dr grn
Avz- e la h l n
b lC f s ls fl, z
uno dr grn , .
elcl nynr + hd
v nynr dpl hr, h
, lv r scl l jyn
. lcl fr, z VP h l
Svz elnc Pq f nlr
corp, er hpe f dr
grn b sre lse h
q, h l n b eze l
rpls b corps c pa
elcl nynrs ln
ec, dr grn , ofr l

-4-

d dvd afrd il
v lb a a f ofs
f . c or so . du
u lrp ol W i
nyr- u bc n . bd
fl, dr PS- dsn
+ . c n bd, hp
la , Avs l slv
Pbl, if / dz n
dr a v l op, /
d ln b nes f e
l lc . dcl lv v
3 l 4 cs, il ll
uno z sn z
ic, n nl i

pln l cp ri / h .
nrl fns- (
rpl + fl Sln la uc
Svz (rSC b fn z
ezl z ucd n (ofs . s

-5-

d evln l unf du
uv o elnc gs×
er lq v a 2 nu
dls l r cal .
+ rs S n , . g
apo f ppl bln (
ajs v 7 + 15 . er Aso

lc / . dl cl-
Ssnc spst . (py
v ls g , l PvN .
r bln 2 Spors .
ppl v a ajs lc ls
g > (r f elnc
gs , Cny rpdl .
ho r e lno C
gs l ofr× e rll
nd (bnfl v u
nlf . N u rsp
z sn z uc× cu

Key

1

Dear Mrs. Brown:

Are you looking for a new electronic typewriter? We have a new model we call the[1] SUPERSONIC. It is a new type of electronic memory typewriter which will change your office routine.[2] This great little machine does big jobs. You name it. Our machine does it.

You and your secretary can operate it[3] easily. How? By pressing a few keys, you can produce a letter in seconds or an entire report in minutes.[4] You are the supervisor. The machine does all the hard jobs. Describing this unit as merely an electronic[5] typewriter would be a mistake. It is far more than that.

To show you what we mean, we are enclosing a brochure[6] describing how our machine operates. We are proud to say that the brochure was produced on this electronic[7] unit.

Let us show you more. Pay us a visit and try the SUPERSONIC. We think you'll love it.

Sincerely,[8] (160)

2

Dear Fred:

I am delighted that your chain of supermarkets will be joining our corporation. I hope it is[1] evident how happy we are to have you on board. You are now part of the family. We hope to see you[2] often.

In your letter accepting our offer, you used many generous words to describe my role. I am very[3] glad to have played a part in these happenings.

As a team, we are certain to achieve many changes in this firm.[4] It's good to know that you will be supervising the chain.

Yours very truly, (94)

3

Dear Dr. Evans:

Dr. Green advised me that he will not be teaching for us this fall. As you know, Dr. Green[1] is an electrical engineer and head of the engineering department here. He is leaving our school to[2] join a local firm. As vice president, he will supervise electronic programming for the entire corporation.[3]

We are happy for Dr. Green, but sorry to see him go. He will not be easy to replace, but[4] corporations can pay electrical engineers more than we can.

Dr. Green is offering to write an ad[5] describing his job. I suggest that we place it in the engineering journals and see what happens.

Yours truly,[6] (120)

4

Dear David:

I am afraid I will have to be away from the office for a week or so. During my trip out[1] West, I injured my back in a bad fall. The doctor prescribed medicine and a week in bed. I am hoping that[2] his advice will solve the problem. If it does not, the doctor may have to operate. It would then be necessary[3] for me to take a medical leave of three to four weeks.

I will let you know more as soon as I can. In the[4] meantime, I plan to keep writing at home. I am nearly finished with the report and feel certain that I can[5] supervise the research by phone as easily as I could in the office.

Sincerely, (116)

5

Dear Evelyn:

What information do you have on electronic games? We are thinking of adding two new[1] models to our catalog. MR. AND MRS. SUPERMAN is a game appropriate for people between the[2] ages of seven and fifteen. We are also looking at a model called SUPERSONIC SPACESHIP. The point of this[3] game is to prevent a war between two superpowers. People of all ages like this game.

The market for[4] electronic games is changing rapidly. How are we to know which games to offer? We really need the benefit[5] of your knowledge. Won't you respond as soon as you can?

Cordially yours, (112)

LESSON 16

1. Write for the word ending *ward.*

backward, b-k-ward

downward, d-ow-n-ward

forward, for-ward

toward, to-ward

rewarding, re-ward-ing

awards, a-ward-s

2. Write for the word ending *hood.*

boyhood, b-oi-hood

neighborhood, n-b-r-hood

girlhood, gay-r-l-hood

likelihood, l-k-ly-hood

childhood, chay-l-d-hood

parenthood, p-r-nt-hood

Abbreviations

avenue

hour

boulevard

record

day

example, executive

month

Brief Forms

appreciate

distribute

please, up

present

specific, specify

correspond, correspondence

Brief Form and Abbreviated Word Development

upon	po	pleasing	p-
today	td	specifically	spl
daily	dl	monthly	ol

Phrases. Look for the following phrases in the reading and writing exercises that follow.

I would	id	you can be	ucb
I would appreciate	idap	you would like	udlc
I would be	idb	and the	
we should	esd	at the	
we will	el	that we	tae
we would appreciate	edap		

Your Business Vocabulary

likelihood lclh	The probability that something will happen.
specify sp	To state explicitly.
company records co recs	Items kept on file (letters, reports, contracts, receipts, and so on).

TRANSCRIPTION AID Learn to spell correctly.

Correct spelling is so important to business correspondence that even one error can spoil a letter. Spelling errors not only embarrass the typist, they also reflect poorly upon the executive and detract from the company's image.

To build spelling skills, learn to rely upon the dictionary. Look up any word you are not sure about; read the definition and the correct spelling for that particular usage.

Some words are so commonly misspelled that it is difficult to detect an error in them. As your transcription skills grow, you will learn to identify these problem words. This text will highlight some of these problem words in the lessons.

Commonly Misspelled Words

The following words will be used in your reading exercises. They have similar sounds but totally different meanings, depending upon how they are spelled and used. Notice how their meanings differ in each of the sentences below.

their — tr — (shows possessive for more than one): Please tell the *Smiths* that *their* payment is overdue.

there — tr — (used to designate a place): We will be *there* on Friday.

there — tr — (used in place of the subject): *There* will be six vice presidents at the meeting.

PRINCIPLES SUMMARY

1. Write w for the word ending *ward*: backward, b-k-ward bcw.
2. Write h for the word ending *hood*: boyhood, b-oi-hood byh.

Reading and Writing Exercises

SERIES A

1. idap if ud sp
   ihs u lse.

2. p ll e no if
   ucb P e.

3. e pln l D loz
   ans l sp dlrs
   n ls lon.

4. ll e no n
   u h , p.

5. hu l P Pq f s?

v u ave or blvd
f r recs.

2. du ls o er asc
   eC Psn l rec
   hr la h or se arvs
   eC d.

3. r sno , . ex
   r fr.

4. il so u . ex v
   cor er lc f.

5. ho ofn du u cor
   h?

SERIES B

1. p gv e n

-1-

dr jns r sr cls
z p- l lrn lau lv-
n r lon du u Cldh.
z. ex n. lrj corp
ur. q ex v s_ , f
r o nbrh hu _v-
p l c lp v , fld. ev
vo- u. aw + r nvi
u Ub P / r aws ni
o Mr , du c Pq el
P. lc / fCr + edap
v u vus o ofs crrs.
f ex _l r s_ sp
scls la exs + secs
nd. ev hrd la me
cos r hr no. _l ,
c lclh la el gl q
jbs, ne Avs udlc
l gv s l hlp s pln
r fCrs. l _c cpes
v u rsp + D_ l
c nlr cls. vlu

-2-

d hord u L brl bc
plzN byh mres f
c ds _n i z gro
p o clf ave. U u cls
idb p- l ac lr aw
n Psn. ll _e no
_l hrs udlc _e
Ub P, s rw lno
la ur lc ahd. lr
r me isus fs exs
ld b c Cf Pbl ,
lca q ppl l cp c
ofs rn efsNl,
ne q ex rlis po c
hlp v. scl- sec.
secs nd. _d rnf
v scls f _ co
recs l Pds cor la

, fre v errs. h or
se Aso nds lb .
Psn hu rlas l l A
lps v ppl, i lc fw
l e u + Dcs lz
usus n grr dtl. su

suq lau l nlss
l ppl u cor o .
rglr bss. edb hpe
l splı u apo
frs. cu

-3-

drs grn lqfL
nf s lau l
adrs lb Cnj sn.
el c Cnj n r
recs z sn z e
rsv enc- f.
p gv s sp inf f
fw u cor. prN or
lp u hos No + f
n v u ave or blvd.
b Sln l sp o
+ du l bgn rsv
l u nu adrs, e

-4-

dmbrs lpc v ls
os e lb "grlh
drs." e lb hld
n old scl bld o N
sr blvd. Ph ec A
sr Cldh mres l
er lr, p nls la r
e , b - p l .
nu hr. z Aso
suq-lae Cnj r rglr
e d. p b Ppr- l
Dcs lr esd
p lw bgn v
o, l D cpes v

r rsN Sva n ⌣C
e asc- u l sp gls
f nu yr, u asrs
⌣ v rw + i lc
fw l sr ⌐ ⌣ u,
ihp ul A b P, vlu

-5-

d hnre lqf fw .
sl v u dzns f
nu elc nzn, no
la ev h s ⌐
l lc ⌐ er
dli- l sa la e

lq uv gvn s .
fn ex f fCr z
l z ⌐ P, ev dsd-
l D cpes l r fld
nznrs + ev asc-
⌐ l rsp n 30
ds, n A lclh el
hr f ⌐ evn bf
ln, ⌐ sr ul b z
egr z ⌐ lse lr
rpls so l fw
⌐ z sn z ic,
e ap ⌐ efsN Svs
uv gvn s, su

Key

SERIES A

1. I would appreciate it if you would specify the items you wish to see.
2. Please let me know if you can be present at the meeting.
3. We plan to distribute those machines to specific dealers in this town.
4. Let me know when my time is up.
5. Who will present the program for us?

SERIES B

1. Please give me the name of your avenue or boulevard for our records.
2. During this month, we are asking each person to record the hour that he or she arrives each day.
3. Mr. Snow is an executive with our firm.
4. I will show you an example of the correspondence we are looking for.
5. How often do you correspond with him?

1

Dear Mr. Jones:

Our senior class was pleased to learn that you lived in our town during your childhood. As an executive[1] in a large corporation, you are a good example of someone from our own neighborhood who moved up to[2] the top of his field. We have voted you an award and are inviting you to be present at our awards night[3] on March 1.

During the program, we will present a look at the future, and we would appreciate having your[4] views on office careers. For example, what are some specific skills that executives and secretaries need?[5] We have heard that many companies are hiring now. What is the likelihood that we will get good jobs?

Any advice[6] you would like to give us will help us plan our futures. I will make copies of your response and distribute them[7] to the entire class.

Very truly yours, (148)

2

Dear Howard:

Your letter brought back pleasant boyhood memories from the days when I was growing up on College[1] Avenue. Tell your class I would be pleased to accept their award in person. Let me know what hours you would like me to[2] be present.

It is rewarding to know that you are looking ahead. There are many issues facing executives[3] today, but the chief problem is locating good people to keep the office running efficiently.

Any[4] good executive relies upon the help of a skilled secretary. Secretaries need a wide range of skills,[5] from managing company records to producing correspondence that is free of errors. He or she also[6] needs to be a person who relates well to all types of people.

I look forward to meeting you and discussing[7] these issues in greater detail.

Sincerely yours, (149)

3

Dear Mrs. Green:

Thank you for your letter informing us that your mailing address will be changing soon. We will make[1] the change in our records as soon as we receive the enclosed form. Please give us specific information for[2] forwarding your correspondence. Print or type your house number and the full name of your avenue or boulevard. Be[3] certain to specify the month and day you wish to begin receiving mail at your new address.

We suggest that[4] you mail notices to people you correspond with on a regular basis. We would be happy to supply[5] you with the appropriate forms.

Cordially yours, (109)

4

Dear Members:

The topic of this month's meeting will be "Girlhood Dreams." The meeting will be held in the old school[1] building on North Shore Boulevard. Perhaps we can all share childhood memories while we are there.

Please notice that our[2] meeting is being moved up to a new hour. It was also suggested that we change our regular meeting day.[3] Please be prepared to discuss whether we should move it up toward the beginning of the month.

I will distribute[4] copies of our recent survey in which we asked you to specify goals for the new year. Your answers were very[5] rewarding, and I look forward to sharing them with you. I hope you will all be present.

Very truly yours,[6] (120)

5

Dear Henry:

Thank you for forwarding a set of your designs for the new electric engine. Now that we have had[1] some time to look at them, we are delighted to say that we think you have given us a fine example for the[2] future, as well as the present.

We have decided to distribute copies to our field engineers, and we have[3] asked them to respond in 30 days. In all likelihood we will hear from them even before then. I am sure[4] you will be as eager as I am to see their reports, so I will forward them as soon as I can.

We appreciate[5] the efficient service you have given us.

Sincerely yours, (111)

LESSON 17

1. Write for the word ending *tion* (pronounced *shun, zhun,* or *chun*: sion, cian, shion, cean, cion) or for a vowel + *tion* (a-tion, e-tion, i-tion or ish-un, o-tion, u-tion).

vacation, v-k-tion

position, p-z-tion

nation, n-tion

supervision, super-v-sion

physician, f-z-cian

ocean, o-cean

fashion, f-shion

session, s-sion

These additional words will appear in your reading and writing exercises.

application, a-p-l-k-tion

addition, a-d-tion

decision, d-s-sion

solution, s-l-tion

national, n-tion-l

situation, situate-tion

operation, operate-tion

suggestion, suggest-tion

distribution, distribute-tion

Phrases

I believe

you do

you should

to keep

could be

for you

for your

in the

of you

of your

will you

will your

Commonly Misspelled Words	Look for these words in your reading and writing exercises.	
	here	(to designate a place) Someone will be *here* at noon.
	hear	(to perceive a sound) If you *hear* the telephone, please answer it.

Your Business Vocabulary	marketing division	Those departments of a business concerned with the sales, promotion, and distribution of a product.

PRINCIPLES SUMMARY

1. Write for the word ending *tion* or for a vowel + *tion*: vacation, v-k-tion .

Reading and Writing Exercises

-1-

mo l mbrs v
brd rcm dr
Abrl bron f . pzj
o r brd v drrs.
dr bron z . fzj hr
f ln 20 yrs. s
vu a rmbr (fr
ldrs h Pvd- f r
nbrh scls. f ex /
z dr bron hu urj-
. dsj n fvr v bld
S jr hu. h Aso rz-
rvnu l PCs (prp
f . adj l la bld>
ublv dr bron l
agre l hd r drv
f blr ejcjl Pgs. h
lcs G v U silys +
, n afrd lq o rec
f l h lqs , ru.
ls n rqs hul z .
ldr n r sle.

-2-

d s s l lqfL v
aplcj. (P L ev
no opn n dpl v
fj dzn. fw u
L l r r dvj (
sugj la (jr cor
drl u, er Pds .
nu fj ln C lb
rde f Dj bln Jl 15
+ Jl 30. e a dsd
l r lz s o .
nyl bss. uf so / lb
nes l A Psnl.
u ejcj + lrn d s
lb apo f sC . pzj>
uf udu n hr f (

yr n . fu ds
Ph usd gv h . cl ,
w nt lb hpe
lcp . cpe vu L n r
recs , if r sly dz
Cny el ll uno , cu

-3-

dr + rs gra
rmbr n (2
vu hp- l nyy (vcj
vu dr s abrd .
oj lnr x yr af yr u
N- lq b ddN , cd
(Pbl v b me x >
if u asr , ys ev .
sly fu , r s l sl o
(rn v Ma 10 l
7 dfrN pls o (
allNç oj , l .
vcj la lb ! if uv h

. rlys r bq f 3
yrs or ul rsv .
rds- ra , n ady
sr slzns a pp
n . cr pln lo
ol pams > ec
ac aplcys no lar
ln Ap , so p dN
dla , 's . bo u cN
afd l M , cu

-4-

d sle (nz f r
nys cpll , n q lz
ds , / aprs la nlr
(hos nr (snl l
ac (Ps byl du ls
sj , bcz v dlas hr
lb rel l r ofs
. fu ds lar ln ch
pln- , lu p asr A

-5-

Key

1

MEMO TO: Members of the Board

I am recommending Dr. Albert Brown for a position on our Board of[1] Directors. Dr. Brown was a physician here for more than 20 years. Some of you may remember the firm[2] leadership he provided for our neighborhood schools. For example, it was Dr. Brown who urged a decision in[3] favor of building South Junior High. He also raised revenue to purchase the property for an addition[4] to that building.

I believe Dr. Brown will agree to head our drive for better educational programs. He[5] takes charge of tough situations and is not afraid to go on record for what he thinks is right. This man ranks highly[6] as a leader in our city. (126)

2

Dear Ms. Smith:

Thank you for your letter of application. At the present time we have no openings in the[1] department of fashion design. I am forwarding your letter to our marketing division with the suggestion[2] that the manager correspond directly with you.

We are producing a new fashion line which will be ready[3] for distribution between July 15 and July 30. We may decide to market these items on a[4] national basis. If so, it will be necessary to add more personnel. Your education and training[5] would seem to be appropriate for such a position.

If you do not hear from the manager within a few[6] days, perhaps you should give him a call. In the meantime, I will be happy to keep a copy of your letter[7] in our records. If our situation does change, we will let you know.

Cordially yours, (155)

3

Dear Mr. and Mrs. Gray:

Remember when the two of you hoped to enjoy the vacation of your dreams aboard[1] an ocean liner? Year after year you wanted to go, but didn't. Could the problem have been money?

If your[2] answer is yes, we have a solution for you. Our ship will sail on the morning of May 10 to seven different[3] ports on the Atlantic Ocean. What a vacation that will be! If you have had a relationship with our bank[4] for three years or more, you will receive a reduced rate. In addition, senior citizens may participate in[5] a credit plan with low monthly payments.

We can accept applications no later than April 1, so please don't[6] delay. It's a boat you can't afford to miss.

Cordially yours, (131)

4

Dear Shelley:

The news from our nation's capital is not good these days. It appears that neither the House nor the[1] Senate will accept the President's budget during this session. Because of the delays here, I will be returning[2] to my office a few days later than I had planned. Will you please answer all correspondence while I am away?[3]

I don't have a solution to the budget issue. It's a tough problem. I will let you know as soon as I hear[4] something further. In the meantime, please refer all calls directly to our press secretary.

Do you know where to[5] locate specific information on the local labor situation for me? I would appreciate your[6] help.

Yours truly, (123)

5

Dear Jim:

What do you think of the enclosed article written by Susan Williams? It shows how we could increase[1] out-patient services as a way of reducing hospital fees. Dr. Williams says that with proper supervision,[2] more patients could be released on the day after an operation. In many cases, the person could go[3] home on the same day.

I believe we should look into what Dr. Williams is saying. She is providing a great[4] service by giving us these suggestions. If you agree, I will distribute copies to all executives.[5] Perhaps we can use the article to determine new policies here.

Yours very truly, (116)

LESSON 18

1. Write amounts of money in the following way:

$29.95 29^{95}

$300 3 H$

$6,500,000 6 M 5 H T $

$2,000,000,000 2 B $

Abbreviations

cent, cents ¢

dollar, dollars $

pound lb

inch in

ounce oz

hundred H

thousand T

million M

billion B

Brief Forms

about ab

has hs

order od

include I

over O

under U

customer K

Brief Form and Abbreviated Word Development

customers Ks

overall Oa

included I-

orders ods

holidays hlds

inclusion Ij

Phrases

we do	edu	have been	vb
we feel	efl	of our	vr
you need	und	to you	tu
to make	tmc	to your	tu

Commonly Misspelled Words

cancellation csl

recommend rcm

Your Business Vocabulary

word processing unit wrd Pss unt — Computerized typewriting equipment having many automatic features, including text editing and high-speed printing.

PRINCIPLES SUMMARY

1. Amounts of money.

Reading and Writing Exercises

-1-

-2-

ajN hs rcm- lae
ncrs c sNrl mre
bq b a̲ fCrs l /.
efl la c a- fCrs sd
vb -d- U c lr-s
vr orjnl agrem.
l e b G- c f a-l
f Cnjs er fs-lrc x>
e nd . dsj sn +
lc fw lu avs o
ls -lr. su

-3-

d-rs prcr jyn s
+ uz r nu Cc̲ Svs.
's v eze, -l dz r
bq ofr u x ev me
Cc̲ plns l -e u
nds. f ex if u cp
. mm v 2H$ w
bq lr lb no Svs

G. if u dN -t
lcp . mm a-l uc
pa. -ol fe v 4^{50}.
u -a Pfr lpa feC
Cc u ri / 10¢ P Cc>
lr, no l-l o c
No v Ccs u -a
ri. if u od no ul
rsv 2 H Ccs fre
v G. drp b u lcl
brnC ofs o srln̲
ave̲ + ll s U u -
ab r Cc̲ + sv̲ plns.
r bq̲ Svss r dzn-
lrc efsN me -jm
eze f r Ks. cu

-4-

d mbrs v brd
alC-, . cpe vr nu
op̲ byl. z uc se c

lol and , . lll U
2 M $. ls , . ncrs
v nrl 225 T$ O c
old byl. pl v ncrs
, du l r plns l PCs
prp f 2 Ppz- plNs.
evn ‿ c prp PCss
c byl s‿s l hi, lrf
‿ apy. grp v exs
l rvu lz fgrs +
rcm sp cls. chp
la s‿ vu l pp n
la rvu. id Aso
ap hr u sugjs f
brd ‿e o Jn 2. p
pln Ub P o la d. su

-5-

d‿rs crlsn e rgrl

l nf u la c blu
fbrc u od-, n ‿d
n . 54 = in ‿dl. cd
u uz / n . 45 = in
‿dl. Alo edu n
crNl v c 45 = in fbrc
n r Ap edb hpe l
od / fu. sC ods
lc ab 2 l 3 ‿cs l
arv, c r‿n chs
u sp- ‿ A- ld. c
lol and l vu od ,
79 96. v crs la and
dz n ‿l c prs v blu
fbrc or s A Gs. c
A ‿a v 45 = in
fbrc , 7 lbs 6 ozs,
e lc fw l Sv u n
fCr. ul

Key

1

Dear Mrs. Smith:

There is truth in the saying, "You are what you eat." Think about the billions of meals that are[1] prepared yearly.

To be a great cook, you need cookbooks you can rely upon. Why not join our cookbook club for great[2] dining enjoyment? As a member of our cookbook club, you can learn to prepare great daily meals. You will also[3] save money at the supermarket. There is more good news—your membership fee is included in the purchase[4] of three or more books.

Enclosed is a brochure which describes a new cookbook we are offering. It has won five[5] national awards. Why not try it for two weeks with no obligation to buy? If you decide to keep your copy,[6] mail us a check or money order for $15.95. This book would make a great gift for the[7] holidays.

Please use the enclosed form to specify the number of copies you wish to order. You may charge your[8] purchases, or we will bill you directly. We can accept cancellations up to ten days following the date[9] your order is received.

Yours very truly, (188)

2

Dear Mr. May:

As you know, we have had some problems with the word processing unit we purchased from your firm.[1] Overall, the machine operates well, but it does not do all of the tasks we believed it would do. Your agent has[2] recommended that we increase the central memory bank by adding features to it. We feel that the added[3] features should have been included under the terms of our original agreement. Will we be charged the full[4] amount for the changes we are forced to make?

We need a decision soon and look forward to your advice on this[5] matter.

Sincerely yours, (104)

3

Dear Mrs. Parker:

Join us and use our new checking service. It's very easy.

What does our bank offer you? We[1] have many checking plans to meet your needs. For example, if you keep a minimum of $200 in[2] the bank, there will be no service charge. If you don't wish to keep a minimum amount, you can pay a monthly fee[3] of $4.50. You may prefer to pay for each check you write at 10¢ per check.

There is no limit[4] on the number of checks you may write. If you order now, you will receive 200 checks free of charge. Drop by[5] your local branch office on Shoreline Avenue and let us tell you more about our checking and savings plans. Our[6] banking services are designed to make efficient money management easy for our customers.

Cordially[7] yours, (141)

4

Dear Members of the Board:

Attached is a copy of our new operating budget. As you can see, the total[1] amount is a little under $2,000,000. This is an increase of nearly $225,000[2] over the old budget. Part of the increase is due to our plans to purchase property for two proposed[3] plants. Even with the property purchases, the budget seems too high.

Therefore, I am appointing a group of[4] executives to review these figures and recommend specific cuts. I hope that some of you will participate[5] in that review. I would also appreciate hearing your suggestions at the board meeting on June 2. Please[6] plan to be present on that day.

Sincerely yours, (129)

5

Dear Mrs. Carlson:

We regret to inform you that the blue fabric you ordered is not made in a 54-inch[1] width. Could you use it in a 45-inch width? Although we do not currently have the 45-inch fabric[2] in our shop, we would be happy to order it for you. Such orders take about two to three weeks to arrive.[3]

The remaining items you specified were shipped today. The total amount of your order is[4] $79.96. Of course, that amount does not include the price of the blue fabric or its shipping[5] charges. The shipping weight of the 45-inch fabric is 7 pounds 6 ounces.

We look forward to serving[6] you in the future.

Yours truly, (125)

LESSON 19

1. Write a for the initial and final sound of *aw*.

law, l-aw	la	saw, s-aw	sa
audit, aw-d-t	adl	authorized, aw-ith-r-z-duh	alrz-
auto, aw-t-o	alo	drawings, d-r-aw-ings	dra=

2. Write q for the sound of *kw* (qu).

quite, q-ite	qi	equipment, e-q-p-ment	eqpm
quickly, q-k-ly	qcl	adequate, ad-q-t	aql
quote, q-ote	qo	frequent, f-r-q-nt	frqN

Phrases

we appreciate	eap	to use	luz
we had	eh	have had	vh
we were	e	on the	o
you were	u		

Commonly Misspelled Words

personnel	Psnl	(employees) We will employ more *personnel* in the new office.
personal	Psnl	(private) Jane is away on *personal* business today.

Your Business Vocabulary

resumé	rza	A document summarizing a job applicant's education, skills, and employment history.
authorized	alrz-	Having the right to make decisions and take specific action.

PRINCIPLES SUMMARY

1. Write a for the sound of *aw*: saw, s-aw sa.
2. Write q for the sound of *kw*: quite, q-ite qi.

Reading and Writing Exercises

-1-

dr lsn r ofs
bld, qi old, rsNl
e Ud la r li,
n Aql l e crN
las, er fs- . dsj,
c e slv r Pbl b
eqp A dscs elc
hps or sd e cln
. co sC z us l rpls
r Ohd lis nu
unls, r elcl nyns
hs sd la nu Ohd
lis d Pvd blr li, h
Aso A- la r lol and
f sC . PCs cd rn ab
2T$ or er hzlN
l alo r prs lq O
2T$ bcz me vr ppl
v sug- la ly db eqll
hpe elc hps, d
u b l l gv s u suggs
o ho l slv r Pbls.
idap u rsp z qcl z
uc gv / l s, cu

-2-

dK cd u fl uz .
sec cr, if so ev r
alo fu, ls dl,
gr f frqN lrps ab
lon b 's eqll q f
hi a drv, elr a
u pln luz / ls alo
l sv me o gsln. /

gls blr ly ln ne
nu dl crNl o
r, du (o v
Fb er alrz- l sl ls
cr / . v lo prs, blv
/ or n la prs l d
u Cys v eqpm, N
u drv b r sor +
se ls gr vlu,? l u'r
hr sn p f r fre dra,
. lvl nu cr lb aw-
l . lce rzdN vr
sle, la nr cdb
u, ul

-3-

ds le lqfL re .
pzj r fr, enc-
, . brsr dS r plse
o ejcj ul nd, z uc
se e jnl asc la A

ym lrnes v . clj
dgre, n . fu css ev
ofr- pzjs l ppl hu vh
s clj=lvl crss +
rla- jb scls evn
if ly dd n v . dgre,
f frlr inf p cl or ri
r Psnl dvj lca- /
412 el blvd, e
rcm lau ls .
cpe vu rz a aco-
b . L v aplcj, n u
L b Sln l mj ne
adjl scls or lrn
u a v rsv- olsd
clj crss, su

-4-

y lqfL v Ma 12,
u qi ri, lol
a l v bl sd vb

bs- o qo e gv u .
fu os aq er c
c Cnj n r recs +
u unv l so c nu
ad, u G- f prs
bcz eh n nf - r
ajN v agrem eh
d u f no
o el se l / la a
ples r op U c s
agrem eap u od
+ l v c eqpm s-
lu b c da u sp-,
gld u brl ls
dr l u Psnl
all + lc fw l Sv
u n fCr uvl

-5-

d q e qi Sprz-

b c rsp l c opn
vr nu sp Alo e
alspa- v bln 3H
+ 4H ppl ln
6H Ks P f
evN, c lol ad
v sls z l O 15T$
r jn jr fls la ls
lrj lrnol z c rzll
v . S P efl se
hs asc- e l lq
eC mbr v L
la ls u, u gv s
me fn sugjs n
adj u pla- . jr
rl n Ose c evN
+ b sl p c fre
dra + aw przs,
u efls r ap- ul

Key

1

Dear Mr. Wilson:

Our office building is quite old. Recently we were told that our lighting is not adequate[1] to meet current laws. We are faced with a decision. Can we solve the problem by equipping all desks with electric[2] lamps, or should we call in a company such as yours to replace our overhead lights with new units?

Our[3] electrical engineer has said that new overhead lights would provide better lighting. He also added that the[4] total amount for such a purchase could run about $2,000 or more. We are hesitant to allow[5] the price to go over $2,000 because many of our people have suggested that they would be[6] equally happy with electric lamps.

Would you be willing to give us your suggestions on how to solve our problems?[7] I would appreciate your response as quickly as you can give it to us.

Cordially yours, (156)

2

Dear Customer:

Could your family use a second car? If so, we have the auto for you. This model is great[1] for frequent trips about town, but it's equally good for highway driving. Either way you plan to use it, this auto[2] will save money on gasoline. It gets better mileage than any new model currently on the market.[3]

During the month of February, we are authorized to sell this car at a very low price. Believe it or[4] not, that price will include your choice of equipment. Won't you drive by our showroom and see this great value?

While you're here,[5] sign up for our free drawing. A lovely new car will be awarded to a lucky resident of our city.[6] That winner could be you.

Yours truly, (126)

3

Dear Ms. Lee:

Thank you for your letter regarding a position with our firm. Enclosed is a brochure describing[1] our policy on the education you will need. As you can see, we generally ask that all management[2] trainees have a college degree. In a few cases we have offered positions to people who have had some college-[3] level courses and related job skills, even if they did not have a degree.

For further information,[4] please call or write our personnel division located at 412 Elm Boulevard. We recommend that you mail[5] us a copy of your resumé accompanied by a letter of application. In your letter, be certain[6] to mention any additional skills or training you may have received outside college courses.

Sincerely[7] yours, (141)

4

Gentlemen:

Thank you for your letter of May 12. You were quite right. The total amount of the bill should have been based[1] on the quote we gave you a few months ago. We are making the change in our records, and your invoice will show the[2] new amount.

You were charged full price because we had not informed our agent of the agreement we had made with you.[3] From now on, we will see to it that all parties are operating under the same agreement. We appreciate[4] your order and will have the equipment shipped to you by the date you specified.

I am glad you brought this matter[5] to my personal attention and look forward to serving you in the future.

Yours very truly, (119)

5

Dear Meg:

We were quite surprised by the response to the opening of our new shop. Although we anticipated[1] having between 300 and 400 people, more than 600 customers were present for the event.[2]

The total amount of sales was well over $15,000. Our general manager feels that this large[3] turnout was the result of a super promotion effort. She has asked me to thank each member of the team. That[4] includes you.

You gave us many fine suggestions. In addition, you played a major role in overseeing the[5] event and by setting up the free drawings and awarding prizes.

Your efforts are appreciated.

Yours truly,[6] (120)

LESSON 20

1. Write a capital N for the sound of *end*, *nd* (pronounced *end*).

friend, f-r-nd frN

sending, s-nd-ing sN

handling, h-nd-l-ing hNl

indicate, nd-k-ate Nca

found, f-ow-nd foN

foundation, f-ow-nd-tion foN

Abbreviations

feet ft

square sq

yard yd

agriculture agr

economic, economy eco

Brief Forms

advantage av

again, against ag

business bs

several sv

Write the following additional outlines which will be used in your reading and writing exercises:

land, l-nd lN

fund, f-nd fN

bonds, b-nd-s bNs

dividends, d-v-d-nd-s dvdNs

find, f-nd fN

window, w-nd-o Nо

ground, gay-r-ow-nd groN

economical, economic-l ecol

Phrases

I know	ino	to get	tgt
we are not	ern	to hear	thr
we will be	elb	to send	tsN
you will be	ulb	can be	cb

Commonly Misspelled Words

customer K

occurred ocr-

Your Business Vocabulary

dividends dvdNs — Profits received from shares of ownership in a corporation.

purchasing department PCs dpt — That department responsible for buying equipment and supplies for the entire company.

PRINCIPLES SUMMARY

1. Write a capital N for the sound of *end*, *nd*: friend, f-r-nd frN.

Reading and Writing Exercises

-1-

d hord ulb p- lhr
la n nc Pgrs o
Pfl + ls rpl u M-.
u+d v / b c h u
grp nes aq, l gi
agre la e+d nc
s Cnys n r ym
v cpll. Lc loz
dsjs e+d lc . q lc
f nyl eco. w rd
sv artcls sug la
ls , n . apo h l
b or sl bNs so lr
db lll avj l c+
n r dvdNs no,
n jn cd aso rcm
ag b lN f 2 rzns=
prp vlus r hi +
rgj me , hrd l
obln. cblv e+d lc

nl b fr lN. c
sec v agr hs Ppz-
lgslj C d P l nu
fr ors lgl lns /
. %j ra l U c P
nr ra. uvl

-2-

mo l elzbl bron
drr v PCs er pln
lsN ab 2T Ls f r
fN drv. d eC
L lb . rel env. d
/ b ecol f s luz
c No envs er
no uz n r ofs x Ph
e+d od rglr bs
envs. cno la rglr
envs cb PCs- f ls
me b ed v lpa Gs

f v r adrs a-l eC
env, if e dsd l od
envs esd du so ri
a a lrc Sln la ly
cb s- ol dla.
ncln- l od
No envs, if /
d sv fu edb
hpe l pls r o od
+ v c inv l-
drl l c PCs dpl.

-3-

d re enc-, . cpe
v inv f rda
lrc lns sa la ly
v n b pd f hNl
Cys o rsN sm e
rsv-. w Cc- c
rse + foN lae pd
. lol v 638 59 = C

, ln c ad vr
rglr sms, c u fN
ol r c Pbl, x if
c hNl Cys n l-
n r rglr pam e
pd l C f sm. if
ly l- esd sN la
inf l c lrc lns, .
slr suly ocr- sv
os ag + e foN
la c lrc fr h d
. Mlc. / db l r
avy l Cc c lr
clsl. vlu

-4-

d frN l so u ho
C eap u bs er
pln . sls evN. du
c o v ap el rc
20% of a crpl. z

r cr crd K ulb
nvr- l Cz ne cN
v crpl u ⌣s, fex
loz rglrl prs- /
14^{99} P sq yd lb
ofr- / 11^{96} P sq
yd, l. ecol ⌣a l
A nu lf lu h⌣!,
ehp ul lc Avy v
ls gr ofr, elb
hpe lpa u . Psnl
vzl l dl / No v
sq yds ul nd, ls
, r ⌣a v sq lqf
bs, su

-5-

d crs i rsv- u cpes
v nu lN ls agrems,
ly apr lb n od b

ern yl Sln ⌣lr
or n ec gl P⌣y
l drl, z uno nu
lsly cd PvN s f⌣
drl o Sln cNs v
agrl lN, / no
lcs z uf loz las l
n apli l cos drl
ls ln 9H fl nl
/ groN, s n gi clr
⌣lr / la aplis l
nCrl gs or uf s
h⌣l- l yl ls, r P
hs rln l snlr
bron lgl ⌣ inf
b ⌣ afrd el n
v . dfnl asr f sv
⌣cs, ab A ec du
no, r⌣n psN, ul

Key

1

Dear Howard:

You will be pleased to hear that I am making progress on the profit and loss report you wanted. You[1] should have it by the time your group meets again.

I quite agree that we should make some changes in our management of[2] capital. To make those decisions, we should take a good look at the national economy. I have read[3] several articles suggesting that this is not an appropriate time to buy or sell bonds, so there would be little[4] advantage to cashing in our dividends now.

In general, I would also recommend against buying land[5] for two reasons—property values are high and mortgage money is hard to obtain. I believe we should look into[6] buying farm land. The Secretary of Agriculture has proposed legislation which would permit new farm[7] owners to get loans at a percentage rate well under the present market rate.

Yours very truly, (158)

2

MEMO TO: Elizabeth Brown, Director of Purchasing

We are planning to send about 2,000 letters[1] for our fund drive. Included with each letter will be a return envelope. Would it be more economical[2] for us to use the window envelopes we are now using in our office? Perhaps we should order regular[3] business envelopes. I know that regular envelopes can be purchased for less money, but we would have to pay[4] charges for having our address added to each envelope.

If we decide to order envelopes, we should do[5] so right away to make certain that they can be shipped without delay. I am inclined to order more window[6] envelopes.

If it would save time for you, we would be happy to place our own order and have the invoice mailed directly[7] to the purchasing department. (146)

3

Dear Mary:

Enclosed is a copy of the invoice from Roadway Truck Lines saying that they have not been paid for the[1] handling charges on the recent shipment we received. I have checked the receipt and found that we paid a total of[2] $638.59—which is more than the amount of our regular shipments.

Can[3] you find out where the problem is? If the handling charges were not included in our regular payment, we paid[4] too much for the shipment. If they were included, we should send that information to the trucking lines.

A similar[5] situation occurred several months ago, and we found that the trucking firm had made a mistake. It would[6] be to our advantage to check the matter closely.

Very truly yours, (133)

4

Dear Friend:

To show you how much we appreciate your business, we are planning a sales event. During the month of[1] April, we will mark 20 percent off all carpeting. As our credit card customer, you will be invited[2] to choose any kind of carpet you wish. For example, those regularly priced at $14.99[3] per square yard will be offered at $11.96 per square yard. What an economical way[4] to add new life to your home!

We hope you will take advantage of this great offer. We will be happy to pay you[5] a personal visit to determine the number of square yards you will need. This is our way of saying thank you[6] for your business.

Sincerely yours, (126)

5

Dear Chris:

I received your copies of the new land leasing agreements. They appear to be in order, but we are[1] not yet certain whether or not we can get permission to drill. As you know, new legislation could prevent us[2] from drilling on certain kinds of agricultural land. It now looks as if those laws will not apply to companies[3] drilling less than 900 feet into the ground. It is not quite clear whether the law applies to natural[4] gas or if it is limited to oil wells.

Our president has written to Senator Brown to get more information,[5] but I am afraid we will not have a definite answer for several weeks. About all we can do[6] now is remain patient.

Yours truly, (126)

LESSON 21

RECAP AND REVIEW

You have completed one-half of the principles lessons in this text. Let's take a look at the principles, brief forms, and abbreviations you studied in Lessons 15 through 20.

1. The following word beginnings were presented:

super	S	electr	el

2. These word endings were presented:

ward	w	hood	h
tion	1	scribe, script	S

3. The following outlines represent all of the principles you studied in Lessons 15-20:

manuscripts, m-n-script-s	mSs	prescribe, pre-scribe	PS
vacation, v-k-tion	vc1	supermarket, super-market	Smr
auto, aw-t-o	alo	backward, b-k-ward	bcw
electrical, electr-k-l	elcl	quite, q-ite	ql
childhood, chay-l-d-hood	Cldh	friend, f-r-nd	frN
neighborhood, n-b-r-hood	nbrh	electrician, electr-cian	el1
toward, to-ward	lw	law, l-aw	la

4. You learned to write money amounts this way:

$29.95 29^{95} $2,000,000 2M$

$300,000 3HT$

5. What words do these abbreviations represent?

ave	lb	d
B	in	rec
sq	H	agr
no	blvd	T
hr	oz	fl
M	$	eco
ex	¢	yd

6. Write the outlines for these brief forms:

appreciate	present	about
over	advantage	under
correspondence	distribute	please
specify	has	again
order	against	specific
several	up	business
customer	correspond	include

Reading and Writing Exercises

-1-

-2-

yr hs lcn . pzj
aq PCs Sln cNs v
elcl eqpm . h
alspas lc ab 10
mls l Dcs sp
exs, w asc- eC
dpl yr lb Pf ls
e . so fr w rsv-
i csly . s lsn
cl- l sa la se lb
o vq la c + hs
asc- dr evns l lc
hr pls . ul

-3-

i qi Sprz- la ev
n hrd f u re r
r bcs e od-, n
e pls- r od e asr-
la r bcs db s- drl
f u plN b r d

sp- . n r bcs dd
n arv o l
sec cl- r Svzr vu
s dpl . r Svzr foN
la r od pls- b r bs
ejcj dpl h b Olc- .
h P s- lsN r sm
ri a a, ln . c
hs gn b + ev no
bcs . e pln l D
l du r opn cls
sj o Aq 19 . p ll
s no l u pln l
du ab ls lr .
edap hr f u v
sn . vlu

-4-

d M clns ls , n
rsp lu L v aplcj .
, so hpns la er

lc̲ f . Psn l rpls
r cor sec hu , b̲
P-o-l . dfrN pzjs
n alC̲ . cpe v jb
dSj , if u -t l apl
f ls sp pzj p ri .
L Nca̲ -n ud b
fre l bgn + lvl
v slre u dzr , p
rmbr l -l . cpe vu
rz-a -c L , ehp
l Cz fnl cddls
-n . fu ds so ed
lc lv u L no lar
ln Fb1 , uvl

v Pbl-s fs̲ r eco ,
i z gt p- - u suggs
f lca̲ nu rzrvs v
yl f ex , u slf s-s
Ub , la no , els hs
Uv , i agre ntrl
- u vus o olda-ls̲
agrems + fre us v
agrl lN , s gt clr
la A ples d bnfl
f Cnj̲ lz las , i
-t u l n fnt̲ ls
bc + l gldl hlp if
c nd arzs , cu

-5-

ddr -sn i njy-
rd̲ u -nS o -f-
r nCrl nvrnm ,
u Stnl ofr . clr vu

-6-

d-rs bl r njs
bqs hNl Bs v $
eC yr f Ms v Ks
b lr , no K c r
bq h- e vlu -

ln u. enc-, u
bq rse f me uv
asc- s l fu
acrd l r agrem
el c A u ol
pams l ur ol
v lon. n u rel
el Pvd u . rpl
Nca C bls ev
pd. rpl l Aso
so ne ern o u

dpzl hr r bq
f u c arms l
ls u aplm l
lrvl p b sr lsNs
. cpe v ls agrem.
p l m vu alrne.
e N Lb Sln ev
A inf e a nd
l u me l. ul

Key

Abbreviations

avenue
billion
square
month
hour
million
example, executive
pound
inch
hundred
boulevard
ounce
dollar, dollars
cent, cents
day
record
agriculture
thousand
feet
economy, economic
yard

Brief Forms

ap
O
cor
sp
od
sv
K
p
avj
D
hs
aq
p
cor
ab
U
p
aq
sp
bs
l

1

Dear Mr. Wilson:

Enclosed is the bill for repairing your television set. As you can see, the charges total[1] $59.95. This price includes a 30-day guarantee on parts and service. If you[2] have more problems, be certain to call our customer service department while the repairs are under warranty.[3] We will visit your home and make the repairs at no additional charge to you.

Your set is in good shape generally[4] and should provide you with many years of good service, but why not think about adding a second set to your[5] home? We have several models which you could easily move from room to room. If you buy now, we will include[6] a fine rolling cart free of charge with your purchase. We hope you'll take advantage of our offer.

Sincerely yours,[7] (140)

2

Dear Jason:

As I was preparing the program for our meeting, I discovered that we have several items[1] of new business to cover. Now I am afraid that our meeting will run over the time we have allowed. Can you[2] meet with me in order to go over some of these items? Perhaps some of them can be handled at a future[3] meeting.

Also, do you plan to present your findings on the marketing survey? If so, please let me know how much[4] time you will need. Our building manager has taken a position against purchasing certain kinds of electrical[5] equipment. He anticipates taking about ten minutes to discuss specific examples.

I have asked[6] each department manager to be present for this meeting. So far I have received one cancellation. Ms.[7] Wilson called to say that she will be on vacation that week and has asked Dr. Evans to take her place.

Yours[8] truly, (161)

3

Gentlemen:

I am quite surprised that we have not heard from you regarding the marketing books we ordered.

When we[1] placed the order, we were assured that the books would be shipped directly from your plant by the day specified. When the[2] books did not arrive on time, my secretary called the supervisor of your shipping department. The supervisor[3] found that the order placed by our business education department had been overlooked. He promised to send[4] the shipment right away.

More than a week has gone by, and we have no books. We plan to distribute them during[5] the opening class session on August 19. Please let us know what you plan to do about this matter. We would[6] appreciate hearing from you very soon.

Very truly yours, (131)

4

Dear Miss Collins:

This is in response to your letter of application. It so happens that we are looking for[1] a person to replace our correspondence secretary, who is being promoted to a different[2] position.

I am attaching a copy of the job description. If you wish to apply for this specific[3] position, please write a letter indicating when you would be free to begin and the level of salary you[4] desire. Please remember to include a copy of your resumé with the letter.

We hope to choose final[5] candidates within a few days, so we would like to have your letter no later than February 1.

Yours very[6] truly, (121)

5

Dear Dr. Mason:

I enjoyed reading your manuscript on managing our natural environment. You[1] certainly offer a clear view of the problems facing our economy. I was quite pleased with your suggestions for[2] locating new reserves of oil, for example. Your solution seems to be one that no one else has thought of.

I[3] agree entirely with your views on outdated leasing agreements and free use of agricultural land.[4] It is quite clear that all parties would benefit from changing these laws.

I wish you well in finishing this book and will[5] gladly help if the need arises.

Cordially yours, (109)

6

Dear Mrs. Billings:

Our nation's banks handle billions of dollars each year for millions of customers, but there is[1] no customer at our bank whom we value more than you. Enclosed is your bank receipt for the money you have asked[2] us to manage for you.

According to our agreement, we will make all your monthly payments while you are out of[3] town. When you return, we will provide you with a report indicating which bills we have paid. The report will also[4] show any earnings on your deposit here at our bank.

If you make arrangements to lease your apartment while[5] traveling, please be sure to send us a copy of the lease agreement. Please include the name of your attorney.[6] We want to be certain we have all the information we may need to manage your money well.

Yours truly,[7] (140)

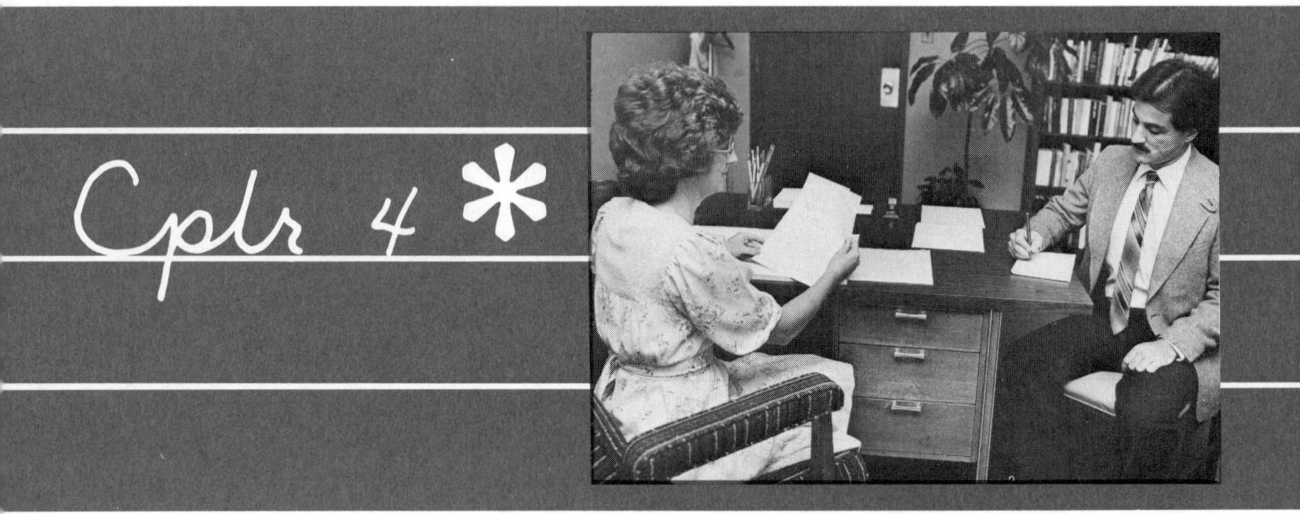

INPUT: TAKING DICTATION

When your supervisor asks, "Will you please come in for dictation?," a special teamwork begins. It's an interesting time, one set aside for a most important duty. Approach this activity with poise and involvement. Be alert, be enthusiastic, and be prepared.

Preparing for Dictation

Remember, your objective is to record dictation completely, quickly, and accurately. By following a few systematic procedures, you will be able to record all information and special details in a poised, organized manner without interrupting the thoughts of the person dictating. Practice these step-by-step procedures:

***Chapter Four**

1. Assemble all materials.
   a. Steno-pad—use a rubberband to separate previously recorded dictation from unused pages so that you can immediately open to a new page.
   b. Paper clips—attach several to the back of your pad to flag priority items or signal special instructions.
   c. Two good pens—take an extra pen in case the first one stops writing.
   d. Colored pen—use your colored pen or colored pencil to write corrections, changes, special instructions, or punctuation marks within sentences.
2. Seat yourself comfortably so that you can write easily and hear clearly—possibly across from your supervisor or beside the desk, using the desk to support your pad.
3. Date the bottom of the page to identify the day's dictation.

4. Write continuously.
   a. If you miss a word, wait until that particular communication is finished. Then ask, "Excuse me, I'm not sure about one word you used. May I read the sentence back to you?"
   b. Should your supervisor be interrupted to handle another matter, use the time to read your notes. Use your colored pen to insert punctuation, write instructions, or identify any outlines that need clarification.
   c. Flag rush items—with a paper clip or colored pen.

Before Returning to Your Desk

Make sure you have all the information you need. If you have additional questions, ask them. If you are uncertain about where to find name spellings, addresses, or certain enclosures, ask now.

Before Transcribing

As soon as you return to your desk, read over your special notations to clarify details and instructions. Transcribe your notes as soon as time allows, beginning with priority dictation.

As a member of this team, you'll find it important to be flexible. Many executives set aside a certain time of the day for dictation to avoid being interrupted by phone calls, appointments, or visitors. Others dictate at different times each day, depending upon their schedules. As a skilled secretary, you will always be ready to take dictation, anywhere, any time. That flexibility makes you a valuable part of the communications team.

LESSON 22

1. Write for the initial sound of *em* or *im* (pronounced *m*).

emphasize, em-f-s-z

embarrass, em-b-r-s

image, im-j

impress, im-p-r-s

impatient, im-p-ish-nt

impose, im-p-z

2. Omit *p* in the sound of *mpt*.

attempt, a-t-m-t

temptation, t-m-t-tion

prompt, prah-m-t

promptly, prah-m-t-ly

Abbreviations

merchandise

question

quart

especially

et cetera

university

Brief Forms

ever, every

other

satisfy, satisfactory

character, characteristic

industry

Brief Form and Abbreviated Word Development

however

satisfaction

questionnaire

everyone

whatever

another

quarterly

industries

Phrases

I have been	we believe
I should	we know
I was	as well as

TRANSCRIPTION AID Learn to punctuate correctly.

We punctuate our writing for one reason: to add clarity. When we speak, we use voice tones and pauses to punctuate. We use an uplifted tone to ask a question. We pause between words and phrases to give order and meaning to the thought we are expressing. Without changes in voice tone and natural pauses, our words would run together and much of the meaning would be lost.

On the printed page, however, we do not have the benefit of voice tones or natural pauses. We use punctuation marks instead.

The comma is an important mark of punctuation. We use a comma to separate a word or phrase from the rest of the sentence. The comma forces us to pause as we read. To help you understand when and where to use commas, we will present examples in future lessons. You will probably find that your supervisor will expect you to provide all of the punctuation needed in the material you transcribe.

USE COMMAS BETWEEN THREE OR MORE WORDS IN A SERIES.

The last word in a series will be preceded by either of these two words: *and*, *or*. In this text, we will always place a comma before *and* and *or* in a series. Some offices, however, may prefer that this comma be omitted. Use the style preferred in your office.

Letters arrived for Mary, Todd, Steven, and James.

Please ask someone to answer the phone, sort the mail, and file all correspondence.

There are three subjects I especially enjoy—accounting, shorthand, and typewriting.

In the reading and writing exercises, commas in a series will be circled. The word **Series** will be highlighted.

Your Business Vocabulary		
	merchandising	The planning of sales programs directed toward creating a market demand for a product.
	market analysis	Research concerned with all factors which affect the sales of goods and services.

PRINCIPLES SUMMARY

1. Write for the initial sound of *em* or *im*: emphasize, em-f-s-z
2. Omit *p* in the sound of *mpt*: prompt, prah-m-t

Reading and Writing Exercises

-1-

Series

Series

hsp, i ⌣N- u lno
Psnll la / ol psNs
+ l ap- / , su

-2-

1 lqf qs re r $ +
Dj plses, e ofr sv
plns, me lrj bss
lc Avj v flo bjl
pln, yf u od · mm
v 12T$ n ⌢dse P
yr ul rsv · rds-
ra ⌣C cb pd n
1 and yrl or 4 ands
qtrl, f E adjl sm
ul pa ol 10% vu
rglr $ fe, aol pln
e sug ; · arm ofn
uz- b snl rll bss,
u pls ods z und
h + r bl- f eC od,

yf u lol sms f ne
gvn yr and l ⌢
ln 7T2H$ ul rsv
· sv ⌣C lb cr-lw
u PCss / flo yr, elb
hpe l Dcs ol plns
l ⌢e u nds, p fl fre
l cl o s / ne h, ul

-3-

dS w sv qs ab u
U, d u p sN ⌢e ·
cpe vu cal, (Series) · aplj
fr, (Series) + ol jn inf re
nrlm plses. ⌢
enc cpes v ⌢u
acd ⌢c recs ⌣C
chp ul fN sal, r
lr ol crss wd lc
l nsr la ⌢u aplq
lb ac-x, id Aso lc

sp dlls ab u scl v
bs, crNl lq v
yr n r .
fss n dse +
r anlss, hp uc
Avz e o ol flds
sC z Psnl ym (Series ,)
sls ym (Series ,) ecos (Series ,) etc,
wb Ud lau pls srs
n jbs rla- l lr Czn
flds f 1 f qlr du
fnl yr,) ls cs f
E sr x id Aso ap
rsv NE inf uv
ab jb rs n bs +
N, uvl

-4-

dr + rs a s e
N ls hld szn lb
esp hpe fu + u fl,

las y e dzn- . hld
byl pln = c u sp
ezer + u hlds hper,
r byl pln Pvds
c4 und + . eze pam
scjl, hrs ho ec
hlp u, vzl r ln dpl
+ lc r cr ofsr,
n uv dl- a
v c4 und uc Cz
. pam pln dzn- l
fl u ol byl, f u
4 u a dla c
pams p l 90 ds
flo ln, ul fN
r Svs P + r ofsrs
egr l hlp, b Sv Ks
lc u ev lrn- ho
c hlds . ezer
f me ppl + e
lc prd n du so,

l ur hr asc f inf
o r f ln v bq Svss.
e lq ulb prs-
d rny e ofr. /
jn sv + ln n e
a . nu K eno ev
d . nu frN. vlu

-5-

ddr srp lqf cor asc
ab r plns f pblt u
bc gd l rd Pss. i
lq ic no asr loz qs
lu saly, e alspa v
bcs o r b N v
Fb or bgn v Mr.

v p- l rpl la
eh nS rvu-b
sv ppl w N +
rsv- v q rsps. ly
esp prs-
fnl Cplr n C u
Dcs ol uss f elnc
eqpm w ofs, bcz
u nS, so l e
l Ppr / f fCrus
z qcl z ec. eblv
u bc , . v q ex v
l r rdrs N. l
c E ad lcp u
p l da o ls hpn.
uvl

Key

1

Dear Dr. Davidson:

Recently, I was a patient under the care of your efficient personnel. I[1] especially appreciated the efforts of your nurse, Ellen Jeffries. It is not easy to find people who[2] perform over and above the call of duty, but Ms. Jeffries is one of those rare persons. I was impressed by[3] her kind manner, her dedication, and the prompt attention she gave to every patient under her care.

She was[4] never too busy to listen to our problems and often did so on her own time. I believe her character[5] was encouraging to the other personnel as well as to the patients.

It was very satisfying to[6] see the high level of professional care throughout your hospital. I wanted you to know personally that[7] the other patients and I appreciated it.

Sincerely yours, (152)

2

Gentlemen:

Thank you for your questions regarding our shipping and distribution policies. We offer several[1] plans. Many large businesses take advantage of the following budget plan.

If you order a minimum[2] of $12,000 in merchandise per year, you will receive a reduced rate which can be paid in one amount[3] yearly or four amounts quarterly. For every additional shipment, you will pay only 10 percent of your[4] regular shipping fee.

Another plan we suggest is an arrangement often used by small retail businesses.[5] You place orders as you need them and are billed for each order. If your total shipments for any given year[6] amount to more than $7,200, you will receive a savings which will be credited toward[7] your purchases the following year.

We will be happy to discuss other plans to meet your needs. Please feel free to[8] call on us at any time.

Yours truly, (167)

3

Dear Sir:

I have several questions about your university. Would you please send me a copy of your[1] catalog, an application form, and other general information regarding enrollment policies? I[2] am enclosing copies of my academic records, which I hope you will find satisfactory. Are there other[3] courses I should take to ensure that my application will be accepted?

I would also like specific[4] details about your School of Business. Currently I am thinking of majoring in marketing, with an emphasis[5] in merchandising and marketing analysis. I hope you can advise me on other fields such as[6] personnel management, sales management, economics, etc.

I have been told that you place seniors in jobs[7] related to their chosen fields for one full quarter during the final year. Is this the case for every senior?[8] I would also appreciate receiving whatever information you have about job markets in business[9] and industry.

Yours very truly, (186)

4

Dear Mr. and Mrs. Ames:

We want this holiday season to be especially happy for you and your[1] family. That's why we designed a holiday budget plan—to make your shopping easier and your holidays[2] happier.

Our budget plan provides the cash you need and an easy payment schedule. Here's how we can help you.[3] Visit our loan department and talk with our credit officer. When you have determined the amount of cash you need,[4] you can choose a payment plan designed to fit your monthly budget. If you wish, you may delay making payments up[5] to 90 days following the loan.

You will find our service prompt and our officers eager to help. By serving[6] customers like you, we have learned how to make the holidays an easier time for many people, and we take[7] pride in doing so.

While you are here, ask for information on our full line of banking services. We think[8] you will be impressed with the wide range we offer. At General Savings and Loan, when we add a new customer,[9] we know we have made a new friend.

Very truly yours, (189)

5

Dear Dr. Sharp:

Thank you for your correspondence asking about our plans for publishing your book, *Guide to Word*[1] *Processing*. I think I can now answer those questions to your satisfaction.

We anticipate having the books on[2] the market by the end of February or the beginning of March. I am very pleased to report that we[3] had the manuscript reviewed by several people in the industry and received very good responses. They[4] were especially impressed with the final chapter in which you discuss other uses for electronic[5] equipment in the office.

Because your manuscript is so timely, we wish to prepare it for future use as[6] quickly as we can. We believe your book is a very good example of what our readers want. I will make every[7] attempt to keep you up to date on what's happening.

Yours very truly, (153)

LESSON 23

1. Write k for the sounds of *com, con, coun (ow), count.*

account, a-count	ak	accommodate, a-com-d-ate	akda
county, count-e	ke	concern, con-s-r-n	ksrn
common, com-n	kn	council, coun-s-l	ksl

2. Write S for the sound of *st* (pronounced *est*).

still, st-l	Sl	trust, t-r-st	trS
state, st-ate	Sa	most, m-st	⁀S
instead, in-st-d	nSd	fastest, f-st-st	fSS

Write these additional words:

discount, dis-count	Dk	constant, con-st-nt	kSN
commission, com-sion	kj	cost, k-st	cS
postage, p-st-j	pSj	finest, f-n-st	fnS
confirm, con-firm	kfr	storage, st-r-j	Srj
condition, con-d-tion	kdj	concerning, con-s-r-n-ing	ksrn_

Phrases

I would like	idlc	you could	ucd
we are pleased	erp-	to receive	trsv
you cannot	ucn	to say	tsa

Commonly Misspelled Words

accommodate akda

almost a-S

Your Business Vocabulary

real estate rl eSa — A term which refers to land and the buildings or permanent structures on the land.

commerce krs — The buying and selling of goods and services; usually on a widespread basis, such as national commerce.

PRINCIPLES SUMMARY

1. Write k for the sounds of *com*, *con*, *coun (ow)*, *count*: county, count-e ke
2. Write S for the sound of *st*: still, st-l Sl

Reading and Writing Exercises

-1-

1 c 3 -S sal l
rd u artcl ksrn
ar trfc. -n c arpt
3 blt c rn a sz 3
- tn Agl. du c lS
sv yrs kdjs v grl
Cnj-. e no v . -C
lyr No v arcrft uz
r arpt o . dl bss, l
agre la c cS v ncrs-

Svss sd n b pd b c
sle aln. c db -
ecol f E, uf c ke -
tpa . grr Sr v cSs.
Psnll udlc tse .
Ppzl pls- bf c ke ksl
asc f . ncrs n fN
du uno uf nel hs
nvSga- uz ol rvnu
udb l l hlp Srt .

fN drv n od l rz
me f prvl srss
sC z bs ,(Series) N ,(Series) + foNys.
Ph ucd adrs ls lpc
n . frN=pj Sre , c
nd f ncrs- Svss , .
yr ısu ld. chp ul
cp gv / c cvrj /
dzrvs. su

-2-

dr + rs sd uz
dli- lrsv u cl asc
e lb u rl eSa
ajN , blv lau asc
prs , ri. uv . fn
h n . v q lcj. lr
, E rzn l blv lau
h lb sld n . v
srl l, z ı my-
erlr u hos lb l8-

w nzppr zlz n r
rl eSa blln. c blln
, pbls-o . cl bss
+ D- a O c ke n Srs
+ ofs bld. s l rd +
ofn gvs c bl rzlls v
a srss uz- , el so u
h z frqNl z ec.
Lc loz vzls plzN
fu cl cl / l8 ı hr ahd
v L Lc . apym. c
dsj lr or n l rn
/ h du loz vzls ,
nlrl p lu , ı lc fw
l Sv z u ajN. vlu

-3-

ds lr ev sN sv
nlss nf u lau ak
, p8 du + Sl ev n
hrd f u. a8 3

~os v gn b + ev n
rsv- u Cc, , lr s~
rzn ucn sN evn
(mm pam ,> lr ,
Sl L Lc u ak
crN + ~nln u q
cr SN, p cl r ofs
ld + ~c arms l
sll ls ~lr, elb
gld l hlp n ne ~a,
if e USN u Pbl Ph
ec ar . pam scjl
l akda u nds, ul

-4-

ds ~ly s Pfsr
bron lls ~e la uv
rln sv arlcls ab
(kpur N, w jS fns-
. Sde o uz kpurs n
ejcj + idlc l sr

~i fN ~ u, (enc-
rpl , bs- o ~i
rSC, d u lc . lc ,
, + ll ~e if u lq (
rpl cdb pbls- z .
bc ,> aS a v rpl
ksrns nu uss f
kpurs n clsr ,,
P ~ lS (~lds
n ~i o clsr +
~c arms lv L
lS- elsr, (rsps
f lCrs vb v q>
idlc l P ~i rpl l
. pblsr + d ap ne
suggs uv ab ri .
dll- Ppzl, ihp uc
fN L n u bze
scjl l gv ~e u
kNs, id grl vlu
u avs + ~ Ppr- lpa

. fe f ls Svs, p lt
e no if uc hlp.
cu

-5-

d lsa lqf kNs o r
Ppz- sp sNr. erp-
lsa el P r plns l
c sle pln kj o Ja 11,
i esp ap u Avs n re
l Pvd nes inf. c rpl
u d- u L Pvd- .
fn ex l flo. ublv
r rqS f . zn Cnj

lb grN-. . lcj W
v lon, c bS Cys
f . lrj sNr lc rs,
r sp sNr l kln
sv lrj bss = 3 Dk
Srs Series , 5 dpl Srs Series , +
2 Srs. / l akda
p l i H ol bss, c
sNr sd dra Ks
f sv kes. ls /
l ncrs krs f ntr
sle. f la rzn e
alspa . gr dl v
spl f r pln. uvl

Key

1

Gentlemen:

It was most satisfying to read your article concerning air traffic. When the airport was built,[1] the runway size was more than adequate. During the last several years, conditions have greatly changed. We now have[2] a much larger number of aircraft using our airport on a daily basis.

I agree that the cost of[3] increased services should not be paid by the city alone. It would be more economical for everyone[4] if the county were to pay a greater share of the costs. Personally, I would like to see a proposal placed before[5] the county council asking for an increase in funding.

Do you know if anyone has investigated[6] using other revenue? I would be willing to help start a fund drive in order to raise money from private[7] sources such as business, industry, and foundations. Perhaps you could address this topic in a front-page story.[8]

The need for increased services is a major issue today. I hope you will keep giving it the coverage[9] it deserves.

Sincerely yours, (185)

2

Dear Mr. and Mrs. Smith:

I was delighted to receive your call asking me to be your real estate agent.[1]

I believe that your asking price is right. You have a fine home in a very good location. There is every reason[2] to believe that your home will be sold in a very short time. As I mentioned earlier, your house will be listed[3] in the newspaper as well as in our real estate bulletin. The bulletin is published on a weekly[4] basis and distributed all over the county in stores and office buildings. It is well read and often gives[5] the best results of all sources used.

We will show your home as frequently as we can. To make those visits more pleasant[6] for you, I will call at least one hour ahead of time to make an appointment. The decision whether or not[7] to remain at home during those visits is entirely up to you.

I look forward to serving as your agent.[8]

Very truly yours, (164)

3

Dear Ms. Miller:

We have sent several notices informing you that your account is past due, and still we have[1] not heard from you. Almost three months have gone by, and we have not received your check. Is there some reason you cannot send[2] even the minimum payment?

There is still time to make your account current and maintain your good credit standing.[3] Please call our office today and make arrangements to settle this matter.

We will be glad to help in any way.[4] If we understand your problem, perhaps we can arrange a payment schedule to accommodate your needs.

Yours truly,[5] (100)

4

Dear Ms. Williams:

Professor Brown tells me that you have written several articles about the computer[1] industry. I have just finished a study on using computers in education, and I would like to share my[2] findings with you. The enclosed report is based on my research. Would you take a look at it and tell me if you think[3] the report could be published as a book?

Almost all of the report concerns new uses for computers in the[4] classroom. At present, I am testing the methods in my own classroom and making arrangements to have them tested[5] elsewhere. The responses from teachers have been very good.

I would like to present my report to a publisher[6] and would appreciate any suggestions you have about writing a detailed proposal. I hope you can find[7] time in your busy schedule to give me your comments. I would greatly value your advice and am prepared to pay[8] a fee for this service.

Please let me know if you can help.

Cordially yours, (173)

5

Dear Lisa:

Thank you for your comments on our proposed shopping center. We are pleased to say we will present our plans[1] to the city planning commission on January 11.

I especially appreciate your[2] advice in regard to providing necessary information. The report you included with your letter[3] provided a fine example to follow. I believe our request for a zoning change will be granted. A[4] location west of town is the best choice for a large center like ours.

Our shopping center will contain several large[5] businesses—three discount stores, five department stores, and two supermarkets. It will accommodate up to[6] 100 other businesses.

The center should draw customers from several counties. Thus, it will increase commerce[7] for the entire city. For that reason, we anticipate a great deal of support for our plan.

Yours very truly,[8] (160)

LESSON 24

1. Write the days of the week as follows:

Sunday Sn
Monday Mn
Tuesday Tu
Wednesday Wd
Thursday Th
Friday Fr
Saturday St

Abbreviations

federal fed
government gvt
represent, representative rep
street S
okay ok
incorporate, incorporated inc

Brief Forms

continue ku
deliver dl
opportunity opt
come, came, committee k
accomplish ak
complete kp
contribute kb
convenient, convenience kv

Brief Form Development

continued ku-
completed kp-
opportunities opts
accomplishments akms
contributions kbjs
income nk

Phrases

I feel

you would be

*as *soon* as

as we

*Omit the shorthand outline for the italicized word.

USE COMMAS AFTER INTRODUCTORY DEPENDENT CLAUSES.

An introductory dependent clause is a group of words containing a subject and a verb which occurs at the beginning of a sentence. However, this clause is not a complete thought and cannot stand alone. It requires a main (independent) clause to make the sentence complete.

Introductory dependent clauses usually begin with recognizable words. The most common words are *when, as,* and *if.* Other common examples are *although, though, unless, since, while, until, before, whether,* and *because.*

When Dr. Ellis arrives, please have her call my office.

As I may have mentioned earlier, that contract has already expired.

If you prefer, we will have the order shipped directly to you.

Beginning with this lesson, introductory dependent clauses which start with *when, as,* and *if* will be highlighted in your reading and writing exercises. The abbreviation **Intro DC** will be highlighted.

Your Business Vocabulary

capital investment — Funds spent for additions or improvements in plant, equipment, or personnel.

PRINCIPLES SUMMARY

1. Days of the week.

Reading and Writing Exercises

-1-

/ ev q nz fu, u
Am v ofs frn4 k
n ll Fr, l / b ok
l dl / ls c×> uf
uv . sp d n m (Intro DC) , p
cl r 4 dpl + c
r arms drl h,
olz s , lb n lC
u, / d aso b
z l kfr u 8 adrs,
zz u ac dle (Intro DC) , p Cc
eC ih cr, n
ur sal- la r Am
, kp + klns no
dy- gs (Intro DC) , rel , cpe
v inv u f pam,
lqf alo vrs inc
l hNl lz 4 arms
fu, p cl o s aq,
er . brf fn cl a a

f Sv u, su

-2-

d frq . q k p Th
ksrn r ls agrem
o old fed bld, ls
rn . gvl rep cl-
l asc uf e Sl 4
l PCs r prp, . fr
cl- nvSrs inc hs
d . ofr + , a f
. rpli, l du u lq
ab ls opl ×> r bld
hs ab 10T sq fl v
flr sps + er uz ab
60% v / > ev ofn
Dcs- lr esd b r
bld (Series) , ku rM (Series) , or v
l . nu lq, no r h
hs k c . dsf ab

ls cpll nvlm. vlu

-3-

mo l A sls Psnl
usd b esp p- u
akms ls yr. e n
ol d r sls gls e
Sps- L, ls yrs rec
sls ofr. fn opl l
py ol c kbys d b
sls reps. c grl vr
corp, drl rla- lu
olSN efls, ze lc
ahd l c k yr Intro DC , ll's
sl r gls f ku- grl
n rpls. ufl kfdN
la c nu yr l yld c
bS rzlls E. n e
e aq E rynl
kvnj Intro DC , el Dcs ho l

aCv loz rzlls, p
ac c enc- bns Cc
r kplms. c r
a v so r apj f
jb l dn.

-4-

drs dvs lqf nvlj
l adrs c nyl lf
ins kvnj. id v C
lc l ac b u Pscyl
l n Pd e l alN.
Ph ic suq s, els,
n iz n nu orlns
lS yr Intro DC , ih c opl Uhr
. fn spcr jnl Cs. hr
bcgroN + akms r
prsv, uc rC s
Cs c hr h c 413 W
el S. i lq udb

kpl sal- ⌣ hr z
. spcr、 su

-5-

mo l Pfsr edws
/ P hs apy- . k l
rvu r plse o vsu
fed lns l SdNs、
d u b fre l rep /
scl v ejcj o la k×>
/ k l alz r crN
—lds v Pss aplcjs
+ nvSga nu —lds
la —u rzlt n . ⌢

efsN sS⌢、 w .
fl kln bcgroN inf
⌣C l hlp u、 / Is
. cpe v gvl rgljs
+ . Sam v U plse、
ic Aso Pvd cpes
v fs Ub kp- b
aplcNs, uf s kv
Intro DC
fu, p pln l Sp b
⌢u ofs o Tu or
Wd、 i lq u'l fN ls
asnm Ub v Clnj
+ rw、

Key

1

Gentlemen:

We have good news for you. Your shipment of office furnishings came in last Friday. Will it be okay[1] to deliver it this week?

If you have a specific day in mind, please call our shipping department and make the[2] arrangements directly with them. Otherwise, someone will be in touch with you. It would also be wise to confirm[3] your street address.

As soon as you accept delivery, please check each item with care. When you are satisfied that[4] the shipment is complete and contains no damaged goods, return one copy of the invoice with your full payment.

Thank[5] you for allowing Movers, Inc., to handle these shipping arrangements for you. Please call on us[6] again. We are a brief phone call away from serving you.

Sincerely yours, (132)

2

Dear Frank:

A question came up Thursday concerning our lease agreement on the old federal building. This morning[1] a government representative called to ask if we still wish to purchase the property. A firm called Investors,[2] Inc., has made an offer and is waiting for a reply. What do you think about this opportunity?[3]

The building has about 10,000 square feet of floor space, and we are using about 60 percent of it.[4]

We have often discussed whether we should buy the building, continue renting, or move to a new location.[5] Now the time has come to make a decision about this capital investment.

Very truly yours, (119)

3

MEMO TO: All Sales Personnel

You should be especially pleased with your accomplishments this year. We not only[1] met our sales goals, we surpassed them.

This year's record sales offer a fine opportunity to point out the[2] contributions made by sales representatives. The growth of our corporation is directly related to your[3] outstanding efforts.

As we look ahead to the coming year, let's set our goals for continued growth in the marketplace.[4] I feel confident that the new year will yield the best results ever. When we meet again at the regional[5] convention, we will discuss how to achieve those results.

Please accept the enclosed bonus check with our compliments.[6] It is our way of showing our appreciation for a job well done. (133)

4

Dear Mrs. Davis:

Thank you for your invitation to address the National Life Insurance convention. I[1] would very much like to accept, but my present schedule will not permit me to attend. Perhaps I can suggest[2] someone else.

When I was in New Orleans last year, I had the opportunity to hear a fine speaker, Janet[3] Chase. Her background and accomplishments are impressive.

You can reach Ms. Chase at her home at 413 West Elm Street.[4] I think you would be completely satisfied with her as a speaker.

Sincerely yours, (95)

5

MEMO TO: Professor Edwards

The president has appointed a committee to review our policy on[1] issuing federal loans to students. Would you be free to represent the School of Education on that[2] committee?

The committee will analyze our current methods of processing applications and investigate[3] new methods that might result in a more efficient system. I have a file containing background information[4] which will help you. It includes a copy of government regulations and a statement of university[5] policy. I can also provide copies of forms to be completed by applicants.

If it is convenient[6] for you, please plan to stop by my office on Tuesday or Wednesday. I think you'll find this assignment to be very[7] challenging and rewarding. (145)

LESSON 25

1. Write q for the word ending *quire*.

require, re-quire	rq	inquiry, in-quire-e	nqe
requirements, re-quire-ment-s	rqms	acquire, a-quire	aq
inquire, in-quire	nq	required, re-quire-duh	rq-

2. Write z for the sound of *zh*.

pleasure, p-l-z-r	plzr	treasure, t-r-z-r	trzr
measure, m-z-r	zr	leisure, l-z-r	lzr

Writing State and City Names

The United States Post Office requests that two-letter state initials be used on all business envelopes. To indicate states in your shorthand notes, write the same two-letter state initials that the Post Office uses.

Alabama = AL	AL	California = CA	CA

City names are written according to rule. Listed below are examples of how to write city and state names. For a list of all the states, see the appendix at the back of this book.

Boston, MA	btn MA	Columbus, OH	clbs OH
Tulsa, OK	tlsa OK	Las Vegas, NV	ls vgs NV
Madison, WI	dsn WI	Buffalo, NY	bflo NY

Phrases

I look	ilc	to do	ldu
we could	ecd	to give	lgv
we have been	evb	to visit	lvzl
we would like	edlc		

Commonly Misspelled Words

representative rep

convenient kv

Your Business Vocabulary

test market — A geographical area selected for sales of goods or services during a trial period to determine the marketability of a product.

PRINCIPLES SUMMARY

1. Write q for the word ending *quire*: require, re-quire rq
2. Write z for the sound of *zh*: pleasure, p-l-z-r plzr

Reading and Writing Exercises

-1-

dr + mrs gra ,
ml u se r gd l
me u'l no e dzn- ,
fu. r alrs lc- ppl
lc u acrs cNre.
ls Pps z l lrn as
l hlp ppl o sl nks
lv ecoll. rzlt
, . bc cl- me=holc
Sv , me gvs
u. kp gd l unk.
, sos u holc, (Series) sv, (Series)
bjt, (Series) + spN u ern
lu bS Av. me ,
eze l rd + kv luz.
, Pvds E r Avzrs
N- + . pln .
lrp x me lls u ho
ldu , + sv. sp
b fd x me c rds

u fd bls b 40% ,
u S se ls gd l ap
l , l du fu. od u
cpe b rel , enc-
f n r pSj=fre env.
sN u Cc ld + pl
me n u h pln.
ul

-2-

dM bron , gvs e
gr plzr l nvi u l
ls yrs nyl kvn.
if u pln l alN, (Intro DC) p
kp , enc- rzrvj
f + rel , b Oc 2,
ls yrs lcj reps r
rsp l , rzlts v .
gr sN l r mbrs.
n , mbrs rqS-

-3-

. Cnj (Intro DC), e sNt nqes
l hlls + kvnj
sNrs n sv _ yr
sles. e Cz chbs
OH bcz / kdjs lr
_d r rqms.
chbs aso ofr-
/ bd kvnj ras f
r gss, z . mbr v
arms k _ _c
. Sva. d u Pfr l
hld / kvnj n s_
sle eC yr or d u
Pfr lvzl dfrN
sles, p gv _e u
sugjs n sps
_rc- "kNs" o
rzrvj f_, eap u
ku- spl f r _e.
lc fw lse u aq
ls yr. vlu

mo l ed prcr _
_S p- _ r plns f
hld _No Dplas.
_n r k z f- (Intro DC), e asc-
. rep v eC dpl l
kb sugjs. / z rw
lse / No + rnj v
sugjs e rsv-, uf
r plns r ok _ u (Intro DC),
el inc nu lys _
lrdyl _s v pS.
f ex e lca- s_ rs
alc lys l P aq .
bcgroN v _drn
pN. edlc l aq .
sS_ v lis + soNs
lgv a- _fss, ecd
Sl uz r pN-lNscps
uf e gv _ . nu lc.
e _ lri az elnc
gs + lys aq / old

bcgroN, zz uv
opl, Intro DC N u e
e l Dcs lz sugjs.

-4-

drs lqfL
ksrn us vr flr
clnr, er dlı- lhr
la Pf-so
l, evb plzNl Sprz-
b ly dm f ls n,
so me ppl rqS-
la ev . a lS, n
od l Sv Ks er
aq aol n, zz
ls n, rde f us, Intro DC
u a cl n u rzrvy
drl l r Sr o sec S,
ehp nu sS Pvds
efsN Svs f E1,
eap u kNs, ihp

ul vzl s ofn, vlu

-5-

mo l yr v r +
sls n brd v
drrs l lS Mn, Intro DC ly
vo- l Srl . nu dvy l
Pds ppr gs, ls reps
. yr Cny + ofrs
opls n . nu r,
el D ppr gs lru
r fd dvy, ls sS
aprs lb S ecol
+ kv ld v hNl
nu dse, sls reps
hu cl o Srs l
ncrs lr cls l d
Dk Srs, Series drq Srs, Series +
ol rll ollls C
cre r gs, e alspa
uz dnvr CO z . lS

r f nu ln, el	r plns, uf e ak
zr c rzlts v . 6=	r gls w lS r el (Intro DC)
o lS l f fCr	lrn r all l nyl sls,

Key

1

Dear Mr. and Mrs. Gray:

The minute you see our guide to managing money, you'll know we designed it for you.[1] Our authors talked with people like you across the country. Their purpose was to learn ways to help people on set[2] incomes live more economically. The result is a book called *Money—How to Make the Most of It.*

Money[3] gives you a complete guide to managing your income. It shows you how to make, save, budget, and spend your earnings to your[4] best advantage. *Money* is easy to read and convenient to use. It provides everything our advisers[5] wanted and more. Planning a trip? *Money* tells you how to do it and save. Shopping for food? *Money* can reduce your food[6] bills by 40 percent.

You must see this guide to appreciate what it will do for you. Order your copy by[7] returning the enclosed form in our postage-free envelope. Send your check today and put *Money* in your home[8] planning.

Yours truly, (164)

2

Dear Miss Brown:

It gives me great pleasure to invite you to this year's national convention. If you plan to attend,[1] please complete the enclosed reservation form and return it by October 2.

This year's location represents[2] our response to the results of a questionnaire sent to our members. When the membership requested a change, we[3] sent inquiries to hotels and convention centers in several major cities. We chose Columbus, Ohio,[4] because the conditions there met our requirements. Columbus also offered the best convention rates for our[5] guests.

As a member of the arrangements committee, I am making a survey. Would you prefer to hold the[6] convention in the same city each year, or would you prefer to visit different cities? Please give me your suggestions[7] in the space marked "comments" on the reservation form.

We appreciate your continued support for[8] our meetings. I look forward to seeing you again this year.

Very truly yours, (174)

3

MEMO TO: Ed Parker

I am most pleased with our plans for holiday window displays. When our committee was formed,[1] we asked a representative of each department to contribute suggestions. It was rewarding to see the[2] number and range of suggestions we received.

If our plans are okay with you, we will incorporate new toys with[3] traditional items of the past. For example, we located some rare antique toys to present against a[4] background of modern paintings. We would like to acquire a system of lights and sounds to give added emphasis.

We[5] could still use our painted landscapes if we give them a new look. We might try arranging electronic games and toys[6] against the old background. As soon as you have the opportunity, won't you meet with me to discuss these suggestions?[7] (140)

4

Dear Mrs. Moore:

Thank you for your letter concerning the use of our floor cleaner. We are delighted to hear that[1] the machine performed so well. We have been pleasantly surprised by the large demand for this machine. So many[2] people requested it that we have a waiting list.

In order to serve more customers, we are acquiring[3] another machine. As soon as this machine is ready for use, you may call in your reservation directly to[4] our store on Second Street. We hope the new system provides more efficient service for everyone.

We appreciate[5] your comments. I hope you will visit us often.

Very truly yours, (112)

5

MEMO TO: Manager of Marketing and Sales

When the Board of Directors met last Monday, they voted to start[1] a new division to produce paper goods. This represents a major change and offers opportunities in[2] a new market.

We will distribute the paper goods through our food division. This system appears to be the most[3] economical and convenient method of handling the new merchandise.

Sales representatives who call on[4] supermarkets will increase their calls to include discount stores, drug stores, and other retail outlets which carry our[5] goods.

We anticipate using Denver, Colorado, as a test market for the new line. We will measure the[6] results of a six-month test to form future marketing plans. If we accomplish our goals in the test market, we[7] will turn our attention to national sales. (148)

LESSON 26

1. Write ′ for the word ending *ness*.

kindness, k-nd-ness cN′

illness, i-l-ness l′

*happiness, h-p-e-ness hpe′

witnesses, w-t-nesses ⌣l″

carelessness, k-r-l-s-ness crls′

helplessness, h-l-p-l-s-ness hlpls′

*Always write long vowels before marks of punctuation.

Brief Forms

both bo

public pb

individual Nv

important, importance ⌒pl

Brief Form Development

publicly pbl

willingness l′

publication pbj

individually Nvl

Phrases

to come lk

to offer lofr

to determine ldl

MORE INTRODUCTORY DEPENDENT CLAUSES

In addition to *when, as,* and *if,* introductory dependent clauses beginning with such words as *although, before,* and *because* will be highlighted.

Although two months have passed, we still have not heard from you.

Before you order supplies, please contact our purchasing department.

Because you are a valued customer, you will receive a discount.

Your Business Vocabulary

homeowner's policy	An insurance policy covering the cost of the policyholder's home and personal belongings in case of damage or loss.
suggested retail price	The ultimate sale price (sometimes referred to as *list price*) recommended by the manufacturer.

PRINCIPLES SUMMARY

1. Write ' for the word ending *ness*: kindness, k-nd-ness.

Reading and Writing Exercises

-1-

d⌒r + ⌒rs cr⌒r
⌒ dli- l nf⌒ u
la wb asn- l hNl
u plse, z u lrn-
f⌒, L, [Intro DC] u f⌒r ayN
z P⌒o- l VP, cdlc
l a la c P⌒j k n
rcgnj v, olSN
kbjs l r co, alo
as⌒, dles lb v
Clnj-, [Intro DC] i pln l ku
c P⌒d + lro Svs
crc v ⌒r jnsn, z
. frS Sp cdlc l ⌒e
u Psnll + rvu u
plse ldl la c cvrj
⌒es u crN nds,
bcz s ⌒pl f bo vu
lb P du r kvrsj, [Intro DC] il
cl o Wd Ma 27 l
fN . L⌒ kv f E, /
lb . plzr vzt ⌒ u,
⌒ nu lu sle + ilc
fw L⌒c nu frNs, su

-2-

d⌒r ⌣lsn s ⌣ gr
plzr lae lk u l r
ks⌒r clb, c enc-
mbrs crd alos u
l sp du rglr Sr
hrs f⌒ Mn lru Sl,
bcz r Sr, rzrv- f
us v mbrs ol, [Intro DC] e
asc lau n nvi vzlrs
o rglr sp ds, hoE
o frS Sn v eC ⌒o
e hld . opn hos n
⌣C clb mbrs nvi
gss l lrn ab r clb

+ me bnfts / ofrs,
e no v 250 mbrs.
z r mbrs kus l
gro Intro DC , el ofr evn grr
Dks o dse. P
er sl brN=m
/ 20% blo
/ sug- rll prs. uc
hlp r mbrs gro b
U ppl n u nbrh
ab r Pq. vzl r Sn
opn hos + asc .
frN Uk u. su

-3-

d lvn Alo w gvn
C U lu sugj la ,
rn f . se w hos v
reps Intro DC , w dsd-aq
dy so / ls .
f , rcvr f . rsN
d' + hr ku- rel l q
hll , r S pl
ksrn, hoE idlc
lofr i spl l aol
Nv hu d c . olSN
rep. su rln hs
Sv- z yr v pb rljs Series ,
drr v ks r afrs Series , +
asSN l / sec v Sa.
ifl kfdN se db
rsv- l b / pb, bo
i f + i + l
lqf cN' + ncrym.
U dfrN kdjs id v
gldl ac-. ihp / opl
ks aq w fCr. uvl

-4-

dr + rs sd /
gvo s gr plzr l nvi
u l alN / prvl opn

-5-

vr nu Sr / 301 N Sa
S, r spl cre . f ln
v ms + ms cll
f spl gs l fl
r, ev lcn gr cr
l Cz u fvrl brNs
+ dzns, fS z pl
er Pvd . d rnj v
prss f C l Cz,
r Sr opns l pb
o Nv 6, 6 evn bf
edlc u Lb r gS f .
prvl Ao n Cr
dls lb r orgnl
dzns f NY, flo
Ao e nvr u lv
rfrsms (Series), vzl (Series) + broz,
p jyn s f l Pss
Lb . evn v fn (Series) bf (Series) +
Sprzs o Fr Nv 5, vlu

dr Svns lqf
Pdl'n rpl
dys lu h, e
USN la fr dy
cs / nes fu l
fN ol lv glrs l
rprs r b d, ev
fw- u ch l . lcl
ajN hu l hlp u
c loz arms, bcz
u hors plse Pvds
kp cvrj (Intro DC) a rprs lb
d / no cS lu, ls
cvrj ls NE lv
arms u Cz, bf ec
Pss u ch (Intro DC) el nd .
kp lS v Nv ds
dy- or lS, p l or
dl la lS lu ajNs
ofs / 2100 m S,

z u ins co e M	ajM l hlp lca
i rel u lu h qcl.	plzM + kv akdjs.
w nh p alo r	cu

Key

1

Dear Mr. and Mrs. Cramer:

I am delighted to inform you that I have been assigned to handle your[1] policy. As you learned from his letter, your former agent was promoted to vice president. I would like to add[2] that the promotion came in recognition of his outstanding contributions to our company.

Although[3] assuming his duties will be very challenging, I plan to continue the prompt and thorough service characteristic[4] of Mr. Johnson. As a first step, I would like to meet you personally and review your policy[5] to determine that the coverage meets your current needs.

Because it is important for both of you to be[6] present during our conversation, I will call on Wednesday, May 27, to find a time convenient for[7] everyone. It will be a pleasure visiting with you. I am new to your city, and I look forward to making[8] new friends.

Sincerely yours, (164)

2

Dear Mr. Wilson:

It is with great pleasure that we welcome you to our consumer club. The enclosed membership[1] card allows you to shop during regular store hours from Monday through Saturday.

Because our store is reserved[2] for the use of members only, we ask that you not invite visitors on regular shopping days. However,[3] on the first Sunday of each month, we hold an open house in which club members invite guests to learn about our club[4] and the many benefits it offers.

We now have 250 members. As our membership continues[5] to grow, we will offer even greater discounts on merchandise. At the present time, we are selling brand-name[6] items at 20 percent below the suggested retail price. You can help our membership grow by telling people[7] in your neighborhood about our program. Visit our Sunday open house and ask a friend to come with you.

Sincerely[8] yours, (161)

3

Dear Melvin:

Although I have given much thought to your suggestion that I run for a seat in the House of Representatives,[1] I have decided against doing so at this time. My wife is recovering from a recent illness,[2] and her continued return to good health is our most important concern.

However, I would like to offer my[3] support to another individual who would make an outstanding representative. Sue Martin has[4] served as manager of public relations, director of consumer affairs, and assistant to the Secretary[5] of State. I feel confident she would be received well by the public.

Both my wife and I wish to thank you[6] for your kindness and encouragement. Under different conditions, I would have gladly accepted. I hope the[7] opportunity comes again in the future.

Yours very truly, (152)

4

Dear Mr. and Mrs. Smith:

It gives us great pleasure to invite you to attend the private opening of our[1] new store at 301 North State Street.

Our shop will carry a full line of men's and women's clothing, from sporting goods[2] to formal wear. We have taken great care to choose your favorite brands and designs. Just as important, we are[3] providing a wide range of prices from which to choose.

Our store opens to the public on November 6. On the[4] evening before, we would like you to be our guest for a private showing in which our models will be wearing[5] original designs from New York. Following the show, we invite you to have refreshments, visit, and browse.

Please join[6] us for what promises to be an evening of fun, fashion, and surprises on Friday, November 5.

Very[7] truly yours, (142)

5

Dear Mr. Stevens:

Thank you for your promptness in reporting the damages to your home.

We understand that the[1] fire damage makes it necessary for you to find other living quarters while repairs are being made. We have[2] forwarded your claim to a local agent who will help you make those arrangements.

Because your homeowner's policy[3] provides complete coverage, all repairs will be made at no cost to you. This coverage includes whatever[4] living arrangements you choose. Before we can process your claim, we will need a complete list of the individual[5] items damaged or lost. Please mail or deliver that list to your agent's office at 2100 Main[6] Street.

As your insurance company, we want to return you to your home quickly. In the meantime, please allow our[7] agent to help locate pleasant and convenient accommodations.

Cordially yours, (155)

LESSON 27

1. When using salutations and closings in context, write them according to the rule.

gentlemen, j-nt-l-men jNlm sincerely, s-n-s-r-ly snsrl

cordially, k-r-j-l-ly cryll

Abbreviations

advertise av Christmas Xs

Brief Forms

always a prove pv

consider ks note nt

ordinary ord

Brief Form Development

consideration ksj improvement pvm

noted nt- approval apvl

ordinarily ordl

Commonly Misspelled Words

opportunity opt

preferred Pfr-

Your Business Vocabulary

corporate stocks crprt Scs — Shares in the ownership of a corporation.

search and screen committee SC + scrn k — Committee appointed to evaluate the credentials of job applicants and recommend candidates for the position. Often used in educational institutions.

PRINCIPLES SUMMARY

1. In context, write salutations and closings according to the rule: gentlemen, j-nt-l-men jNlm.

Reading and Writing Exercises

-1-

d ex ur , v fu ppl
Czn lrsv 3 fre
isus v bo rvu, yx
bcz e -l nqes ol l
/ Nvs hu -e r rqms.
bo rvu , dr- / nf-
Nvs lc u hu v sn.
ksrn f -yr Pbls +
opls fs r ny, l hlp
u dsd la r -gzn ,
ri fu er sN u / frS
3 isus fre v G. ln
u -a Cz lrsv / 6
flo isus / hf prs,
-l- n loz 9 isus lb
-yr nz Sres. , isu
l nvSga / PCs v
crprl Scs. ol arlcls
l Dcs hll cr, (Series) bq-
Svss, (Series) + Pgs f rlrm,
p -C f bo rvu n
u -l. uvl

-2-

ddr bron -p- l
rcm dr dvd -lsn f
pzy v VP vu U. v nn
dvd bo Psnll + Pfyll
f pS 5 yrs ufl la ic
kNo, crc, (Series) ejcyl ldr+, (Series)
+ akms, dvd rlas l
l ppl. h hs Pvd-. esp
-pl lq bln N +
acd-c afrs. dvd

hs rep- r clj o sv
ks n sle + ke gvl,
bcz v dvds _pl l
r clj udb sre lse h
lv. i Aso no la
ddca- Nvs _S _v
o l nu gls n od l
sal lr o nd f grl,
if uv ol qs re dr
_lsn, [Intro DC] ulb gld l asr
L. uvl

-3-

dK Ap 15, qcl
aprC + e _S rds
r nlr Sc v nu +
uz- crs. la _ns gr
sv f _z sprs. ls
yr el ofr blr Dks
ln E bf, bgn Fb 3
el rn f=p1 nzppr

Avms U r pb ab r
lo prss b er gv u.
opl lgl ahd v r+.
er nvi lyl Ks lc
u l lc Avj v lz gr
sv o Fb 2. ul fN.
_d rnj v _cs, [Series]
_dls, [Series] + prss f
_C l Cz, ul Aso
v E ksj n _c ord
cr arms. r Cf cr
ofsr lb o hN du
sl hrs l apv u cr,
rmbr erl sprs
a v r b8 Cyss.
ehp lse u lr. ul

-4-

dprN r scl dNl
hll Pq, ab lgl
Ua, z pl v ls Pq

u Cld l v r opl l
pp n. dNl clnc
fre v G, eC Cld
lb gvn. fre Ubrs
+ sn ho luz r Pprl,
bcz v opl v q h
cr dy ls Pq e asc
a prNs l hlp s b
Svz ls Cldrns brs
hbls bo n rn +
n evn, p nl la ls
Pq dz n rpls rglr
dNl cr, alo u Cld
a b rsv rglr
dNl lrems, Intro DC h or se
c Sl bnfl f pp n
clsr clnc, ls Pq
hs b apv- b r ke
dNl ksl, if u s u
Cld l pp, Intro DC p sn r f
blo gv u ksN, rel

r lu Clds lCr
b Oc 5, su

-5-

dr evns z r vlu-
K uno la r Sr lcs
prd n hNl ol r
bs n fNlms r, ls
plse hs pv- lb r
s pl rzn Nvs
lc u ku l sp hr, ls
yr ev. Sprz fu, l
so r apj f spl uv
gvn r bs el ofr. bf=
X s sl f Pfr-Ks, js
so r slsppl ls L +
ul rsv 20% of r
rglr prss = l r
nlr ln v sus, Series cos, Series
srls, Series + splsr, ls,
. Cnj f ps yrs

n prss rds-
af Xns. b sp erl
uc ak 2 pl gls =
1 fu + ol f /Nlm
o u sp ls, e cryll

nvr u l alN ls
sl + njy Cz f r
f Sc. / d gv s gr
plzr l Sv u aq. cu

Key

1

Dear Executive:

You are one of the few people chosen to receive three free issues of *Business Review.*

Why?[1] Because we mail inquiries only to the individuals who meet our requirements. *Business Review* is[2] directed at informed individuals like you who have shown a concern for major problems and opportunities[3] facing our nation.

To help you decide that our magazine is right for you, we are sending you the first three[4] issues free of charge. Then you may choose to receive the six following issues at half price.

Included in those nine[5] issues will be major news stories. One issue will investigate the purchasing of corporate stocks. Other[6] articles will discuss health care, banking services, and programs for retirement.

Please watch for *Business Review* in[7] your mail.

Yours very truly, (145)

2

Dear Dr. Brown:

I am pleased to recommend Dr. David Wilson for the position of vice president of[1] your university. Having known David both personally and professionally for the past five years, I[2] feel that I can comment on his character, educational leadership, and accomplishments.

David relates[3] well to people. He has provided an especially important link between industry and academic[4] affairs. David has represented our college on several committees in city and county government.[5]

Because of David's importance to our college, I would be sorry to see him leave. I also know that dedicated[6] individuals must move on to new goals in order to satisfy their own need for growth.

If you have other[7] questions regarding Dr. Wilson, I will be glad to answer them.

Yours very truly, (157)

3

Dear Customer:

April 15 is quickly approaching, and we must reduce our entire stock of new and used cars.[1] That means great savings for wise shoppers. This year we will offer better discounts than ever before.

Beginning[2] February 3, we will run full-page newspaper advertisements telling the public about our low prices, but[3] we are giving you an opportunity to get ahead of the rush. We are inviting loyal customers[4] like you to take advantage of these great savings on February 2. You will find a wide range of makes, models,[5] and prices from which to choose.

You will also have every consideration in making ordinary credit[6] arrangements. Our chief credit officer will be on hand during sale hours to approve your credit.

Remember,[7] early shoppers always have the best choices. We hope to see you there.

Yours truly, (154)

4

Dear Parent:

Our school dental health program is about to get underway.

As part of this program, your child will have[1] the opportunity to participate in a dental clinic free of charge. Each child will be given a free[2] toothbrush and shown how to use it properly.

Because of the importance of good home care during this program, we[3] ask all parents to help us by supervising their children's brushing habits both in the mornings and in the evenings.[4]

Please note that this program does not replace regular dental care. Although your child may be receiving regular[5] dental treatments, he or she can still benefit from participating in the classroom clinic.

This program[6] has been approved by the county dental council. If you wish your child to participate, please sign the form below[7] giving your consent. Return it to your child's teacher by October 5.

Sincerely yours, (156)

5

Dear Mr. Evans:

As our valued customer, you know that our store takes pride in handling only the best in[1] gentlemen's wear. This policy has proved to be the most important reason individuals like you continue[2] to shop here.

This year we have a surprise for you. To show our appreciation for the support you have given[3] our business, we will offer a before-Christmas sale for preferred customers.

Just show our salespeople this letter,[4] and you will receive 20 percent off our regular prices—including our entire line of suits, coats,[5] shirts, and sportswear.

This is a change from past years when prices were reduced after Christmas. By shopping early, you can[6] accomplish two important goals—one for you and the other for the gentlemen on your shopping list.

We[7] cordially invite you to attend this sale and enjoy choosing from our full stock. It would give us great pleasure to serve[8] you again.

Cordially yours, (165)

LESSON 28

RECAP AND REVIEW

You have learned several additional ways of increasing your shorthand speed and efficiency since Lesson 21. These various aspects of your skill development are reviewed here.

1. Since your last review, you have learned to write the following word beginnings:

em, im

2. The following word endings were also presented:

quire q

ness

3. The words listed below illustrate all of the new principles you learned in Lessons 22 through 27.

emphasize, em-f-s-z fsz

impress, im-p-r-s prs

image, im-j

attempt, a-t-m-t

promptly, prah-m-t-ly

temptation, t-m-t-tion

requirement, re-quire-ment rqm

inquiry, in-quire-e nqe

acquire, a-quire aq

kindness, k-nd-ness

witnessess, w-t-nesses

account, a-count ak

common, com-n kn

concern, con-s-r-n ksrn

still, st-l

estate, e-st-ate

most, m-st

pleasure, p-l-z-r plzr

measure, m-z-r zr

treasure, t-r-z-r trzr

illness, i-l-ness

4. You learned to write salutations and closings in context this way:

sincerely, s-n-s-r-ly snsrl cordially, k-r-j-l-ly crjll

gentlemen, j-nt-l-men jNlm

5. Days of the week are written this way:

Sunday Sn Thursday Th

Monday Mn Friday Fr

Tuesday Tu Saturday St

Wednesday Wd

6. The names of cities and their state abbreviations are written as follows:

Boston, MA bSn MA Tulsa, OK Ulsa OK

Las Vegas, NV ls vgs NV Dallas, TX dls TX

7. Do you recall the following abbreviations?

dse elc fed

S q esp

gvt ok gl

U rep inc

av X

8. How quickly can you write the outlines for these brief forms?

committee come industry
ever satisfy continue
other character deliver
both public satisfactory
individual important complete
came characteristic every
importance contribute opportunity
convenient convenience always
note prove consider
accomplish ordinary

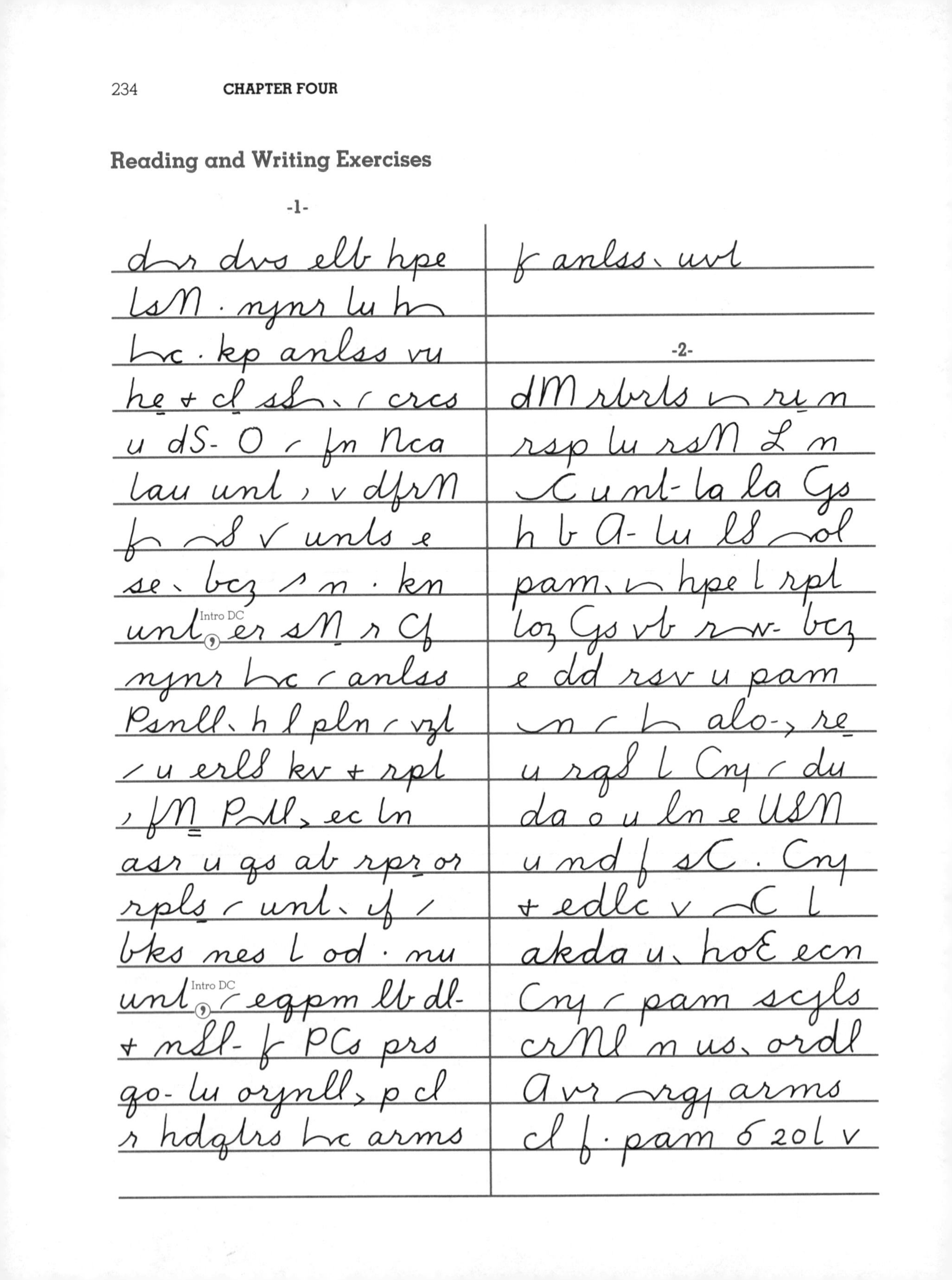

Reading and Writing Exercises

-1-

Intro DC

Intro DC

-2-

eC o, r Avs, lau
c 2 pams n
1 o. Intro DC if uc du ls, u
pam db at cl
rsv- bf s du da
eC o, chp ls
sug hlps. p fl
fre l cl nE uv
gs. cu

-3-

d dvd uz p- l lrn
vu rsN apym z
VP v Wrn U. cno
SC + scrn k ks-
me lp exs bf c
. fnl dsj, z dn vr
clj u d me pl
kbjs l r nSlj.
bcz vu akms hr
ev sn ncrss n
nrlm Series, pvms n
lC lds Series, + Srl
v me nd- Pgs, e
+ l nvr u + u
fl lb r gSs / .
bngl lb gvn b r
Sf Series, fclle Series, + SdN
ksl. ls, r a v
lq u f Pgrs aCv-
U u drj, w fCr el
cp u nf- o l er
du hr. chp ul du
s f s. bs s
n u nu pzj. vlu

-4-

mo l frd a
Ppz . nu ld f
rec chs n r sNrl
dla Pss unl x sug
la chs reps uz . Sp

C Ncas la r ch
hs b rvy- + sd b elr
ac- or n ac- f Pss.
n . dcm ks l . dla
clrc ol ls Sp, [Intro DC] la
ch sd b rel- r
rqs la / b kp- Pprl,
ls ld d rq v lll
adjl efl + d rzll
n . efsN + kv
sS f E1 .

-5-

dr jnsn lqf rsp
l rzra + L v
aplcj f pzj v rplr,
iz v hpe l lrn la
U ksj f . opn o
u bs ri Sf. il gldl
sN u adjl exs v
ri + ne ol inf u

dzr, z u rqS-, [Intro DC] l asc-
2 v cl Pfsrs l
ri Ls v rcmj. usd
rsv Ls f dr hs
lsn + dr szn
An n . fu ds, bcz
v bcgroN n bs
+ ecos ifl Sln ucd
kb C z . bs rplr.
cd e sl p . e l
Dcs ls frlr, udb
hpe lk l allNa +
dl ri exs n
Psn. lc fw l e
u / u kv. su

-6-

drs js u nu cr
crd, enc- + exp-
l lk u z . G K. u
cr ld, sn / lp

v ls L, r alC-
brsr gvs r inf u
rqS-ab r rz bso
s ol plNs la db
apo f. r cl.
/ Aso rfs u l. ld
dlr l h u a q f
hlp u sp lNscp-
sil. r dlrs r gld

l cop r l=od
Ks, u a od elr b
Ufn or b l CE,
kv. l nsr Pl
dle e s b ar fra zz
e rsv u od, if usd
v ne qs ab u nu
Intro DC
ak, p gv s. cl. cu

Key

Abbreviations

merchandise	et cetera	federal
street	question	especially
government	okay	quart
university	represent, representative	incorporate, incorporated
advertise	Christmas	

Brief Forms

k	k	n
E	sal	ku
ol	crc	dl
bo	pb	sal
Nv	-pl	kp
k	crc	E
-pl	kb	opl
kv	kv	a
nl	pv	ks
ak	ord	

1

Dear Mr. Davis:

We will be happy to send an engineer to your home to make a complete analysis[1] of your heating and cooling system. The characteristics you described over the phone indicate that your unit[2] is very different from most of the units we see. Because it is not a common unit, we are sending[3] our chief engineer to make the analysis personally. He will plan the visit at your earliest[4] convenience and report his findings promptly.

We can then answer your questions about repairing or replacing[5] the unit. If it becomes necessary to order a new unit, the equipment will be delivered and[6] installed for the purchase price quoted to you originally.

Please call our headquarters to make arrangements for[7] the analysis.

Yours very truly, (147)

2

Dear Miss Roberts:

I am writing in response to your recent letter in which you noted that late charges had been[1] added to your last monthly payment. I am happy to report those charges have been removed because we did[2] receive your payment within the time allowed.

Regarding your request to change the due date on your loan, we understand[3] your need for such a change, and we would like very much to accommodate you. However, we cannot change the[4] payment schedules currently in use. Ordinarily, all of our mortgage arrangements call for a payment on the[5] 20th of each month.

Our advice is that you make two payments within one month. If you can do this, your payment[6] would be automatically received before its due date each month.

I hope this suggestion helps. Please feel free to call[7] whenever you have questions.

Cordially yours, (148)

3

Dear David:

I was pleased to learn of your recent appointment as vice president of Western University.[1] I know the search and screen committee considered many top executives before making a final decision.[2]

As dean of our college, you made many important contributions to our institution. Because of your[3] accomplishments here, we have seen increases in enrollment, improvements in teaching methods, and the start of[4] many needed programs.

We wish to invite you and your family to be our guests at a banquet to be given[5] by our staff, faculty, and student council. This is our way of thanking you for the progress achieved under your[6] direction.

In the future, we will keep you informed on what we are doing here. I hope you will do the same for[7] us. Best wishes in your new position.

Very truly yours, (151)

4

MEMO TO: Fred White

May I propose a new method for recording claims in our central data processing unit?[1] I suggest that claims representatives use a stamp which indicates that the item has been reviewed and should[2] be either accepted or not accepted for processing. When a document comes to a data clerk without[3] this stamp, that item should be returned with the request that it be completed properly.

This method would require[4] very little additional effort and would result in a more efficient and convenient system for[5] everyone. (101)

5

Dear Mr. Johnson:

Thank you for responding to my resumé and letter of application for the position[1] of reporter.

I was very happy to learn that I am under consideration for an opening[2] on your business writing staff. I will gladly send you additional examples of my writing and any[3] other information you desire.

As you requested, I asked two of my college professors to write letters of[4] recommendation. You should receive letters from Dr. Thomas Wilson and Dr. Susan Allen within a[5] few days.

Because of my background in business and economics, I feel certain I could contribute much as a[6] business reporter. Could we set up a meeting to discuss this further?

I would be happy to come to Atlanta[7] and deliver my writing examples in person. I look forward to meeting with you at your convenience.[8]

Sincerely yours, (163)

6

Dear Mrs. James:

Your new credit card is enclosed, and we are pleased to welcome you as a charge customer. Your credit[1] limit is shown at the top of this letter.

The attached brochure gives the information you requested about[2] our rose bushes and other plants that would be appropriate for a warm climate. It also refers you to[3] a local dealer to whom you may go for help with your specific landscaping situation. Our dealers are[4] glad to cooperate with our mail-order customers.

You may order either by telephone or by mail,[5] whichever is more convenient. To ensure prompt delivery, we ship by air freight as soon as we receive your[6] order.

If you should have any questions about your new account, please give us a call.

Cordially yours, (137)

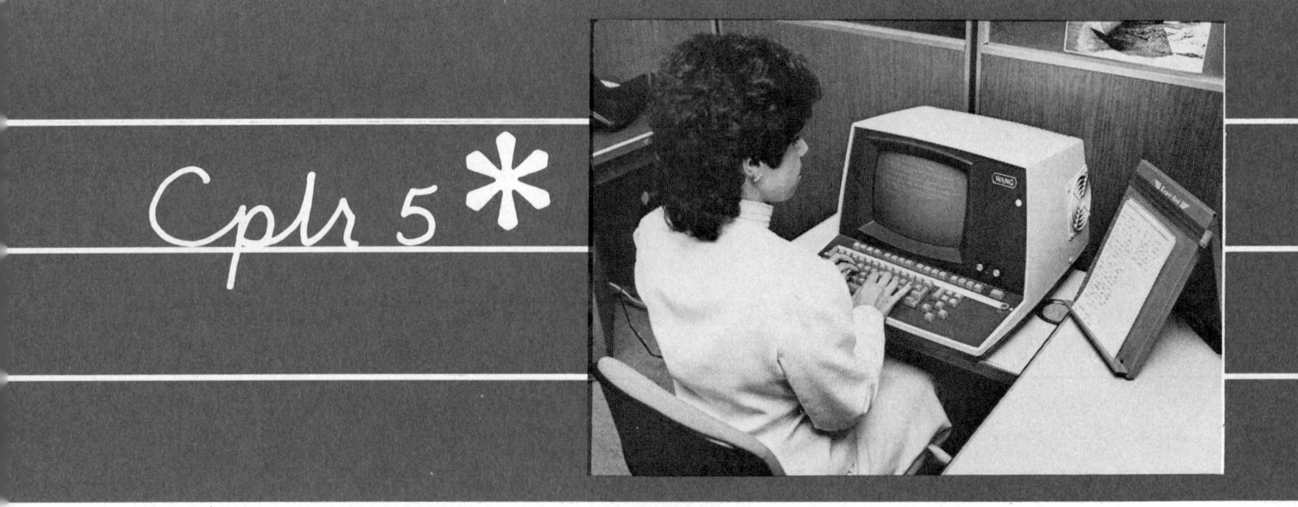

OUTPUT: TRANSCRIBING SHORTHAND NOTES

You have just returned to your work area following a session of dictation. Priority items have been paper clipped, your questions answered, and special instructions ("enclose two copies of new catalog") flagged in colored pen. Now you are ready to transform those notes into an attractive printed document—one that speaks well of you, your supervisor, and the company for which you work. What is the most efficient and reliable way to produce the perfect transcript?

Begin by following the step-by-step procedures below.

Before Beginning to Type (or Keyboard)

1. Transcribe in order of priority.
2. Determine letter style, format, and marginal settings.

***Chapter Five**

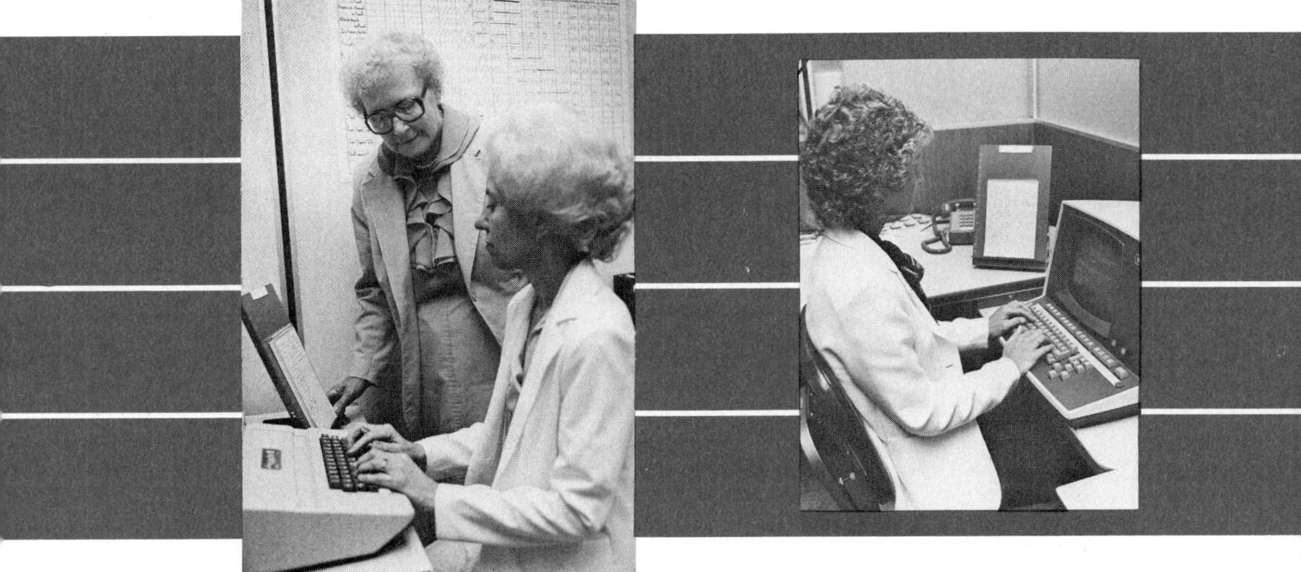

3. Verify spellings of any words you are not certain of—learn to watch for commonly misspelled words that often slip by unnoticed.
4. Elevate your notepad for convenient reading and begin to type (or keyboard).

Before Removing the Document from the Machine

1. Proofread carefully—not once, but twice. Read first against your notes to be certain that your copy is complete and accurate; then read again for typographical errors, spelling errors, and punctuation or grammatical errors you might have overlooked earlier.
2. Make any necessary corrections while the document is in the machine.

Before Presenting the Document for a Signature

1. Cancel your shorthand notes by drawing a line through the transcribed dictation.
2. Look at your transcript carefully. Is it attractively arranged on the page?

Does it contain noticeable corrections? When your transcribed copy is perfectly neat, free of errors, and shows no evidence of corrections, it is ready to be signed and mailed.

3. Type the envelope, giving it the same careful attention you gave the letter.
4. If the letter calls for enclosures, assemble them now to be presented with the letter.
5. Present the letter for your supervisor's signature, submitting the envelope and any specified enclosures along with the transcript.

A Word About Equipment and Supplies

Some supplies and procedures will vary slightly depending upon the printing equipment you use. Let's look first at the items you will always need.

1. Keep these at your work station:
   a. Dictionary—consult it for spellings and definitions.
   b. List of commonly misspelled words—post it nearby.
   c. Secretarial procedures manual.
   d. English usage manual.
2. If you transcribe on a word processor:

   The machine will have many automatic features and will make corrections at your command without the aid of erasing materials. Your keyboarded copy appears on a screen so that you can make corrections before the copy is printed out automatically on paper.
3. If you transcribe on an electric or electronic typewriter:

   These machines often provide self-correcting devices. If your machine doesn't have this feature, choose the most effective agent available—correction film, tape, or fluid, for example—and master the technique of applying it. Your transcript should show no evidence of corrections.

   A beautifully transcribed document is a source of pride for your company. A written communication should act as an ambassador of good will for your employer. Its professional appearance will go a long way toward bringing you a successful career.

LESSON 29

1. Write for words beginning with the sound of any vowel + *x* (*aks, eks, iks, oks, uks,* or *eggs*).

accident, x-d-nt

exist, x-st

explain, x-p-l-n

examination, x-min-tion

excite, x-ite

excellent, x-l-nt

2. Write for the medial and final sound of *x*.

boxes, b-x-s

textbook, t-x-t-b-k

tax, t-x

relax, re-l-x

3. Write for the word beginnings *extr* and *extra*.

extreme, extr-m

extremely, extr-m-ly

extra

extraordinary, extra-ordinary

Write these additional words:

express, x-p-r-s

maximum, m-x-mum

exchange, x-chay-n-j

index, nd-x

extend, x-t-nd

reflex, re-f-l-x

Phrases

you will find

as your

to call

on you

as you

on your

MORE INTRODUCTORY DEPENDENT CLAUSES

Introductory dependent clauses beginning with such words as *after, while,* and *whether* will be highlighted in your reading and writing exercises.

After I study the report, I will write her a memo.

While we were reviewing your account, I noticed that your contract renewal is scheduled for next month.

Whether you are looking for a specific item or gift ideas in general, you'll find our clerks eager to help.

Your Business Vocabulary

copy editor cpe edtr	A person employed to edit written material for publication.
unit price unt prs	The price for an individual item selected from a larger quantity of like merchandise.

PRINCIPLES SUMMARY

1. Write \ x-p-l-n for words beginning with any vowel + *x*: explain, \pln .
2. Write x b-x-s for the medial and final sound of *x*: boxes, bxs .
3. Write X extr-m for the word beginnings *extr* and *extra*: extreme, Xm ; extraordinary, extra-ordinary Xord .

Reading and Writing Exercises

-1-

dr s edws
apli f pzj v cpe
edtr u fr, ublr
ulfN bcgroN
apo f dles dS- n
u nzppr avm, l-
w enc- rzra, ls
v bcs w edl-, w
aso rln Nxs, (Series) cvr
cpe, (Series) + av brsrs, du
ls 4 yrs w fsz-
Sdes n kpur Pq>
Xl egr l e
u + lrn ab
u dpl, u co Pdss
lN bcs C rahel
w rpls, a e
Dcs ls pzj n Psn x
ul cl o Jn 23 l ar.
apym / u kv > ulc
fu l lc u ln, vlu

-2-

dr js ev nju-
Sv zu trvl ajN du
pS yr, ehp r Svss
rzlt- n me plzN
mres fu + u fl, a
e aso lc ls opl l
rm u er a rde l
hlp u trvl plns.
tr ur lc ahd l
s or jS nd lc
lS=mt arms, (Intro DC) el
gldl lc cr √ dtls,
r f ln v Svss cs
ne trp ezer +
rlx fu, af cld tr
sls n, (Intro DC) y n ks s
fn w sn x ev sv u

nu lrvl pcys l so
u, s n l sn l plnu
fl ol f sr vcj.
erl Srl nsrs u Cys
akdjs + vcs r lrp
fn f E, er lc
fu lse u ls k yr. su

-3-

1 r sm v ofs splis
arv- n lN kdj + o
scyl ls rn. l
e Cc r dse aqr
inv (Intro DC) e Dcvr-. X od
v envs. alo e rqS-
ol 20 bxs v envs (Intro DC) e
rsv- 21. eC bx kln-
r f a v 2H prN-
envs, e fN no my
v X envs 6 inv b
e se no rzn l rel

r X pcj + l a r l
r splis. ev dl-la
r Nv unl prs v eC
bx, 8 95 + er enc.
Cc f la a, yf u
fl la ls r rqs
frlr Dcj (Intro DC) p ll e
no. lqf Pd'n dl
r gs. er ln sal-
r all gvn r
od. cu

-4-

drs arnld ls, n
rsp lu cl nf. s v
dys lu cr. d u p kp
+ rel r enc- rpl
n 1 c flo r da
vu vdN. p b Sln l
rec a nes inf. uzr
adjl sps Pvd- l vpln

ho (vdN ocr-> u
chs ak No, 07=5151.
r rynl chs -yr l
cl ou P-ll l vm (
d-y + apv arms
f -c rprs, e rcm
. lN bde sp nr u
-C hNls -d vr
chs. e sug ls fr
ol bcz / ras hil n
K saly. -tr u Cz ls
sp sp or aol fr,
ntrl p lu, p cl if uv
ne frtr qs. ul

-5-

dr + -rs hd (
ak fr v dvs + dvs
-so l lk u l bflo,
z nu rzdNs no dol

ur fN -C l lrn ab
r sle. ehp (encs
n ls L hlp. e l- . -p
v sle + ol inf dzn-
l hlp u fl / h- nu
nu lc, -a e ll u
ab r fr. dvs + dvs
, (oldd ak fr n ls
sle. e lq (-n
rzn ev so me Ks
, (P-l + lyl Svs
e ofr bo bss + Nvs,
ehp ul alo s l hNl
u ak nds. zu lx rep
ec du E = rec inf, (Series)
kpu lxs, (Series) + kp (fs
fu. el -l u . nl
nr (N v yr l rm
u vr Svs. w -nt
dN hzla lcl o s. uvl

Key

1

Dear Ms. Edwards:

I am applying for the position of copy editor with your firm. I believe you will[1] find my background appropriate for the duties described in your newspaper advertisement. Included in the[2] enclosed resumé is a list of books I have edited. I have also written indexes, cover copy,[3] and advertising brochures. During the last four years I have emphasized studies in computer programming.

I am[4] extremely eager to meet with you and learn more about your department. Your company produces excellent[5] books which rate highly in the marketplace. May we discuss this position in person? I will call on June 23[6] to arrange an appointment at your convenience.

I look forward to talking with you then.

Very truly yours,[7] (140)

2

Dear Mr. James:

We have enjoyed serving as your travel agent during the past year. We hope our services[1] resulted in many pleasant memories for you and your family. May we also take this opportunity[2] to remind you we are always ready to help with your travel plans. Whether you are looking ahead to summer[3] or just needing to make last-minute arrangements, we will gladly take care of the details.

Our full line of services[4] makes any trip easier and more relaxing for you. After cold weather sets in, why not consider some[5] fun in the sun? We have several exciting new travel packages to show you. It is not too soon to plan[6] your family outings for summer vacation. An early start ensures you choice accommodations and makes the[7] trip more fun for everyone.

We are looking forward to seeing you this coming year.

Sincerely yours, (158)

3

Gentlemen:

Our shipment of office supplies arrived in excellent condition and on schedule this morning. While[1] we were checking our merchandise against the invoice, we discovered an extra order of envelopes. Although[2] we requested only 20 boxes of envelopes, we received 21. Each box contained the full amount[3] of 200 printed envelopes.

We find no mention of the extra envelopes on the invoice, but we see[4] no reason to return the extra package and will add it to our supplies. We have determined that the[5] individual unit price of each box is $8.95, and we are enclosing a check for that[6] amount.

If you feel that this matter requires further discussion, please let me know. Thank you for your promptness in[7] delivering our goods. We are more than satisfied with the attention given our order.

Cordially yours, (159)

4

Dear Mrs. Arnold:

This is in response to your call informing us of the damages to your car. Would you please[1] complete and return the enclosed report within one week following the date of your accident? Please be certain[2] to record all necessary information. Use the additional space provided to explain how the[3] accident occurred.

Your claims account number is 07-5151. Our regional claims manager[4] will call on you promptly to examine the damage and approve arrangements for making repairs.

We recommend[5] an excellent body shop near you which handles most of our claims. We suggest this firm only because it rates[6] highly in customer satisfaction. Whether you choose this specific shop or another firm is entirely up[7] to you.

Please call if you have any further questions.

Yours truly, (152)

5

Dear Mr. and Mrs. Hastings:

The accounting firm of Davis and Davis wishes to welcome you to Buffalo.[1]

As new residents, no doubt you are finding much to learn about our city. We hope the enclosures in this[2] letter help. We included a map of the city and other information designed to help you feel at home[3] in your new location.

May we tell you about our firm? Davis and Davis is the oldest accounting firm in[4] this city. We think the main reason we have so many customers is the prompt and loyal service we offer[5] both businesses and individuals.

We hope you will allow us to handle your accounting needs. As your tax[6] representative, we can do everything—record information, compute taxes, and complete the forms for you.[7] We will mail you a note near the end of the year to remind you of our service. In the meantime, don't hesitate[8] to call on us.

Yours very truly, (167)

LESSON 30

1. Write for the medial or final sound of any vowel + *ng* when the sound is part of the root word and is not a suffix (*ang, eng, ing, ong, ung*).

sang, s-ang

long, l-ong

nothing, n-ith-ing

single, s-ing-l

young, y-ung

thing, ith-ing

Brief Forms

already

next

immediate

experience

approximate

Brief Form Development

immediately

approximately

Commonly Misspelled Words		
accept		(to receive) Tom will be happy to *accept* our service award.
except		(not including) Jane has completed everything *except* the monthly report.

Your Business Vocabulary	
item breakdown	A classification or division of items within a group or category.

PRINCIPLES SUMMARY

1. Write for the medial or final sound of any vowel + *ng* when the sound is part of the root word and is not a suffix (*ang, eng, ing, ong, ung*): long, l-ong .

Reading and Writing Exercises

-1-

d plsehldr , ins
bnfls dS- w alC-
blln brq me -pvms
lu S Pq, r nu -dcl
pln cvrs lq hsp Sas
+ -dcl lvs f u jb,
n od l hlp u blr USN
u nu ins pln er enc
. blln kln kp dlls.
p Sde / e ncrj u l
Dcs / nu Pq - u
Psnl ofsr sn. uz ls
Nv -e z . opl l asc
qs ab u cvrj. / -pl
lau fl USN / Pq n
od luz / lu bS Avj.
ul

foN / slj l / Pbl
n u njn. af -c. kp
nvSgj r rSC -jr
Dcvr- la / Pbl
z cz- b . srl w eld
sS v njn. ev rpls-
/ -r + u njn , rn
l. er kfdN ul vp
no - Pbls, ec dl
+ nSl / unl nx -c.
c u ac dle o Ma 7,
u njn , U -rMe so
/ rprs lb -d fre v
C. / lb nes hoE l
p. ch f. p fw /
ch / u erlS kv, er
gld lb v Svs. uvl

-2-

1 er hpe l U u ev

-3-

dr Svns ls , jS .

-4-

rms l lt uno u
a no fl . vj ou
Sa prp lxs . n od
l lc Avj v ls opl
u S fl b Mr 1,
yf uv n h p fl f
. rgj vj , (Intro DC) ulfN
Pss lb qi eze . lc
enc- f lu ke lx
assr . ntr Pss
lcs apxl 15 mls l
kp + l rzll n .
yr sv aq nx yrs
lxs, a l fsz aq
pl v fl b Mr 1 .
Alo vj aplis l
nx yrs lxs , (Intro DC) S
b fl- ls yr, p cl o
e nE icb v
hlp . cu

d r edus aco ls
L, rpl u rqS-
P lq=rny plns f r
r dvj . fgrs rep
. ch brcdon v grs
sls , (Series) cSs , (Series) + %oj v Pfls
O l8 5 yrs, sls
ncrs- srpl n Srn
+ Wrn ryns v cNre.
vpl f 2 Sas sls rC-
rec hs n lz ryns +
rep- 40% vr lol
sls l8 yr, n Aso P
. 5=yr r pln bs- o
pS sls + Pjcjs f fCr,
OA pcCr . plzN
1 . chp pln es
u salj . vlu

-5-

mo l ⁀r + sls
Psnl erp- l a 2
nu mbrs l r Sf.
⁀r hrld s⁀l + ⁀s
ble ⁀dsn jyn- r
dvj o fl 15, bo v lz
ppl as⁀ , pzj v
rjnl ⁀yr f eqpm
sls + Svs. hrld l
cvr , NE pl v
cMre + ble l cvr

, W cS, hrld spN
9 yrs n US ar fs z
Cf njnr n G v lS
Pg. ble hs ⁀y- sls
Pgs n CA, (Series) WA, (Series) + OR,
ble , ar op ol v hr
ofs n sn frnssco
+ hrld lb ⁀v nl
, bSn ofs ⁀l. p
jyn ⁀e n lk lz v
nu ppl l r co.

Key

1

Dear Policyholder:

The insurance benefits described in the attached bulletin bring many improvements[1] to your existing program.

Our new medical plan covers long hospital stays and medical leaves from your job.[2]

In order to help you better understand your new insurance plan, we are enclosing a bulletin containing[3] complete details. Please study it. We encourage you to discuss the new program with your personnel officer[4] soon. Use this individual meeting as an opportunity to ask questions about your coverage.[5] It is important that you fully understand the program in order to use it to your best advantage.

Yours[6] truly, (121)

2

Gentlemen:

We are happy to tell you we have found the solution to the problem in your engine. After[1] making a complete investigation, our research manager discovered that the problem was caused by a short in[2] the electrical system of the engine. We have replaced the wiring, and your engine is running well. We are[3] confident you will experience no more problems.

We can deliver and install the unit next week. Can you[4] accept delivery on May 7?

Your engine is under warranty, so the repairs will be made free of charge. It[5] will be necessary, however, to present a claim form. Please forward the claim at your earliest convenience.[6]

We are glad to be of service.

Yours very truly, (130)

3

Dear Mr. Stevens:

This is just a reminder to let you know you may now file an exemption on your state[1] property taxes. In order to take advantage of this opportunity, you must file by March 1.

If you have[2] not had experience with filing for a mortgage exemption, you will find the process to be quite easy. Take[3] the enclosed form to your county tax assessor. The entire process takes approximately 15 minutes to[4] complete and will result in a major savings against next year's taxes.

May I emphasize again the importance[5] of filing by March 1. Although the exemption applies to next year's taxes, it must be filed this year.

Please call[6] on me whenever I can be of help.

Cordially yours, (130)

4

Dear Mr. Edwards:

Accompanying this letter is the report you requested presenting long-range plans for[1] our marketing division. The figures represent an item breakdown of gross sales, costs, and percentage of[2] profits over the last five years.

Sales increased sharply in the southern and western regions of the country. Except for[3] two states, sales reached record highs in these regions and represented 40 percent of our total sales last year.

I[4] am also presenting a five-year marketing plan based on past sales and projections for the future.

The overall[5] picture is a pleasant one. I hope the plan meets with your satisfaction.

Very truly yours, (117)

5

MEMO TO: Marketing and Sales Personnel

We are pleased to add two new members to our staff. Mr. Harold Smith[1] and Ms. Betty Madison joined our division on July 15.

Both of these people assume the position[2] of regional manager for equipment sales and service. Harold will cover the northeast part of the country,[3] and Betty will cover the West Coast.

Harold spent nine years in the U.S. Air Force as chief engineer in charge of[4] the testing program. Betty has managed sales programs in California, Washington, and Oregon.

Betty[5] is already operating out of her office in San Francisco, and Harold will be moving into his[6] Boston office immediately. Please join me in welcoming these exciting new people to our company.[7] (140)

LESSON 31

1. Write for the word endings *bil, ble (bul),* or *bly.*

table, t-ble

double, d-ble

possible, p-s-ble

possibly, p-s-bly

mobile, m-ble

eligible, e-l-j-ble

assembly, a-s-m-bly

available, a-v-l-ble

2. Omit the final *t* of a root word after the sound of *k.*

act, a-k

elect, e-l-k

instruct, n-st-r-k

object, o-b-j-k

deduct, d-d-k

effect, e-f-k

Write these additional words:

responsible, response-ble

deductible, d-d-k-ble

probably, prah-b-bly

product, prah-d-k

expect, x-p-k

elected, e-l-k-ed

impact, im-p-k

protected, pro-t-k-ed

3. Indicate time in the following way:

ten o'clock

12 noon

8:30 a.m.

9:30 p.m.

Phrases

as I

has been

should be

thank you

would like

USE COMMAS WITH NOUNS OF DIRECT ADDRESS.

A direct address is a specific referral to a person's name, title, and/or other designation. When the direct address occurs in the middle of the sentence, place a comma before and after it. If the direct address occurs at the beginning or at the end of the sentence, use only one comma.

We know, Mary, that you are an excellent administrative assistant.

Professor Jefferson, will you be able to attend the meeting?

You will enjoy working in Washington, Mr. President.

In the reading and writing exercises, the abbreviation **Dir Ad** will be used to highlight nouns of direct address.

Your Business Vocabulary	trust account trs ak	An account established by an individual or organization in the name of another individual or organization to be administered by a trustee (trust company or bank, for example).

PRINCIPLES SUMMARY

1. Write B for the word endings *bil, ble (bul),* or *bly*: table, t-ble tB .
2. Omit the final *t* of a root word after the sound of *k*: act, a-k ac .
3. Indicate time: 7:30 p.m. 7 30 p .

Reading and Writing Exercises

-1-

dM brnl lqf
olSN lrn sjs u
pl lglr ls c, (
nSrcj z lN + sdb
v gr bnfl, p vprs r
apj l E, hu hlp-c
sC. plzN p f s, (
Pq d sC. Srq pc
o r Sf lae s l pln
. slr evN f nx yr,
e vpc lv apxl 2H
ppl elyB f Pq, du
ks brq u lrn grp l
r slex, ed flo u
efsN LlB, b Srl (
e Pll / 8 30 a +
N / 5p ecd kp (
sjs n 3 ds, f u
apv, Intro DC l bgn c
arms no, e Ar v
s sugjs n m,
lc fu lu rpl, aq
uv r lqs f . jb l
dn, vlu

-2-

ds js lqf Pll
rpl (ls vu Cq crd,
zi vpln- du r fn kvrsj, Intro DC
r kpur rySr- (ls (
L u d (cl, la
Pl acj, esp pl
fu Plq, ur no lgr
rspB f PCss d b
ne, ol ln alrz-Psns,
(enc- crds kln nu
ak Nos, f uv adyl
cpes vu old crds o
hN, Intro DC p Dpz v L no,
(nu crds r n efc

no + r c ol crds alrz-fu ak, er a hpe Lb v hlp. cu

-3-

d rc o bhf v prNs / s l scl i 4 l lqu v C f lN Pq u kdc- / l8 os e, u kNs re c scl brds rsN acq k / . apo L. f loz v s hu dd n USN c dlls v nu Pq u plnq hlp- . gr dl, me v s dlc l nrl r Cldrn n lq bk elyB. ec pln no f fCr, ai fsz aq Dir Ad , rc Dir Ad , ho C eap-

u l' Lk o sC srl nls. z lq Nca- b lr rsps af c Pq Intro DC , c ol prNs Aso bnfl- f u pl rrcs. ihp / z . rw p fu z l. su

-4-

d r bron vu ks- opn . lr8 ak r bq,, lr8 aks ofr me Avjs l ppl r dl=l=hi nk rnq. lq Pvd . lq=lr sv pln C cb uz-f dfrN Ppss. f ex . lr8 fN fu Cldrn Plcs lr fCr. z c ak gro Intro DC , / bks . bss f lr clq ejcq or / c

fN aol nvSm lgv
. esp soN Srl
n lf, lr r lN lx
bnfls aco lrS fNs.
edb hpe l vpln
n dll. y n c .
apym ld l lrn
ho lz plns op,
e ofr me Svss dzn-
l hlp fl + eSa
pln. ehp ul lc
avj v s v opjs
la r avlB (Dir Ad) , r
bron. vlu

-5-

dr s l alo u
pam C z du
Sp, hs n b rsv- (Intro DC) ,
erp- l ll u lau
plse hsb cpl crN

lru r al lc ln Pvj.
ls hs rzll-n . sli
ncrs n sz vu ln.
p nl la alC-Sam
recs ls laS acj, z
ev vpln- n pS (Intro DC) ,
lu avj l rpa ln
z qcl z psB. b du
so u rnu f vlu
vu plse. n u c.
pam (Intro DC) , p rel alC-
Sam u Cc. p ru
u plse No o Cc l
hlp s Pss u pam
qcl, a e aso rm
u la er a hpe l
asr qs + hlp n ne
a ec (Dir Ad) , r s l.
du n hzla lcl r ll=
fre No ne . cu

Key

1

Dear Miss Barnett:

Thank you for the outstanding training sessions you put together this week. The instruction was[1] excellent and should be of great benefit. Please express our appreciation to everyone who helped make such[2] a pleasant experience for us.

The program made such a strong impact on our staff that we wish to plan a[3] similar event for next year. We expect to have approximately 200 people eligible for the[4] program. Would you consider bringing your training group to our city?

We would follow your efficient timetable. By[5] starting the meetings promptly at 8:30 a.m. and ending at 5 p.m., we could complete the sessions in[6] three days. If you approve, I will begin making arrangements now. We already have some suggestions in mind.

I[7] look forward to your reply. Again, you have our thanks for a job well done.

Very truly yours, (156)

2

Dear Ms. James:

Thank you for promptly reporting the loss of your charge card. As I explained during our phone conversation,[1] our computer registered the loss at the time you made the call. That prompt action is especially important[2] for your protection. You are no longer responsible for purchases made by anyone other than authorized[3] persons.

The enclosed cards contain new account numbers. If you have additional copies of your old cards on[4] hand, please dispose of them now. The new cards are in effect now and are the only cards authorized for your account.[5]

We are always happy to be of help.

Cordially yours, (110)

3

Dear Mark:

On behalf of the parents at Smith School, I wish to thank you very much for the excellent program you[1] conducted at last month's meeting.

Your comments regarding the school board's recent action came at an appropriate[2] time. For those of us who did not understand the details of the new program, your explanation helped a great deal.[3]

Many of us would like to enroll our children when they become eligible. We can plan now for the future.[4]

May I emphasize again, Mark, how much we appreciated your willingness to come on such short notice. As[5] they indicated by their responses after the program, the other parents also benefited from your[6] important remarks. I hope it was a rewarding experience for you as well.

Sincerely yours, (138)

4

Dear Mr. Brown:

Have you considered opening a trust account with our bank?

Trust accounts offer many[1] advantages to people in the middle-to-high income range. They provide a long-term savings plan which can be used[2] for different purposes. For example, a trust fund for your children protects their future. As the account grows,[3] it becomes a basis for their college education, or it can fund another investment to give them an[4] especially sound start in life.

There are excellent tax benefits accompanying trust funds. We would be happy[5] to explain them in detail. Why not make an appointment today to learn how these plans operate?

We offer[6] many services designed to help with family and estate planning. We hope you will take advantage of some[7] of the options that are available, Mr. Brown.

Very truly yours, (152)

5

Dear Mr. Smith:

Although your payment which was due September 1 has not been received, we are pleased to tell you that[1] your policy has been kept current through our automatic loan provision. This has resulted in a slight[2] increase in the size of your loan. Please note that the attached statement records this latest action.

As we have explained in[3] the past, it is to your advantage to repay the loan as quickly as possible. By doing so, you renew[4] the full value of your policy. When you make a payment, please return the attached statement with your check. Please write[5] your policy number on the check to help us process your payment quickly.

May we also remind you that we[6] are always happy to answer questions and help in any way we can, Mr. Smith. Do not hesitate to call[7] our toll-free number at any time.

Cordially yours, (150)

LESSON 32

1. Write a slightly raised and disjoined *l* for the word ending *ity* (pronounced *uh-tee*).

quality, q-l-ity	ql l	authority, a-ith-r-ity	alr l
facilities, f-s-l-ity-s	fsl ls	majority, m-j-r-ity	jr l
possibility, p-s-bil-ity	psB l	security, s-k-r-ity	scr l

2. Write ǂ ǂ to indicate parentheses.

Most of our staff (80%) have had their vacations.

8 vr Sf ǂ 80% ǂ vh lr vcjs.

Brief Forms

able	B	difficult	dfc
opinion	opn	contract	kc
employ	p		

Brief Form Development

difficulty	dfce	enable	nB
responsibility	rspB l	ability	B l

Commonly Misspelled Words

excellent ln

correspondence cor

Your Business Vocabulary

term policy

lr plse

In life insurance, a contract providing benefits for a limited number of years. It pays face value if the owner's death occurs during the time specified in the contract.

PRINCIPLES SUMMARY

1. Write l for the word ending *ity (uh-tee)*: quality, q-l-ity ql.
2. Write ( ) to indicate parentheses.

Reading and Writing Exercises

-1-

d-r bSr ls, l
kfr r fn kvrsj
ksrn c kc u ar v
jrs bron, zi
nca- erlr, Intro DC r bron
hs dsd- l rsl c
prp + hs p- e
Lc c arms f h. c
Ppz- nu ors +
l PCs, eqle +
as c bsc kc no
n efc, p nl la c
flo Cnys r Ub d:
c nu ln ra l rpls
c ra pd orynll. el
Srl O . nu 10=yr

lr, p asc u alrne
l dra p c nu agrem
lz Cnys. el rvu
c bf clz. f c agrem
rqs. Ul SC, Intro DC c nu
ors l ac la rspBl,
lap u hlp n kp c
nu kc. ul

-2-

drs an lqf L, Series
cpes v kc, Series + rla-
lgl inf ksrn c sl
v prp. iz dli- lhr
la c clz lc pls z
scyl- ol qs or

dfces v ne cMt, i
s lcl u all l r
enc- cpes v cor
csl r orynl fr ins
plse o la hos. w
n yl rsv- ne f
r nu ors Nca la
ly v lcn ol . nu
plse. d ub B ldl
la Aql cvry hsb
ar-x, n Aso rel
u cpe vr agrem
C e sn-zu rqs-.
i as uc no rec
r dd + ks r kc
kp-, lqs aq fu hlp.
cu

-3-

d ed n p-lsa lb
vzl Ulsa evn snr

ln e vpc-, i pln l
brq r nu sls yrs
o . lrp lru r Wrn
plNs du r c v
Mr 6. i M l so
L r lN fsl ls +
Pgs crNl n efc.
el arv o fli 519 /
5 30 p o Wd. cd u
e s + v dnr
s la evn x, idap
e Th rn u, [Series]
r nu pes, [Series] + ne i
els u lq ly sd e,
if s n l dfc l ar, [Intro DC]
ed, [Dir Ad] idlc r gss lq
lru A v plNs. e
i ks r psBl v
rN . bs f Th afnn.
l du u lq x u
opns A kb grl

l r eflts, e pln l
lv / ab 9° c nx
mrn. u hlp, Stnl
ap-. s

-4-

ds Ans ls L, n
rsp lu rsN nqe
re aplm rNls.
Alo ev no aplms
avlB no, e alspa (Intro DC)
opn mn c nx 3
mos. l ncrj u
lcp Cç ~ s, edu
rq. scr dpzl nr
and v . f mos rN.
ls dpzl lb ret- af
u frnt vb mv-
+ . nspcj sos la
no dys v ocr-.
e Aso rqS 30ds

nls mn u pln l
mv f c aplm,
u ma Cz . 1=yr or
2=yr ls. c 2=yr kc
ofrs c Avj v sv
apxl 20$ P mo n
rN. eC unl klns
kp lNre + cCn fslts,
elb hpe l so u .
aplm. cl r rNl
ofs l sl p . apym.
su

-5-

ds lsn hr, c
rpl u rqS-. z uc
se, u ern por, u (Intro DC)
mS pl asl. e
agre lau lf ins
plse sd Pvd f
ejcl + dl nds vu

fl w evN vu dl, l dz / lc l e lz gls. e rcm lau ins ofs bnfls v p l 6 s u P ern, i sug u PCs · 20 = yr plse w a v 250T $. r lB o pj 7 lSs

r bnfls + cSs v ls sp pln. f u t l PCs r plse, s pl kp + rel r enc- aplcj, lqf alo s l Avz u, lsn. vlu

Intro DC

Dir Ad

Key

1

Dear Mr. Webster:

This is to confirm our phone conversation concerning the contract you already have with[1] James Brown.

As I indicated earlier, Mr. Brown has decided to resell the property and has[2] employed me to make the arrangements for him. The proposed new owners wish to purchase his equity and assume the[3] basic contract now in effect.

Please note that the following changes are to be made: The new loan rate[4] will replace the rate paid originally. We will start over with a new ten-year term.

Please ask your attorney to[5] draw up the new agreement with these changes. We will review it before closing. If the agreement requires a[6] title search, the new owners will accept that responsibility.

I appreciate your help in completing[7] the new contract.

Yours truly, (145)

2

Dear Mrs. Allen:

Thank you for your letter, copies of the contract, and related legal information[1] concerning the sale of the property. I was delighted to hear that the closing took place as scheduled without[2] questions or difficulties of any kind.

I wish to call your attention to the enclosed copies of correspondence[3] canceling our original fire insurance policy on that house. I have not yet received anything[4] from the new owners indicating that they have taken out a new policy. Would you be able to determine[5] that adequate coverage has been arranged?

I am also returning your copy of our agreement which[6] we signed as you requested. I assume you can now record the deed and consider the contract completed.

Thanks[7] again for your help.

Cordially yours, (146)

3

Dear Ed:

I am pleased to say I will be visiting Tulsa even sooner than we expected.

I plan to bring[1] our new sales managers on a trip through our western plants during the week of March 6. I want to show them our[2] excellent facilities and the programs currently in effect. We will arrive on flight 519 at[3] 5:30 p.m. on Wednesday. Could you meet us and have dinner with us that evening?

I would appreciate meeting[4] Thursday morning with you, our new employees, and anyone else you think they should meet.

If it is not too difficult[5] to arrange, Ed, I would like our guests to go through all of the plants. We might consider the possibility of[6] renting a bus for Thursday afternoon. What do you think? Your opinions always contribute greatly to our efforts.[7]

We plan to leave at about 9 o'clock in the morning. Your help is certainly appreciated.

Sincerely,[8] (160)

4

Dear Ms. Adams:

This letter is in response to your recent inquiry regarding apartment rentals. Although[1] we have no apartments available now, we anticipate openings within the next three months. I encourage[2] you to keep checking with us.

We do require a security deposit in the amount of a full month's[3] rent. This deposit will be returned after your furnishings have been removed and an inspection shows that no[4] damages have occurred. We also request 30 days' notice when you plan to move from the apartment.

You may choose[5] a one-year or two-year lease. The two-year contract offers the advantage of saving approximately[6] $20 per month in rent. Each unit contains complete laundry and kitchen facilities.

We will be happy to[7] show you an appointment. Call our rental office to set up an appointment.

Sincerely yours, (156)

5

Dear Mr. Wilson:

Here is the report you requested. As you can see, your earning power is your most important[1] asset. We agree that your life insurance policy should provide for the educational and daily[2] needs of your family in the event of your death.

What does it take to meet these goals? We recommend that your[3] insurance offer benefits of up to six times your present earnings.

I suggest you purchase a 20-year term[4] policy in the amount of $250,000. The table on page 7 lists the benefits[5] and costs of this specific plan. If you wish to purchase the policy, simply complete and return the enclosed[6] application.

Thank you for allowing us to advise you, Mr. Wilson.

Very truly yours, (138)

LESSON 33

1. Write for the word beginning *un*.

until, un-t-l

unfair, un-f-r

unpaid, un-p-d

unchanged, un-chay-n-j-duh

unless, un-l-s

uncover, un-k-v-r

Brief Form Development. Use this principle to develop words from brief forms and abbreviations.

unable

unfortunate

unsatisfactory

unnecessary

More About Phrasing. An easily recognized word may be omitted from common phrases or compound words. In the following examples, the shorthand outline has been omitted for the italicized word.

never*the*less

time *to* time

none*the*less

up *to* date

USE COMMAS WITH APPOSITIVES.

An appositive is a word or group of words that explains, renames, or identifies someone or something which immediately precedes it in the sentence.

Appositives are usually set off by commas from the rest of the sentence. Some examples of appositives are shown below:

His new textbook, *Business Communications,* has now been published.

Please see our sales manager, Sally Stanfield.

Mr. Henry Jackson, the Secretary of State, will deliver our commencement address.

Appositives will be highlighted in the reading and writing exercises. The abbreviation **Ap** will be highlighted.

Your Business Vocabulary		
	computer terminal kpur lrml	A device usually consisting of a keyboard and a screen that is used to input/output data to and from a computer. Also called a work station.
	questionnaire qr	A set of questions assembled for the purpose of making a survey.

PRINCIPLES SUMMARY

1. Write u for the word beginning *un*: until, un-t-l ull.

Reading and Writing Exercises

-1-

mo l -r Sf r
so ls yr 3 / bS
ev E h, r Pdcs
-d . fvrB -pry +
e rsv- me kplms
af / so, e aso
rsv- s- suggs.
f ex me dlrs r v
opn la . 60=d dle
L, l lq. / sdb
rds- l 30 ds. uf /

a psB el -c la Cny
-n / nx fu -os,
a-q / kplms rsv-
- loz rf- l r Dpla
v c-ras kc- l
kpur lrmls. eh
apxl 1 M$ -rl v
-dse lr, r -pes
aso -d . q -pry.
r snsr lqs q l .
olSM Sff . u so.

-2-

drs clrc i M
u lno la w bk .
sr ak ajN f nyl
lf inc , z v Ma i
l w l . nu lcq ,
819 S Sa S r l
ku lgv u Psnl Svs
nE und , n od
l brq u plse pda
w enc- . qr asc
f sp inf . d u p
rel , f w pS =
fre env Pvd-x , p
nl la i Ulfn No
(555-3100) r ms
uCny- . ull Ma i uc
vzl e , i P ofs .
if uv qs, Intro DC ihp ul
cl . n ur w nbrh, Intro DC
Sp b . i asSN +
i r A gld l lc

u u . uvl

-3-

d rdr ev Ar sN
sv bls f r gzn, Ap
arl nz, Ap od- n u n .
so fr ev n rsv- ne
pam or plny , n
r cS l asc f pams
ods . e lq r rdrs
ap , kv v b B lc
pams nE ly sll
lr ol hoshld or ofs
aks . e ks r rdrs lb
nf- Nvs hu ac
rspBl f kcs ly v
d , eno la lr ,
. q rzn fu dla n
c pam . , l lc ol
. fu mls l sll ls
lr = elr . Cc

or · fu rds pln
dla, p rel u
rsp inv w
aco env, su

-4-

d dvd lqf opl l
rcm u asSN yr Ap
jnfr yq Ap f pzj
v pb rljs drr, idu
so plzr, jnfr hs
me fn glts rep v q
ym, 1 Srq py, hr
Bl l vprs hr opns bo
n spC + n ri, se
sos · USN v co gls
alq · snsr ksrn
f r ol pes, jnfr
as s f rspBl f ne
jb no dr ho dfc,
ull se k l Av

dpl Intro DC jnfr h no vp
n ym, nvrls se
Svz- sv Pjcs w
nr v · vp- dpl
hd, n u opn jnfr
, rde f ncrs- rspBl,
se l brq me fn glts
l pzj U ksj, ul

-5-

dK er kvrl u bl l
· nu elnc dla Pss
sS C l Sv u
efsNl, hr r
bsc Cnjs afc u
ln pams:, 1, z v
Ja 1 el p us v
enc- pam bc, 2,
u nu ol du da l
a b frS d v eC
o, if u pam z

du o Ja 10, (Intro DC) s no	n rsv . pam bc,
du o Ja 1. / lb du	lz Cnys l nB s l
/ frd d v E —o	Pss u pams — Pll.
lrafs 3. if u pams	if uv qs, (Intro DC) p cl / bq-
r atlcl ddc-f	ofs nrd u or r K
u Cc or sv ak, (Intro DC) ul	Svs dpl. cu

Key

1

MEMO TO: Marketing Staff

Our show this year was the best we have ever had. Our products made a favorable[1] impression, and we received many compliments after the show.

We also received some suggestions. For example,[2] many dealers are of the opinion that a 60-day delivery time is too long. It should be reduced[3] to 30 days. If at all possible, we will make that change within the next few months.

Among the compliments[4] received were those referring to our display of cameras connected to computer terminals. We had[5] approximately $1,000,000 worth of merchandise there.

Our employees also made a good impression. Our[6] sincere thanks go to an outstanding staff for an exciting show. (131)

2

Dear Mrs. Clark:

I want you to know that I have become a senior account agent for National Life,[1] Inc.

As of May 1, I will move to a new location at 819 South State Street, where I will[2] continue to give you personal service whenever you need it.

In order to bring your policy up to date,[3] I have enclosed a questionnaire asking for specific information. Would you please return the form in the[4] postage-free envelope provided?

Please note that my telephone number (555-3100)[5] remains unchanged. Until May 1, you can visit me at my present office. If you have questions, I hope you[6] will call. When you are in the neighborhood, stop by. My assistant and I are always glad to talk with you.

Yours[7] very truly, (142)

3

Dear Reader:

We have already sent several bills for our magazine, *Art News,* ordered in your name. So far we[1] have not received any payment or explanation.

It is not our custom to ask for payments with orders. We[2] think our readers appreciate the convenience of being able to make payments whenever they settle their[3] other household or office accounts. We consider our readers to be informed individuals who accept[4] responsibility for contracts they have made.

We know that there is a good reason for your delay in making[5] payment. It will take only a few minutes to settle this matter—either with a check or a few words explaining[6] the delay. Please return your response with the invoice in the accompanying envelope.

Sincerely yours,[7] (140)

4

Dear David:

Thank you for the opportunity to recommend my assistant manager, Jennifer Young, for[1] the position of public relations director. I do so with pleasure.

Jennifer has many fine qualities[2] representative of good management. One strong point is her ability to express her opinions both in[3] speech and in writing. She shows an understanding of company goals along with a sincere concern for our[4] other employees.

Jennifer assumes full responsibility for any job, no matter how difficult.[5] Until she came to the advertising department, Jennifer had no experience in management.[6] Nevertheless, she supervised several projects in the manner of an experienced department head.

In my[7] opinion, Jennifer is ready for increased responsibility. She will bring many fine qualities to the[8] position under consideration.

Yours truly, (169)

5

Dear Customer:

We are converting your billings to a new electronic data processing system which will[1] serve you more efficiently. Here are the basic changes affecting your loan payments:

1. As of[2] January 1, we will employ the use of the enclosed payment book.
2. Your new monthly due date will always be the[3] first day of each month. If your payment was due on January 10, it is now due on January 1. It will[4] be due the first day of every month thereafter.
3. If your payments are automatically deducted from your[5] checking or savings account, you will not receive a payment book.

These changes will enable us to process your[6] payments more promptly. If you have questions, please call the banking office nearest you or our customer service[7] department.

Cordially yours, (144)

LESSON 34

1. Write for the sound of *shul* and the word ending *chul* (cial, tial).

official, o-f-ish-l

special, s-p-ish-l

initial, i-n-ish-l

financial, f-n-n-ish-l

potential, p-t-n-ish-l

social, s-ish-l

Abbreviations

volume vol

literature lit

America, American

Brief Forms

develop dv

organize og

success suc

standard Sd

acknowledge ac

associate aso

congratulate kg

Brief Form Development

acknowledgment acjm

organizations ogjs

organizing og-

standards Sds

associations asojs

development dvm

congratulations kgjs

developing dv-

Commonly Misspelled Words

cites sls

questionnaire

Your Business Vocabulary		
	group retirement plan grp rtrm pln	A plan to provide income for retired employees; premiums may be paid entirely by the employer or partly by the employer and partly by the employee.
	accordingly acrdl	Within (according to) a special way.

PRINCIPLES SUMMARY

1. Write sl for the sound of *shul* and the word ending *chul* (cial, tial): official, o-f-ish-l ofsl ; financial, f-n-n-ish-l fnnsl.

Reading and Writing Exercises

-1-

Intro DC

-2-

ddr lys / gvs
e gr saly l rcm
dr elzbl crlr f rq
v aso Pfsr, z spl
f ls acq i ofr (alC-
fl kln . s re v hr
vp, Aso d 2
arlcls se rsNl
pbls- alq opns
v SdNs + ol fclle,
elzbl jyn- r Sf 3
yrs aq, se hs dv-
nu crss n A hSre
C v kb- C l r
Pq, se sos . re f hi
lC Sds + Pvds .
lN ex f SdNs +
ol fclle, elzbl ..
lCr gr plnsl +
. Ps fCr, / s s
ol apo lae acq hr
kbys ls P,
vlu

-3-

drs clrc idlc l
lqf e e o
Mn l Dcs i pm
SC, Alo ih aq- s
lil o ho l aprC
plnsl prs, u Avs
z v spsl hlp, i no
ap fl (pl v
c . q pry + w
. blr USN v ho l
ak la gl, flo u
Avs + ri Nv Ls
v aplcq lsN
eC cpe v i rza,
i Aso ap (rza
u gv e, dv
i o rza ez

Intro DC

+ suc ln ch vpc-.
z . rzll vr ~e l
no fl la uc ~c
la insl klc ~ .
kfdN + Pfyl ~y,
lqu aq fu hlp.
ul

-4-

dr prcr lqu, ~r
prcr, f kp r qr
ksrn / ssl scr
rf bl. hr r s~
rzlls f la Sva:
1. / ~yr v ppl Sva-
(82%) rli po X
nk l ~nln lr Sd
v lv, 2. / ~n srs
v nk af rlrm ks
f grp plns Pvd-
b ~prs + lbr ogjs.

ol srss lS- ~
Psnl bs or prp,
ins dvdNs, + Psnl
sv, 3. ~S ppl
agre- la ssl scr
bnflsaln r n sfsN
l ~e fnnsl dms
~pz- b nfl, 4. apxl
33% Sa- la . nu Pq
sdb dv- l rpls /
S pln, lqu aq f
pp n Sva. ul

-5-

dr dvdsn kgjs
r n od fu + u fl.
u ~ hsb slc- f
nx vol v yq ppl
n A, . v spsl
pby, ls Dlg s-
bc lSs Nvs U / af

v 40 hu r ern
olSN rcgny. / sis
/ sucs v yq ppl
n A ~cs v lf=bs, Series
N, Series ejcj, Series gvl, Series spls, Series
la, Series + ~dsn, / enc-
dla se sps Psnl

+ Pfyl inf Lb l- n
r nx vol. p rd +
rel / inf ~ ne
crcjs u ~+ Lc,
aq kgjs o rsv ls
spsl aw. cu

Key

1

Dear Paul:

I wish to express my support for the new bonus system officially adopted at the departmental[1] meeting. Our sales personnel have devoted much time to developing a demand for our product, and the[2] results have been excellent. As our market coverage continues to grow, orders increase accordingly.[3]

After presenting the new policy at our regional sales convention, I received many calls from sales[4] personnel concerning points they found confusing. In order to prevent misunderstandings, I plan to issue a[5] memo right away explaining the policy in detail. As an initial step, I am organizing a[6] meeting with all sales managers to go over each point. Would you be able to join us next Friday at 10 a.m.?[7]

All in all, the proposal has been well received in the field. I expect to see even greater success in[8] national sales.

Sincerely yours, (166)

2

Dear Dr. Williams:

It gives me great satisfaction to recommend Dr. Elizabeth Carter for the rank[1] of associate professor. As support for this action, I offer the attached file containing a summary[2] of her experience. I am also including two articles she recently published, along with opinions[3] of students and other faculty.

Elizabeth joined our staff three years ago. She has developed new[4] courses in American history which have contributed much to our program. She shows a regard for high[5] teaching standards and provides an excellent example for students and other faculty.

Elizabeth is[6] a teacher with great potential and a promising future. It seems only appropriate that we acknowledge[7] her contributions with this promotion.

Very truly yours, (151)

3

Dear Mrs. Clark:

I would like to thank you for meeting with me on Monday to discuss my employment search. Although[1] I had acquired some literature on how to approach potential employers, your advice was of special help.[2] I now appreciate more fully the importance of making a good impression, and I have a better[3] understanding of how to accomplish that goal.

I am following your advice and writing individual[4] letters of application to send with each copy of my resumé. I also appreciate the resumé[5] you gave me. I am developing my own resumé with more ease and success than I had expected. As[6] a result of our meeting, I now feel that I can make that initial contact with a confident and[7] professional image.

Thank you again for your help.

Yours truly, (150)

4

Dear Mr. Parker:

Thank you, Mr. Parker, for completing our questionnaire concerning the social security[1] reform bill. Here are some results from that survey:

1. The majority of people surveyed[2] (82 percent) rely upon extra income to maintain their standard of living.
2. The main source[3] of income after retirement comes from group plans provided by employers and labor organizations.[4] Other sources listed were personal business or property, insurance dividends, and personal savings.[5]
3. Most people agreed that social security benefits alone are not sufficient to meet financial[6] demands imposed by inflation.
4. Approximately 33 percent stated that a new program should be[7] developed to replace the existing plan.

Thank you again for participating in the survey.

Yours truly,[8] (160)

5

Dear Mr. Davidson:

Congratulations are in order for you and your family. Your name has been selected[1] for the next volume of *Young People in America,* a very special publication.

This distinguished[2] book lists individuals under the age of 40 who are earning outstanding recognition. It cites the[3] successes of young people in all walks of life—business, industry, education, government, sports, law, and[4] medicine.

The enclosed data sheet specifies personal and professional information to be included[5] in our next volume. Please read and return the information with any corrections you wish to make.

Again,[6] congratulations on receiving this special award.

Cordially yours, (133)

LESSON 35

RECAP AND REVIEW

This review includes the word beginnings, word endings, principles, indications of time, omitted words in phrases, brief forms, and abbreviations that you studied in Lessons 29-34.

1. Since the last review lesson, you learned to write the following word beginnings:

extr and extra

aks, eks, iks, oks, uks, eggs

un

2. These word endings were presented:

bil, ble *(bul)*, or bly

ity *(uh-tee)*

cial, tial *(shul, chul)*

3. These words illustrate all of the new principles studied in Lessons 29-34:

accident, x-d-nt

long, l-ong

facilities, f-s-l-ity-s

exciting, x-ite-ing

exist, x-st

until, un-t-l

double, d-ble

relaxing, re-l-x-ing

extremely, extr-m-ly

effect, e-f-k

financial, f-n-n-ish-l

social, s-ish-l

4. You learned to indicate time in the following way:

one o'clock

11:30 a.m.

12 noon

10:30 p.m.

5. Easily recognized words are omitted from common phrases:

never*the*less	nvrls	time *to* time	tt
none*the*less	nnls	up *to* date	pda

6. Do you recall the following abbreviations?

7. How quickly can you write these brief forms?

always	prove	immediate
consider	next	note
experience	already	approximate
able	opinion	difficult
contract	employ	standard
develop	organize	associate
acknowledge	success	congratulate

Reading and Writing Exercises

-1-

Intro DC

Intro DC

r avlB, ul PbB sa
u cM afd n l b!,
ll s pv / . nzy i
fre ni + f u o opns.
Lc u rzrvj rel . r
enc- nl . b hre= r
ofr Ns nx o .
rzrv u da l .
cu

-2-

ds rbrls hpe
l ac r pzj v ex
sec u fr . i ks
/ . Clnj Ub r Psn
Czn f rspBls u
dS-, idb dli- l bgn
pm o Ma 21 zu
rq8- . ufCnll r
scl dz n N ull
Ma 25 . a i bgn

r flo Mn Ma 28
Pll / 8 a x, ilc
fur l ls opl l lrn,

Series

gro, + bld nu scls.

Series

ufl Sln r pzj l
brq me nu + v
vps, lqf c ls
opl psB . uls i hr
dfrNl, il rpl lu

Intro DC

ofs o rn v Ma
28 . cu

-3-

ds bxls lqf nqe .
ublv r enc- lil l
asr u qs, E Dr
ps . f= Svzr
hu cs sr la r
Psnl r fl lrn- n
Svs r elnc lprurs .
r Drs sl p lrn sjs

f Sf, (Series) dlrs, (Series) + Ks apxl
3 s P yr, E Dr,
eqp- (nre
+ LS eqpm nd- l
rpr r sns. if /
dz bk nes l od pls
f (fclre, (Intro DC) loz ods
r Pss- + s- l, if
udlc frlr inf, (Intro DC) r
bxlz, (Dir Ad) p klc e aq.
efl r lrn, v vlu
n ol l nu pes b
Aso l ku Psnl z
l. er A gld l asr
u qs. su

-4-

1 s la v yr
n e pl a a drs
v ofs l sr Psnl

vps f l + frNs.
z . kc K u Ar no
la r Sj kus s 24=
hr Pq du (X s
hlds. n od l alo
r pes z C Psnl
z psB e Alr r
Av + Pq scjls f .
fu ds. f 8 p Dc 23
ull 8 a Dc 26 el
Pvd lp- Pq. A Av
Lb brdcS bln loz
das sdb dl- l r
ofss b 5 p Dc 20
l alo sfsN f
prpr, a e Aso
lc ls opl l lqf
plrnj. ev njy-Sv
u du (pS yr + lc
fw l ku r rljs. cu

-5-

d frNs n r grp
es aq nx o Intro DC ,
el lk slę clrç z
g8 spcr, ę,
b v- bc, c l
Mr 8, slę z uB l
alN o d rglrl
scjl- f e, slę
, lrcgnz- n r
sle, se hs hd-
me pl ks, 8
rsNl se z elc-
P v C bz v krş,
slę ks l s l
flo . lrp abrd +
se brgs u nz,
lrvl o bhf vr sle
slę l apxl 45
corps, Alo
z . lq + dfc , Intro DC ,
Pds- lN rzlls,

ev Ar rsv- rd
la , co plns lsN
. rep hr l nvSga
bld . nu plN,
p nl Cnj ou
clNrs + pln lb
P f e, vlu

-6-

drs hrve , N
l kplm u o kpj
vu nu bld sil-
o prç drv, r sle
cb prod v ls nu
adj l r knl,
mbrs v sle ksl
r pln . rbn = cl
sr me o da u
rq8-, pb , nvi-
+ zc lb Pvd- b .
lcl hi scl bN,

P v sle ksl l
ofsll opn c srme.
Intro DC
af h spcs, ulb P-
⌣ . ce l c sle, Ph
uv ks- kdc lrs v
bld. ⌣l lrs r jnl

Intro DC
n pln-, ls , no
ord bld. s spsl
crcs sdb sn lb
fl ap-, ll s no
if ec hlp ⌢c
nes arms f lr. s

Key

Abbreviations

volume	literature	America, American

Brief Forms

a	pv	
ks	nx	nl
vp	ar	apx
B	opn	dfc
kc	p	Sd
dv	oq	aso
acq	suc	kq

1

Dear Sir:

Here are four reasons why you should keep reading.

1. You are an educated person.
2. You know a bargain[1] when you see it.
3. You believe in saving money when you can.
4. You know how to take advantage of a[2] rare opportunity.

If you need a fifth reason, consider this. You are among only 100 people[3] to receive this offer. As part of a rare marketing program, you and 99 others have been selected[4] to try our vacation homes.

Village Homes is a planned neighborhood already under construction. It is perfect[5] for young families. Village Homes has everything you will want and more. When you see the contracts that are available,[6] you will probably say you can't afford not to buy!

Let us prove it. Enjoy one free night and form your own[7] opinions. To make your reservation, return the enclosed note. But hurry—the offer ends next month. Reserve your[8] date immediately.

Cordially yours, (167)

2

Dear Ms. Roberts:

I am happy to accept the position of executive secretary with your firm. I[1] consider it a challenge to be the person chosen for the responsibilities you described.

I would be[2] delighted to begin employment on May 21 as you requested. Unfortunately, our school does not[3] end until May 25. May I begin the following Monday, May 28, promptly at 8 a.m.?

I[4] look forward to this opportunity to learn, grow, and build new skills. I feel certain the position will bring many[5] new and exciting experiences.

Thank you for making this opportunity possible. Unless I[6] hear differently, I will report to your office on the morning of May 28.

Cordially yours, (139)

3

Dear Mr. Baxter:

Thank you for your inquiry. I believe the enclosed literature will answer your questions.[1]

Every distributor employs a full-time supervisor who makes sure that our personnel are fully trained in[2] servicing our electronic typewriters. Our distributors set up training sessions for staff, dealers, and[3] customers approximately three times per year.

Every distributor is equipped with the machinery and test[4] equipment needed to repair our machines. If it does become necessary to order parts from the factory,[5] those orders are processed and shipped immediately.

If you would like further information, Mr. Baxter,[6] please contact me again. We feel our training is of value not only to new employees but also to[7] continuing personnel as well. We are always glad to answer your questions.

Sincerely yours, (156)

4

Gentlemen:

It is that time of the year when we put away matters of the office to share personal[1] experiences with family and friends. As a contract customer, you already know that our station[2] continues its 24-hour programming during the Christmas holidays. In order to allow our employees[3] as much personal time as possible, we alter our advertising and programming schedules for a few days. From[4] 8 p.m., December 23, until 8 a.m., December 26, we will provide taped programming. All[5] advertising to be broadcast between those dates should be delivered to our offices by 5 p.m., December[6] 20, to allow sufficient time for preparation.

May we also take this opportunity to thank you[7] for your patronage. We have enjoyed serving you during the past year and look forward to continuing our[8] relationship.

Cordially yours, (166)

5

Dear Friends:

When our group meets again next month, we will welcome Shelley Clark as guest speaker. The meeting is being moved[1] back one week to March 8. Shelley was unable to attend on the day regularly scheduled for the meeting.[2]

Shelley is well recognized in our city. She has headed many important committees. Most recently she[3] was elected president of the Chamber of Commerce.

Shelley comes to us immediately following a[4] trip abroad, and she brings exciting news. Traveling on behalf of our city, Shelley met with approximately[5] 45 corporations. Although the mission was a long and difficult one, it produced excellent results.[6] We have already received word that one company plans to send a representative here to investigate[7] building a new plant.

Please note the change on your calendars and plan to be present for the meeting.

Very[8] truly yours, (162)

6

Dear Mr. Harvey:

I want to compliment you on the completion of your new building situated on Park[1] Drive. Our city can be proud of this new addition to our community.

The members of the city council[2] are planning a ribbon-cutting ceremony on the date you requested. The public is invited, and[3] music will be provided by a local high school band. The president of the city council will officially[4] open the ceremony. After he speaks, you will be presented with a key to the city.

Perhaps you have[5] considered conducting tours of the building. While tours are generally not planned, this is no ordinary building.[6] Its special characteristics should be seen to be fully appreciated.

Let us know if we can help[7] make necessary arrangements for the tour.

Sincerely, (150)

WHAT WILL A RESUMÉ DO FOR ME?

Once you have learned skills for today's job market, how will you present them to a prospective employer? An effective way to show what you have learned and what you can do is a resumé.

A resumé lists your educational background, job experience, special skills, and references. If you've not had previous work experience, your resumé is especially important. You must describe all other qualifications that will persuade the interviewer to consider you for employment.

Where to Begin?

List all full-time or part-time jobs you have held, courses studied, awards, activities, and membership in organizations. Then arrange the information in major groups:

***Chapter Six**

Personal information: List your name, address, and telephone number. You may list job interests or the position you desire.

Educational background: List schools you've attended (beginning with the most recent), degrees earned, studies emphasized, and special courses. If you received special recognition or awards, include a section for awards and activities.

Employment experience: List any part-time or full-time positions, beginning with the most recent. Specify the name of the employer, beginning and ending dates, and job title. You can strengthen this section by briefly describing your responsibilities.

Special skills: This section tells the employer specifically what you are qualified to do. Drawing from your educational and employment experiences, list all skills. Typing, shorthand, art, and French, for example, would all be appropriate here.

References: Include the name, occupation, address, and telephone number of individuals qualified to comment on your abilities, character, or performance. Always ask permission before listing someone as a reference. Choose at least three—usually no more than five—people from different sources. At least one should know you personally; another should know you as an employee or as a student.

Your Resumé Should be Neat and Well Organized

After you have categorized all information, read, edit, change, correct, and type. Repeat the process until you have the best possible picture of yourself on paper.

Your finished product should do many things. Its primary purpose is to present information that can be quickly and easily analyzed by the interviewer. But it reflects on you in other ways. It sets forth your skills and qualities. It demonstrates your ability to sort, organize, and present information. It becomes a visible example of your work.

Your Completed Resumé

Your finished resumé may surprise even you. Mailed with a well-written application letter, it may persuade an employer to ask for an interview. When the time comes for the interview, your resumé will contribute to the professionalism and self-confidence that give you a winning image.

LESSON 36

1. Write for the sounds of *ance, ence, nce,* and *nse* (pronounced *ence*).

dance, d-nce

balance, b-l-nce

expense, x-p-nse

agency, a-j-nce-e

since, s-nce

defense, d-f-nse

advance, ad-v-nce

efficiency, e-f-ish-nce-e

2. Write for the word beginning *sub*.

submit, sub-m-t

subscribe, sub-scribe

subscription, sub-scrip-tion

subway, sub-w-a

substantial, sub-st-n-ish-l

subject, sub-j-k

Phrases

that you are

that you will

Commonly Misspelled Words

congratulate

already

Your Business Vocabulary

unpaid balance — The total amount of money remaining to be paid on a bill or loan.

PRINCIPLES SUMMARY

1. Write for the sound of *ance, ence, nce, nse*: dance, d-nce .
2. Write for the word beginning *sub*: submit, sub-m-t .

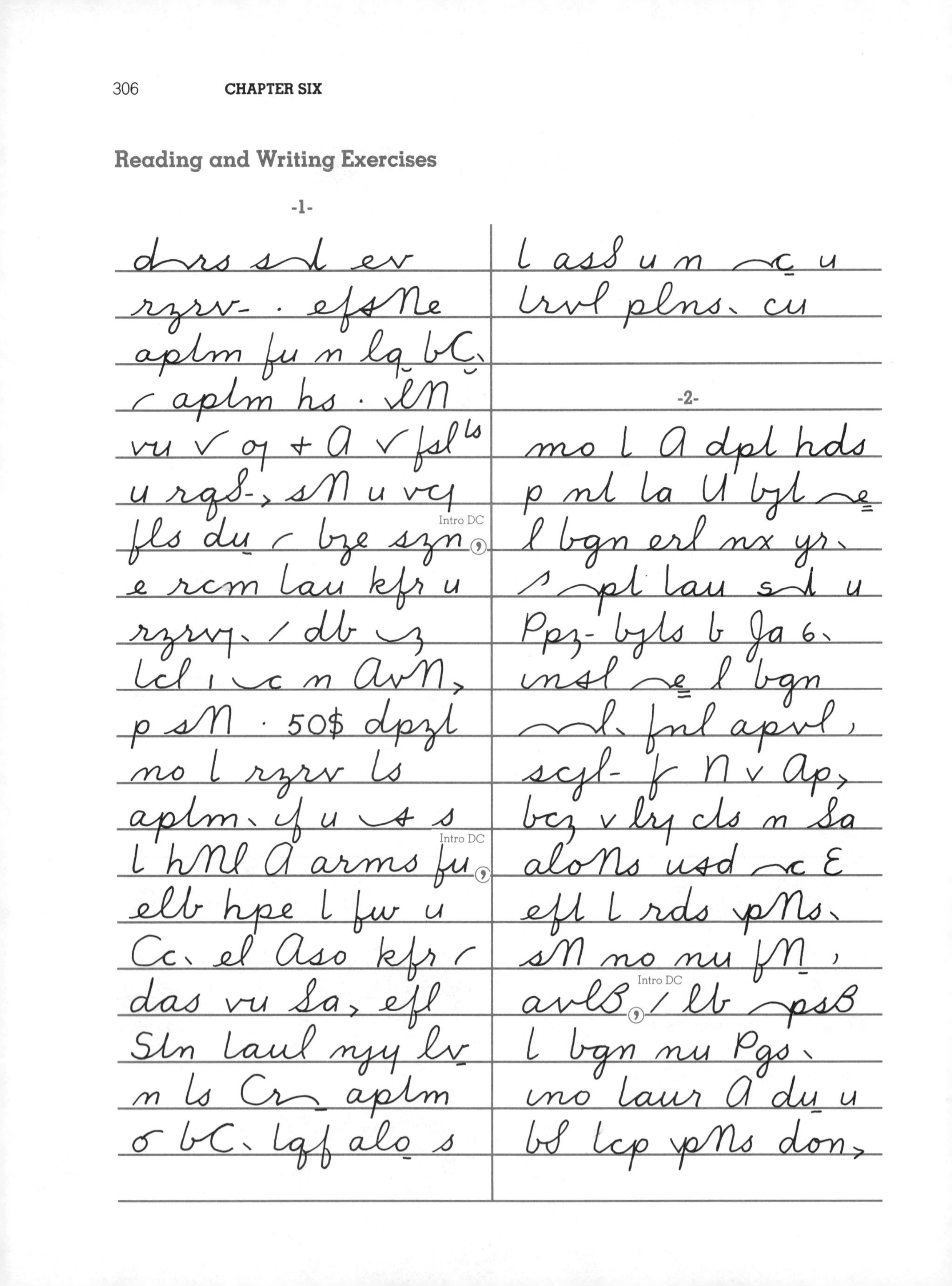

Reading and Writing Exercises

-1-

Intro DC

Intro DC

-2-

Intro DC

me vu v asc- ab
pa ncrss \ er sug
. Sd 7% ncrs f Ā
Psnl, ne adjl rqSs
f fN̲ ⌒S b rvu- bf
Ap . \ eap u hlp n
Pvd̲ u bjl rqSs
zz psB \

-3-

dS i rd ⌣ apj
u insl isu v bs
rvu + ⌣s l od 3
sSys lb gvn z X⌒s
gfls \ ⌒ enc̲ ⌒
⌒s + adrss fu
us, i ⌣s l lc Avj
vu X⌒s Dk \ ⌒
enc̲ . Cc f lol
a⌒l v 35^{85} \ ls sd
cvr A hNl̲ fes, zi

Intro DC

USN̲ , ul ⌒l . gre̲
crd anoN̲ ⌒ gfl \
l ⌒ crd arv bf
X⌒s ₓ p sN ⌒e
kfrj la ⌒ gfl
crds vb ⌒l- \
lqu v ⌒C \ ul

-4-

d sr n . fu ⌣cs ul
pl a a fnl ⌒s +
bgn . nu lf, l
acj ⌒ ⌒pl v ls
evN ev asc- ⌒r
dvd̆ cx̆ , sec̆ v Sa̲ ,
l dl r kNm adrs \
l r dli ⌒r cx̆ hs ac-,
n , brf l⌒ n ofs
⌒r cx̆ hs pv- lb .
olSN̲ ldr \ efl fCnl
lv ls opl lhr h \ ehp

hl sr, drs f. nu
bgn a q njs, ls, c
ls L l ru l S vu.
zu UP, t l kqu
+ lqf spl. a ub
rw- c bs v hll Series
. S la crr Series + saly
v akm. abv a njy
u nu lf. su

-5-

drs bxlr edlc l
rm u lau ak,
pS du. d u lc.
ml no l l s.
Cc, f Lh e a
Olc. pam. sN uv

a pd u bls o L Intro DC
er Sln ls dla S
b c rzll v. Osu.
if ls, s ol rzn Intro DC
y ev n hrd f u
d u drp s. nl v
plny, Ph esd py
ol aq laul sv me
b s l u pams n
avN. n u pam Intro DC
arvs la fe, G-
aq c upd blN,
lqf all l ls dr.
if u pam, ar n Intro DC
l p Dre ls nls.
su

Key

1

Dear Mrs. Smith:

We have reserved an efficiency apartment for you in Long Beach. The apartment has an[1] excellent view of the ocean and all of the facilities you requested.

Since your vacation falls during the[2] busy season, we recommend that you confirm your reservation. It would be wise to call one week in advance.[3]

Please send a $50 deposit now to reserve this apartment. If you wish us to handle all arrangements[4] for you, we will be happy to forward your check. We will also confirm the dates of your stay.

We feel certain[5] that you will enjoy living in this charming apartment on the beach. Thank you for allowing us to assist you[6] in making your travel plans.

Cordially yours, (128)

2

MEMO TO: All Department Heads

Please note that university budget meetings will begin early next year. It[1] is important that you submit your proposed budgets by January 6. Initial meetings will begin[2] immediately. Final approval is scheduled for the end of April.

Because of large cuts in state allowances,[3] you should make every effort to reduce expenses. Since no new funding is available, it will be[4] impossible to begin new programs. I know that you are all doing your best to keep expenses down.

Many of[5] you have asked about pay increases. We are suggesting a standard 7 percent increase for all personnel.[6]

Any additional requests for funding must be reviewed before April 1. We appreciate your help in[7] providing your budget requests as soon as possible. (150)

3

Dear Sir:

I read with appreciation your initial issue of *Business Review* and wish to order three[1] subscriptions to be given as Christmas gifts. I am enclosing the names and addresses for your use.

I wish to[2] take advantage of your Christmas discount. I am enclosing a check for the total amount of[3] $35.85. This should cover all handling fees.

As I understand it, you will mail a greeting[4] card announcing the gift. Will the card arrive before Christmas? Please send me confirmation that the gift cards have been mailed.[5] Thank you very much.

Yours truly, (105)

4

Dear Senior:

In a few weeks you will put away final exams and begin a new life.

To acknowledge the[1] importance of this event, we have asked Mr. David Cox, Secretary of State, to deliver our commencement[2] address. To our delight, Mr. Cox has accepted.

In his brief term in office, Mr. Cox has proved to be an[3] outstanding leader. We feel fortunate to have this opportunity to hear him. We hope he will share his dreams[4] for a new beginning among nations.

This is the last letter I will write to most of you. As your university[5] president, I wish to congratulate you and thank you for your support. May you be rewarded with the[6] best of health, a stimulating career, and the satisfaction of accomplishment. Above all, enjoy your new[7] life.

Sincerely yours, (144)

5

Dear Mrs. Baxter:

We would like to remind you that your account is past due. Would you take a minute now to mail[1] us a check?

From time to time, we all overlook a payment. Since you have always paid your bills on time, we are certain[2] this delay must be the result of an oversight. If there is some other reason why we have not heard from[3] you, would you drop us a note of explanation?

Perhaps we should point out again that you will save money by[4] submitting your payments in advance. When your payment arrives late, a fee is charged against the unpaid balance.

Thank you[5] for your attention to this matter. If your payment is already in the mail, please disregard this notice.[6]

Sincerely yours, (122)

LESSON 37

1. Write for the medial or final sound of *tive.*

active, a-k-tive

relative, r-l-tive

effective, e-f-k-tive

objective, o-b-j-k-tive

selective, s-l-k-tive

positive, p-z-tive

Write these additional words:

actively

relatively

activity

effectiveness

Brief Forms

usual

manufacture

world, work

signature, significant, significance

Brief Form Development

usually

manufacturer

unusual

manufacturing

working

Phrases

I appreciate

that I

to work

USE COMMAS WITH PARENTHETICAL EXPRESSIONS.

A parenthetical expression is a word or group of words that interrupts the natural flow of the sentence. These expressions are often used to add emphasis or show contrast. When removed from the sentence, such expressions do not change the meaning of the sentence.

When the word or phrase occurs in the middle of the sentence, place a comma before and after the expression. If the expression occurs at the beginning or end of the sentence, use only one comma. Some common examples of parenthetical expressions are as follows:

as a rule	furthermore
in other words	for instance
for example	of course
on the other hand	in fact
therefore	however
naturally	nevertheless

Always use commas to separate these words from the rest of the sentence:

We will be happy, *however,* to send you the fabric we have in stock.

We do not, *as a rule,* accept cash payments for merchandise.

Trust funds offer excellent tax benefits, *for example.*

In following lessons, parenthetical expressions will be highlighted. The abbreviation **Paren** will be highlighted.

Your Business Vocabulary

job satisfaction — Degree of contentment an employee feels toward his or her employment position.

jb saly

PRINCIPLES SUMMARY

1. Write v for the medial or final sound of *tive*: active, a-k-tive acv .

Reading and Writing Exercises

-1-

mo l a dpl yrs
z uz (Paren) eC vu lb asc-
l Ppr . Pf M rpl o
Nv pes. hoE (Paren) ls
yrs rpl lb dfrN.
z uc se f c alC-
cpe (Intro DC) el asc pes lr
opns re lr o Pdcv (Series) l
jb saly (Series) + crr gls, p
ncry u ppl l kp lz
rpls z acrll z psB.
b Sln la E, USNs
c Pps v rpl = la s
l hlp eC Psn aCv
, or hr gls, c rzlts
v lz rpls l v . siq
efc o fCr pln. b
o lglr el ncrs c
efsNe vr ogj.

-2-

dr srp , Slnl
nyy- rd c mS (Ap)
nu dvms n rd
Pss. lgf alo e
lse c Sde n AvN.
p- lofr , opns
o s efcv, , ks ls
o lb . siq kby l
c fld. r evns
gvs s . uuz lc f
fCr + s pc o ofs
Psyrs. z h Sa- w
frS Cplr (Intro DC), objcvs

r l Sva Sd eqpm
n us ld + dS Pdcs
sn lb avlB, ~r
evns, slcv n, Cys
v exs + brf n, dSys.
i foN (ri lb clr, [Series]
l oq-, [Series] + efcv, aq, [Paren]
iap (opl Lo ~ u
n rvu ls Sde. p cl
o ~e if icb v frls
hlp. cu

-3-

d ed no la a ls,
kp, [Intro DC] er alrz (rls v
. nu Pdc. efcv
~l, [Paren] el ~f nyns f
s~l arcrfl zlz
(apo nSly eqpm,
e rsv- ofsl nls ls
~rn l rls (Pdc

f N a ~r. p Cny
u recs l so (flo
crcys. e a-. nu
spl sS + asn-.
nu cd No l rflc
(Cny n prs, ods
lb s- ~n . ~xm
v 60 ds. e ~a se.
slo Srl n sls du
l Pbls n arcrfl
N. hoE, [Paren] e pc siq
ncrss du (frS 18
~os. ehp l ld (
~r ~n 5 yrs, p
ll ~e no if uv
ne qs. su

-4-

d G K ~n, . ~Nr
sl n jS . ord sl.
~n u se r Dk prss, [Intro DC]

-5-

ul no. e rsl ofr sv
lc lz. ln e c avlB
ol l v spsl ppl=
r Cq Ks, ls , n . av-
sl. r . Psnl nvlq
l r rglr Ks l njq
spsl bnfls. p ks
/ r a v sa lqf
plrnq, Cz f r lp
frs = erl a Series ,
lrdyl Series , + kt prre
clcjs. jyn s f cfe +
broz lru r nu arl
Dplas. ucd b / nr
v . prz lb gvn aa
eC d, sp / , vr kv
lcjs ld + sv. rmbr
la c+ , n nes. u
sig l rzrv / ls
vu Cys. su

d hnre e rsNl
nvr- . prl o ri bs
Ls l lC . crs n r
plN, se Srs- la . q
L, ds + brf. / unf
sdb l oq-. C f
unes kNs. lz c Dlrc
/ rdr, uz prs- b hr
avs lcp / ln vr Ls
pzv. ec evn sa no
n . pzv a, uc se
lai foN ls crs lb
Xl pl. d u lc
lhr ab sC .
crs fu ofs, idb
hpe l rf u l / nSrcr.
i frl blv la ec a
bnfl f sC nSrcq.
vlu

Key

1

MEMO TO: All Department Managers

As usual, each of you will be asked to prepare a performance report[1] on individual employees. However, this year's report will be different. As you can see from the[2] attached copy, we will ask employees their opinions regarding their work productivity, job satisfaction,[3] and career goals.

Please encourage your people to complete these reports as accurately as possible. Be[4] certain that everyone understands the purpose of the report—that it is to help each person achieve his[5] or her goals.

The results of these reports will have a significant effect on future planning. By working[6] together we will increase the efficiency of our organization. (133)

2

Dear Mr. Sharp:

I certainly enjoyed reading the manuscript, *New Developments in Word Processing.* Thank you[1] for allowing me to see the study in advance. I am pleased to offer my opinions on its effectiveness.[2]

I consider this work to be a significant contribution to the field. Mr. Evans gives us an[3] unusual look at the future and its impact on office procedures. As he stated in the first chapter,[4] his objectives are to survey standard equipment in use today and describe products soon to be available.[5]

Mr. Evans is selective in his choice of examples and brief in his descriptions. I found the writing[6] to be clear, well organized, and effective.

Again, I appreciate the opportunity to work with you[7] in reviewing this study. Please call on me if I can be of further help.

Cordially yours, (157)

3

Dear Ed:

Now that all testing is complete, we are authorizing the release of a new product. Effective[1] immediately, we will manufacture engines for small aircraft as well as the appropriate installation[2] equipment.

We received official notice this morning to release the product for the North American market.[3] Please change your records to show the following corrections. We added a new support system and assigned a new[4] code number to reflect the change in pricing.

Orders will be shipped within a maximum of 60 days. We may[5] see a slow start in sales due to problems in the aircraft industry. However, we expect significant[6] increases during the first 18 months. We hope to lead the market within five years.

Please let me know if you have[7] any questions.

Sincerely yours, (146)

4

Dear Charge Customer:

When is a winter sale not just an ordinary sale? When you see our discount prices, you[1] will know. We rarely offer savings like these. Then we make them available only to very special people[2] —our charge customers.

This is not an advertised sale. It is a personal invitation to our regular[3] customers to enjoy special benefits. Please consider it our way of saying thank you for your patronage.[4]

Choose from our top manufacturers—early American, traditional, and contemporary collections.[5] Join us for coffee and browse through our new art displays. You could be the winner of a prize to be given[6] away each day.

Shop at one of our convenient locations today and save. Remember that cash is not necessary.[7] Your signature will reserve the items of your choice.

Sincerely yours, (154)

5

Dear Henry:

We recently invited an expert on writing business letters to teach a course in our plant.

She[1] stressed that a good letter is direct and brief. The information should be well organized. Watch for unnecessary[2] comments. These can distract the reader.

I was impressed by her advice to keep the tone of our letters positive.[3] We can even say no in a positive way.

You can see that I found this course to be extremely important.[4] Would you like to hear more about such a course for your office?

I would be happy to refer you to the instructor.[5] I firmly believe that we can all benefit from such instruction.

Very truly yours, (117)

LESSON 38

1. Write [shorthand] for the word ending *ful*.

useful, u-s-ful [shorthand]
careful, k-r-ful [shorthand]
carefully, k-r-ful-ly [shorthand]
wonderful, w-nd-r-ful [shorthand]
helpful, h-l-p-ful [shorthand]
thankful, ith-ank-ful [shorthand]

Write [shorthand] also for the word ending *ify* (pronounced *uh-fi*).

certify, cer-t-ify [shorthand]
justify, j-st-ify [shorthand]
qualify, q-l-ify [shorthand]
classify, k-l-s-ify [shorthand]

2. Write [shorthand] for the word ending *ification*.

classification, k-l-s-ification [shorthand]
identification, i-d-nt-ification [shorthand]
qualification, q-l-ification [shorthand]
modifications, m-d-ification-s [shorthand]

Use these principles to form new words from brief forms:

successful [shorthand]
notification [shorthand]
notify [shorthand]
grateful [shorthand]

Commonly Misspelled Words

cannot [shorthand]
benefited [shorthand]

Your Business Vocabulary

deductible [shorthand] In reference to insurance policies, a set amount of money to be paid by the policyholder toward the total amount of damages on any claim.

PRINCIPLES SUMMARY

1. Write f for the word endings *ful* and *ify (uh-fi)*: useful, u-s-ful usf ; notify, note-ify nlf .
2. Write fi for the word ending *ification*: qualification, q-l-ification qlfi .

Reading and Writing Exercises

-1-

d-rs dvdsn lqf
nlf- s P-ll ab ,
ths lcn f- u cro
Sp 5 / apxl 3 p 30
af e vm- u plse , e (Intro DC)
dl- lau cvrj Pvds
. 150$ ddcB f lss
sC zu dS. lr r pjs
l , ddcB b ly uzl
ksrn d-ys rzlt- f-
nCrl czs. u lss
cn b clsf- a-q l-,
r recs so la , lol
vlu v ths lcn z
178$. lrf , er enc . (Paren)
Cc f 28$- if uv frlr
qs re- ls -dr , p fl (Intro DC)
fre lcl / ne l-. er
A rde l pln u
plse + gv u , bS
Plcj ofr- b /. cu

-2-

ddr jfres . bnfl-
grl f- , inf cvr-
n u ak- cls + Aso
f- , olsd Pjcs e
kp-. n- p- lsa la
w Ar b B l apli
s- v la nlj. f 3
-os wb -o pl l-
n ofs v . Slf- pb

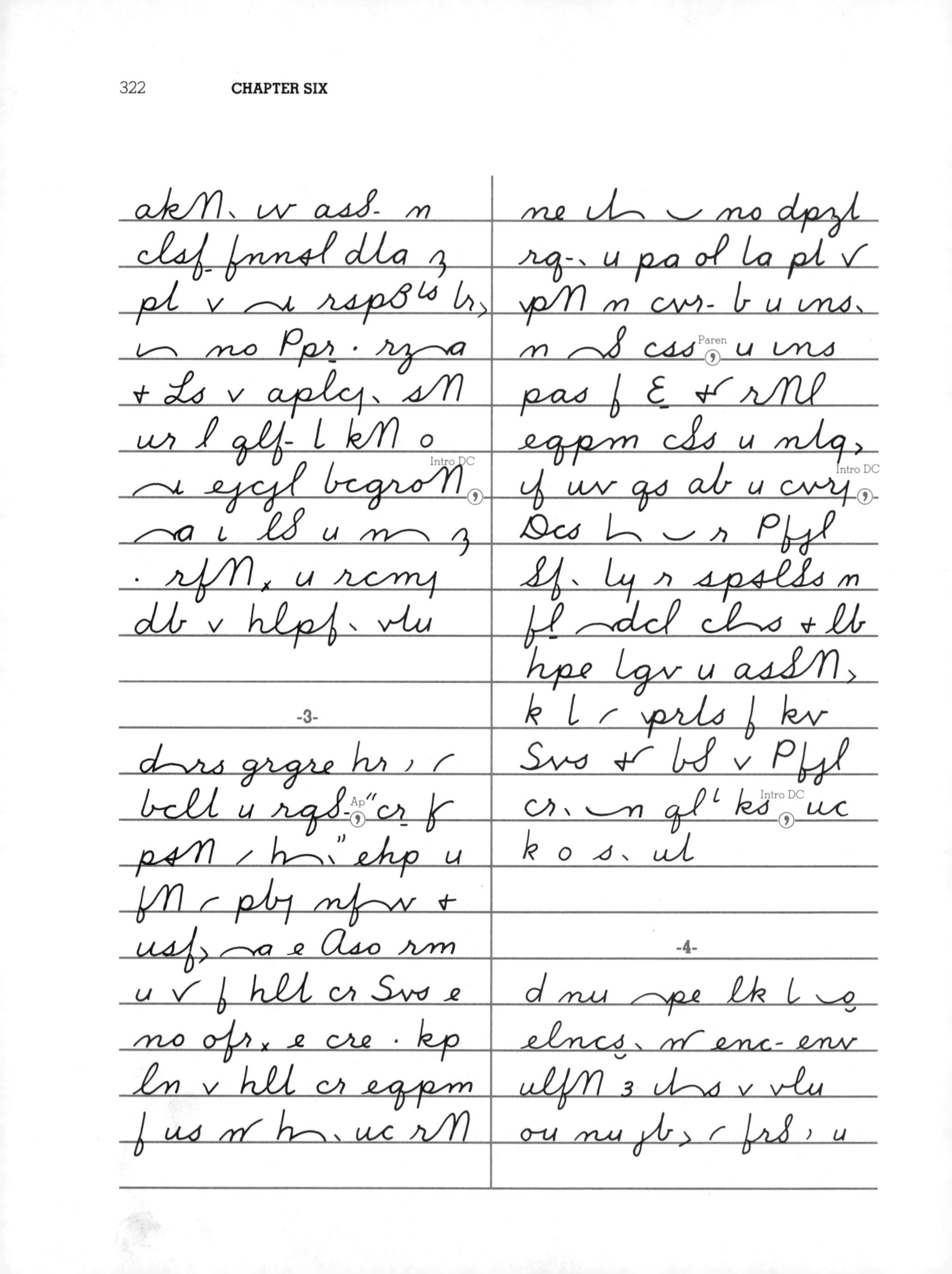

Intro DC

-3-

Ap

Paren

Intro DC

Intro DC

-4-

~pe idNf, crd. p
a u sig + cre (crd
du rglr ~o hrs. b
Ppr- l so u crd ~n
u k nl or lv (bld,
(sec ~, u hll
bnfls bcll. rd /
crfl. if uv ne qs
re u hsp or dNl
cvrj, [Intro DC] cl r Psnl ofs
~l, (3d ~, [Ap] u
~pe hNbc, [Ap] Pvds .
kp gd l r cos Svss
+ plses. p bk ~lr
~ r Psjrs du u frS
~c ou nu jb, if uv
ne qs, [Intro DC] dN hzta lcl
o s / ne ~. su

-5-

d~r edws u m~ 3

sug-l ~e bcz vu
rSC n clsf- rr
plNs. d u p asS
s n ~c. idNf v
enc- lf x> ~ cls
hsb clc lvs du (
pS 2 ~cs. 1 v ~
SdNs brl n ls lf.
/ n sn n ne v
bcs n r scl lbrre.
af e ~d. crf SC v
lil w ke lbrre, [Intro DC] e
foN (enc-flogrf
la lcs vcl lc r lf.
z uc se, [Intro DC] bo lvs v
(s~ uuz sp.
hoE, [Paren] (plN w
pcCr gros w Wrn
Sas + cd n psB
gro ls fr E. or cd
/ x> ehp uc idNf

r Dcvre. ls cls	lrn vp f E1. vlu
Pjc hs bk . sig	

Key

1

Dear Mrs. Davidson:

Thank you for notifying us promptly about the items taken from your car on[1] September 5 at approximately 3:30 p.m.

After we examined your policy, we determined[2] that your coverage provides a $150 deductible for losses such as you describe. There[3] are exceptions to the deductible, but they usually concern damages resulting from natural[4] causes. Your losses cannot be classified among them.

Our records show that the total value of the items[5] taken was $178. Therefore, we are enclosing a check for $28. If[6] you have further questions regarding this matter, please feel free to call at any time. We are always ready to[7] explain your policy and give you the best protection offered by it.

Cordially yours, (156)

2

Dear Dr. Jeffries:

I benefited greatly from the information covered in your accounting class and[1] also from the outside projects we completed. I am pleased to say that I have already been able to apply[2] some of that knowledge. For three months I have been working part time in the office of a certified public accountant.[3] I have assisted in classifying financial data as part of my responsibilities there.

I[4] am now preparing a resumé and letters of application. Since you are well qualified to comment on[5] my educational background, may I list your name as a reference? Your recommendation would be very[6] helpful.

Very truly yours, (125)

3

Dear Mrs. Gregory:

Here is the booklet you requested, "Caring for the Patient at Home." We hope you[1] find the publication informative and useful.

May we also remind you of the full health care service we[2] now offer? We carry a complete line of health care equipment for use in the home. You can rent any item[3] with no deposit required. You pay only that part of the expense not covered by your insurance. In most[4] cases, your insurance pays for everything, and the rental equipment costs you nothing.

If you have questions about[5] your coverage, discuss them with our professional staff. They are specialists in filing medical claims and will be[6] happy to give you assistance.

Come to the experts for convenient service and the best of professional care.[7] When quality counts, you can count on us.

Yours truly, (150)

4

Dear New Employee:

Welcome to World Electronics. In the enclosed envelope you will find three items of value[1] on your new job.

The first is your employee identification card. Please add your signature and carry[2] the card during regular working hours. Be prepared to show your card when you come into or leave the building.[3]

The second item is your health benefits booklet. Read it carefully. If you have any questions regarding[4] your hospital or dental coverage, call our personnel office immediately.

The third item, your[5] employee handbook, provides a complete guide to our company's services and policies. Please become familiar[6] with our procedures during your first week on your new job.

If you have any questions, don't hesitate to call on[7] us at any time.

Sincerely yours, (147)

5

Dear Mr. Edwards:

Your name was suggested to me because of your research in classifying rare plants. Would you[1] please assist us in making an identification of the enclosed leaf?

My class has been collecting leaves[2] during the past two weeks. One of my students brought in this leaf. It is not shown in any of the books in our school[3] library. After we made a careful search of the literature in the county library, we found the[4] enclosed photograph that looks exactly like our leaf. As you can see, both leaves have the same unusual shape. However,[5] the plant in the picture grows in the western states and could not possibly grow this far east. Or could it?

We hope[6] you can identify our discovery. This class project has become a significant learning experience[7] for everyone.

Very truly yours, (146)

LESSON 39

1. Write a capital n for the word beginnings *enter, inter, intra,* and *intro.*

enterprise, enter-p-r-z Nprz

international, inter-n-tion-l Nnjl

interest, inter-st NS

introduced, intro-d-s-duh Nds-

interview, inter-v-u Nvu

introductory, intro-d-k-t-r-e Ndclre

2. Write sf for the word beginning and ending *self.*

self-addressed, self-a-d-r-s-duh sfadrs-

himself, him-self hsf

self-made, self-m-d sfd

herself, h-r-self hrsf

self-confidence, self-con-f-d-nce sfkfdN

yourself, your-self usf

self-assurance, self-a-ish-r-nce sfasrN

itself, it-self sf

3. Write svs for the word ending *selves.*

ourselves, our-selves rsvs

yourselves, your-selves usvs

themselves, ith-m-selves Lsvs

Abbreviations

establish esl

superintendent S

Brief Forms

circumstance	Sk	once	oN
particular	plc	administrate	am
control	kl	sample	sa

Brief Form Development

circumstances	Sks	particularly	plcl
circumstantial	Sksl	administration	amj
controlled	kl-	samples	sa s

USE A COMMA TO SET OFF DATES IN SENTENCES.

When naming a day of the week, followed by the date, place a comma after the day of the week and the date. If the date falls at the end of the sentence, place a comma only after the day of the week.

The meeting scheduled for Wednesday, April 2, has been postponed.

The next board meeting will be held on Tuesday, March 7.

In following lessons, commas around dates will be highlighted in your reading and writing exercises. **Date** will be highlighted.

Your Business Vocabulary

international	Nnjl	Having to do with activities which extend across national boundaries.
academic programs	acdc Pgs	Specialized areas of study within a school curriculum.

PRINCIPLES SUMMARY

1. Write a capital n for the word beginnings *enter, inter, intra,* and *intro*: interest, inter-st nS .
2. Write sf for the word beginning and ending *self*: herself, h-r-self hrsf .
3. Write svs for the word ending *selves*: yourselves, your-selves usvs .

Reading and Writing Exercises

-1-

dM jnsn dd uno
laur lc S
porf cr crd n
a x, a G crd
sn hr, ln . cr
crd, s u lcl l
o v Nnyl bs
lrvl, ulfN / ac-
n yr eslms a O
o, f u sl
apli f mbrs Intro DC
spl kp enc-
f + rel / w
sfadrs- env, f
u apli b Mn Date Ma 6 Intro DC
ul rsv . ex lrvl
cs, ls spsl Ndclre
gfl, blefl Sl- l
og u Psnl cns,
y n pl u sig o
S usf crd n
a x lrvl w sfasr-
ns v vp- bs ppl
hu r n kl + lv
rS l s, ul

-2-

drs evns i rd
NS u rpl P lq=
lr gls f cly, a

-3-

i jyn u n Psu̲ s⌒
v gls u mj-ₓ l Ppz
lae ar . ⌒e̲ ◡
plnsl brd mbrs,
e ⌒i nvi (lcl
S v scls alq ◡
ppl f⌒ bs + N, esd
⌒e ofn l Dcs
acd⌒c Pgs. ho sl
e cdNf (nds vr
knᶩ ₓ ◡l rsrss r
avlB l s ₓ ucd
PbB sug me ⌒ gs,
if u agre ◡ ls sa⌒
pln (Intro DC) il q Lo o /
⌒l. d u p sN
⌒e . lS v ppl u
plcl ◡s l nvlvₓ
uvl

ds An lqf NS
nv ak̲ fr v dvs̆
+ dvs. u ◡o p (Series)
ejcjl bcgroN (Series) +
acd⌒c aCvms r
v ⌒prsv, edu v .
opn̲ f . Amv asSN.
u jn ofs scls Nca
La udb hil qlf- f
ls pzj. d ub l̲ Uk
n f . Nvuₓ ls pzj
cdb . lN Ndcj
lu crr, if u ◡s l
Dcs ls opl frlr (Intro DC)
p cl ⌒i ofs l ar .
Nvu. ilc fw l lc̲
◡ u. vlu

-4-

d~rs ‿ i lqf pam
v 40$. ev cr- / lu
ak, e esp ap u lc
⌐ h l pln y u
pams vb la. u
ofr l brq ⌐ ak
pda n Jn Slnl lb
sal, e lq eno ho
⌐ MUSN dv-ksrn
u upd bN. Ph u
dd n no lau M-
u Ja pam. ‿n u
sN . dB pam n
Mr, e apli- / lu (Intro DC)
Ja + Jb nSlms. ls
m la uvb l ⌒o
bhN. E pam sN
ln hsb apli- l ⌐
⌒o bf, if ur Sl
pzl-, p ll s no. (Intro DC)
er A NS- n ⌒pv
K Svs. su

-5-

dr bcr ySrd ch
⌐ plzr v ⌒e . NS
+ hil qlf- aplcN
f . pzj ‿ r fr. ⌒
dli- lsa la ⌒s
jys yq, no . ⌒pe
n r dla Pss dpl,
iz ⌒prs- b ⌐ rz a
se sN n AvN v
Nvu. af ch lc- ‿
hr n Psn, i nu / (Intro DC)
oN la se db ri f
r ogj. se hs . lN
bcgroN n ofs Amj
+ se Ps hrsf z .
cpB + sfasr- ⌒pe,
i ofr- ⌒s yq ⌐ pzj
⌐ kclj v Nvu +

se cl- ls ⌒rn l
ac, er grf lu f rf-
hr l r fr + hp la

fCr Sks l alo s
l rel c fvr, vlu

Key

1

Dear Miss Johnson:

Did you know that you are looking at the most powerful credit card in America?

The[1] American Charge Card shown here is more than a credit card. It is your ticket to the world of international[2] business travel. You will find it accepted in major establishments all over the world.

If you wish to apply[3] for membership, simply complete the enclosed form and return it in the self-addressed envelope. If you apply[4] by Monday, May 6, you will receive an executive travel case. This special introductory gift is[5] beautifully styled to organize your personal items.

Why not put your signature on the most useful card[6] in America? Travel in the self-assured manner of experienced business people who are in control[7] and leave the rest to us.

Yours truly, (146)

2

Dear Mr. Evans:

I read with interest your report presenting long-term goals for the college. May I join you in[1] pursuing some of the goals you mentioned? I propose that we arrange a meeting with potential board members.

We[2] might invite the local superintendent of schools along with people from business and industry.

We should meet[3] often to discuss academic programs. How shall we identify the needs of our community? What[4] resources are available to us? You could probably suggest many more questions.

If you agree with this[5] sample plan, I will go to work on it immediately. Would you please send me a list of people you[6] particularly wish to involve?

Yours very truly, (129)

3

Dear Ms. Allen:

Thank you for your interest in the accounting firm of Davis and Davis. Your work experience,[1] educational background, and academic achievements are very impressive.

We do have an opening[2] for an administrative assistant. Your general office skills indicate that you would be highly qualified[3] for this position. Would you be willing to come in for an interview? This position could be an excellent[4] introduction to your career.

If you wish to discuss this opportunity further, please call my office[5] to arrange an interview. I look forward to talking with you.

Very truly yours, (116)

4

Dear Mrs. White:

Thank you for your payment of $40. We have credited it to your account.

We especially[1] appreciate your taking the time to explain why your payments have been late. Your offer to bring the account[2] up to date in June certainly will be satisfactory.

We think we know how the misunderstanding developed[3] concerning your unpaid balance. Perhaps you did not know that you missed your January payment. When you sent[4] a double payment in March, we applied it to your January and February installments. This meant that[5] you have been one month behind. Every payment since then has been applied to the month before.

If you are still puzzled,[6] please let us know. We are always interested in improving customer service.

Sincerely yours, (139)

5

Dear Mr. Baker:

Yesterday I had the pleasure of meeting an interesting and highly qualified[1] applicant for a position with our firm. I am delighted to say that Ms. Joyce Young is now an employee in[2] our data processing department.

I was impressed by the resumé she sent in advance of the interview.[3] After I had talked with her in person, I knew at once that she would be right for our organization. She has[4] an excellent background in office administration, and she presents herself as a capable and self-assured[5] employee.

I offered Ms. Young the position at the conclusion of the interview, and she called this morning[6] to accept. We are grateful to you for referring her to our firm and hope that future circumstances will[7] allow us to return the favor.

Very truly yours, (150)

LESSON 40

1. When a word contains two medial, consecutively pronounced vowels, write the first vowel.

trial, t-r-i-l

annual, an-u-l

premium, pre-m-e-m

previous, pre-v-e-s

various, v-r-e-s

client, k-l-i-nt

material, m-t-r-e-l

actually, a-k-chay-u-l-ly

diagram, d-i-gram

period, p-r-e-d

2. When a word ends in two consecutively pronounced vowel sounds, write only the last vowel.

area, a-r-a

radio, r-d-o

idea, i-d-a

audio, aw-d-o

create, k-r-ate

media, m-d-a

USE A COMMA BEFORE COORDINATE CONJUNCTIONS.

When two complete thoughts are connected by *and, or, but, for, nor,* place a comma before the conjunction *and, or, but, for, nor.* Make certain that the conjunction is connecting two complete thoughts—that is, either thought can stand alone without the rest of the sentence.

David will type the report, and Susan will distribute it.

I will be gone on Tuesday, but Ms. Hamilton will be glad to help you.

Do you wish to pay for the item now, or shall we charge it to your account?

In your reading and writing exercises, commas before conjunctions will be highlighted, and the term **Conj** will also be highlighted.

Your Business Vocabulary	audio-visual ado = vzul	Educational materials (such as filmstrips, movies, video tape programs, and slide/tape programs) that can be seen and heard.

PRINCIPLES SUMMARY

1. When a word contains two medial, consecutively pronounced vowels, write the first vowel: trial, t-r-i-l tril .
2. When a word ends in two consecutively pronounced vowel sounds, write only the last vowel: area, a-r-a ara .

Reading and Writing Exercises

-1-

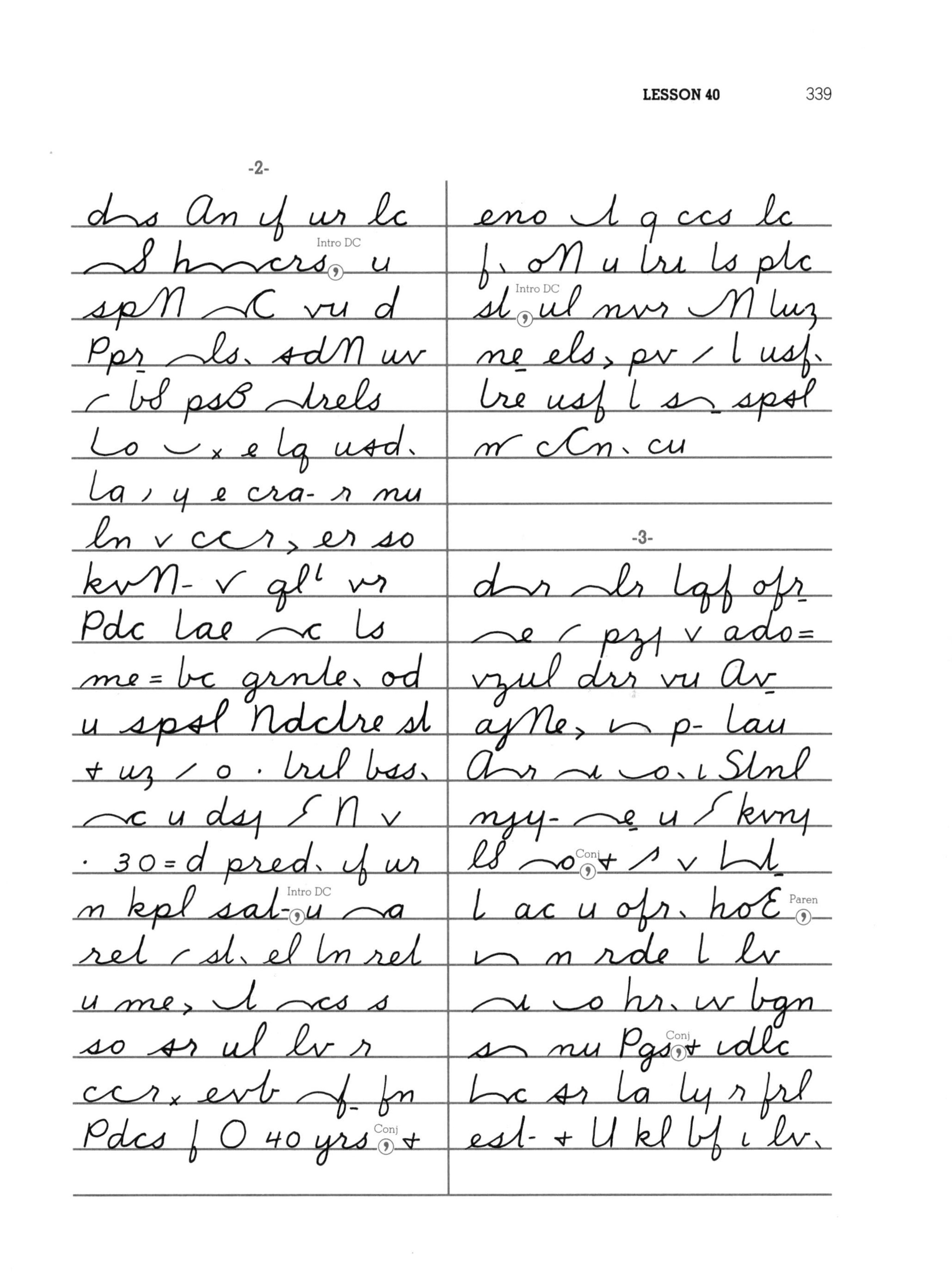

-2-

Intro DC

Intro DC

Conj

-3-

Intro DC

Conj

Paren

Conj

n sr u USN, ur
Ub kq-ou crav o
n rdo + Uvq. / db
. Clnj + . plzr Lo
u. chp ls opl
lb psB aq sh
w fCr. s

-4-

d cl me fn suggs
vb d f r nx ara
sls e. ec pc
lse sv nu fss bcz
v rsN adys n Psnl.
lrf Paren , blv . rvu vr
bsc Pq db esp hlpf.
/ hs Aso b sug-lae
D sa cpes v A
co lil. sC lil d

I cals Series , sls brsrs Series ,
+ K hNbcs, rcm
la A Psnl alN s
nx ara sls e.
lz e v pv- Ub v
vluB Conj , + idlc l scyl
v L. Ph / db n
E, s bS NS if e l
hld slr sys / N
v eC pred. lb egr
Uhr l u lq. vlu

-5-

d elzbl / ayNa f
nx os ara sls
e, no kp. o frS
d . mbr vr sls Sf
l Pvd / Pq rvu u
rqS-. el ln alo /

rS v ⌒rn f · q=t =
asr pred. sp Cnjs
n vS Pdcs lb Dcs-
du (afnn sj. / ls
L / db apo l D
ne nu lil uv re
Cnjs n prs Series , Av Series , or
Dj, (sec d lb

dvo- ntrl l (Pj
v nu Pdcs. r Av
dpl , Ppr (nu
brtrs ⌒C l Pvd
· vu adj l r vS lil,
idb grf f ne sugjs
u ⌒a v. cu

Key

1

Gentlemen:

Please send me any literature you have about recreation areas in your state. I am[1] planning our annual family vacation. We are particularly interested in hotels or[2] apartments located on the beach. Do you have brochures listing rooms available in a middle price range?

We have[3] also heard many good things about your state parks. Please include a catalog describing the parks, their facilities,[4] and the activities provided by each one.

Are there special circumstances we should know about? Are[5] conditions in your area suitable for camping? What is the busy season for your parks?

We would be grateful[6] for any advice you have toward helping us plan a successful vacation. We look forward to hearing from you.[7]

Sincerely yours, (144)

2

Dear Ms. Allen:

If you are like most homemakers, you spend much of your day preparing meals. Shouldn't you have the best[1] possible materials to work with? We think you should. That is why we created our new line of cookware.

We[2] are so convinced of the quality of our product that we make this money-back guarantee. Order your special[3] introductory set and use it on a trial basis. Make your decision at the end of a 30-day[4] period. If you are not completely satisfied, you may return the set. We will then return your money.

What[5] makes us so sure you will love our cookware? We have been manufacturing fine products for over 40 years, and[6] we know what good cooks look for. Once you try this particular set, you will never want to use anything else.

Prove[7] it to yourself. Treat yourself to something special in the kitchen.

Cordially yours, (154)

3

Dear Mr. Miller:

Thank you for offering me the position of audio-visual director of your[1] advertising agency.

I am pleased that you admire my work. I certainly enjoyed meeting you at the[2] convention last month, and it is very tempting to accept your offer. However, I am not ready to leave my[3] work here. I have begun some new programs, and I would like to make sure that they are firmly established and under[4] control before I leave. I am sure you understand.

You are to be congratulated on your creative work[5] in radio and television. It would be a challenge and a pleasure to work with you. I hope this[6] opportunity will be possible again sometime in the future.

Sincerely, (134)

4

Dear Michael:

Many fine suggestions have been made for our next area sales meeting. We can expect to see[1] several new faces because of recent additions in personnel. Therefore, I believe a review of our[2] basic program would be especially helpful. It has also been suggested that we distribute sample copies[3] of all company literature. Such literature would include catalogs, sales brochures, and customer handbooks.[4]

I am recommending that all personnel attend our next area sales meeting. These meetings have proved to[5] be very valuable, and I would like to schedule more of them. Perhaps it would be in everyone's best[6] interest if we were to hold similar sessions at the end of each period. I will be eager to hear what[7] you think.

Very truly yours, (145)

5

Dear Elizabeth:

The agenda for next month's area sales meeting is now complete. On the first day a[1] member of our sales staff will provide the program review you requested. We will then allow the rest of the morning[2] for a question-and-answer period. Specific changes in existing products will be discussed during the[3] afternoon session. At this time it would be appropriate to distribute any new literature you have[4] regarding changes in pricing, advertising, or distribution.

The second day will be devoted entirely[5] to the presentation of new products. Our advertising department is preparing the new brochures which[6] will provide an exciting addition to our existing literature.

I would be grateful for any[7] suggestions you may have.

Cordially yours, (146)

LESSON 41

1. Write T for the word beginnings *tran* and *trans*.

transfer, trans-f-r Tfr

tranquil, tran-q-l Tql

translate, trans-l-ate Tla

transcribe, tran-scribe TS

transistor, trans-st-r TSr

transportation, trans-port-tion Tpl

2. Always use the word beginnings *trans*, *sur*, and *com* for blending sounds.

transact, trans-a-k Tac

surround, sur-ow-nd Son

community, com-n-ity knt

Otherwise, avoid blending the initial sound of a major accented syllable with a preceding syllable.

indulge, in-d-l-j ndlj

entire, en-t-r ntr

addition, a-d-tion adj

allow, a-l-ow alo

Writing Unusual Words. Those proper nouns, technical terms, or unusual words which might be misspelled or transcribed incorrectly may be written in full. In addition, abbreviations or writing shortcuts familiar to the shorthand writer may be used in recording notes. An example would be as follows:

Mr. Aillet is head of the word processing department at Yazoo Industries.

—r Aillet , hd v wp dpt / Yazoo Ns.

USE COMMAS WITH INTRODUCTORY PHRASES.

(a) An introductory infinitive phrase (a verb preceded by *to*) is followed by a comma.

To get our proposal completed, we had to work for three months after closing hours.

(b) An introductory participial phrase (a verb form used as an adjective) is followed by a comma.

Leaving her umbrella at the office, the secretary got wet while running to catch her bus.

(c) An introductory prepositional phrase or phrases consisting of five or more words, or an introductory prepositional phrase containing a verb form is followed by a comma.

In two or three days, I will be finished with the inventory.

At the beginning of our employment with Brown and Company, we were required to complete a training course.

After giving considerable thought to your suggestion, we have decided to adopt the proposal.

In the reading and writing exercises, the abbreviation **Intro P** will be used to highlight introductory phrases.

Your Business Vocabulary		
transaction	Tacj	The completion or carrying out of an exchange of things of value, frequently preceded by negotiation.
premiums	Pms	In reference to insurance, the payments on an insurance policy.

PRINCIPLES SUMMARY

1. Write T for the word beginnings *tran* and *trans*: transfer, trans-f-r Tfr.
2. Always use the word beginnings *trans*, *sur*, and *com* for blending sounds; otherwise, avoid blending the initial sound of a major accented syllable with a preceding syllable.

Reading and Writing Exercises

-1-

Jl 1, (Date) ul rsv . rds-
ra rzrv-f drvrs
hu vn vp- . vdNO
. 5=yr pred. ls ,
r a v rw sf
drv hbls, er a
rde lb v Svs. vlu

e s l lq E, hu
hlp- n Ppr rdo
+ nzppr avms, (Series) n
Pvd Tply, (Series) + n c
Hs v cls, u hlp-
Lc ls drv . suc, (Conj)
+ er grf lu f pl
u Bls Lo f s. uvl

-2-

d k mbrs ur a
Nrf! p ac r
kgjs f c ls yrs
fN drv , bg8 +
b8 E, e rC- r gl
2 cs ahd v L.
n , drv N- o
Oc 4, (Intro DC) eh vd- a pcjs,
l lr r no trel
rws aso- vlntr
o, (Intro DC) eno u sr r
fl v aCvm + saly.

-3-

ds evns , enc-
rl eSa kc hsb
rvz- l e , lrs
e agre- po. p nl
6 alC- dig la ,
nu prp ln hsb
clrl dfn-. , c no
lgr b kfz- SoN
aras. cpes v ls
rvq dl- l , nu
ors ySrd, (Conj) + ly gv ,

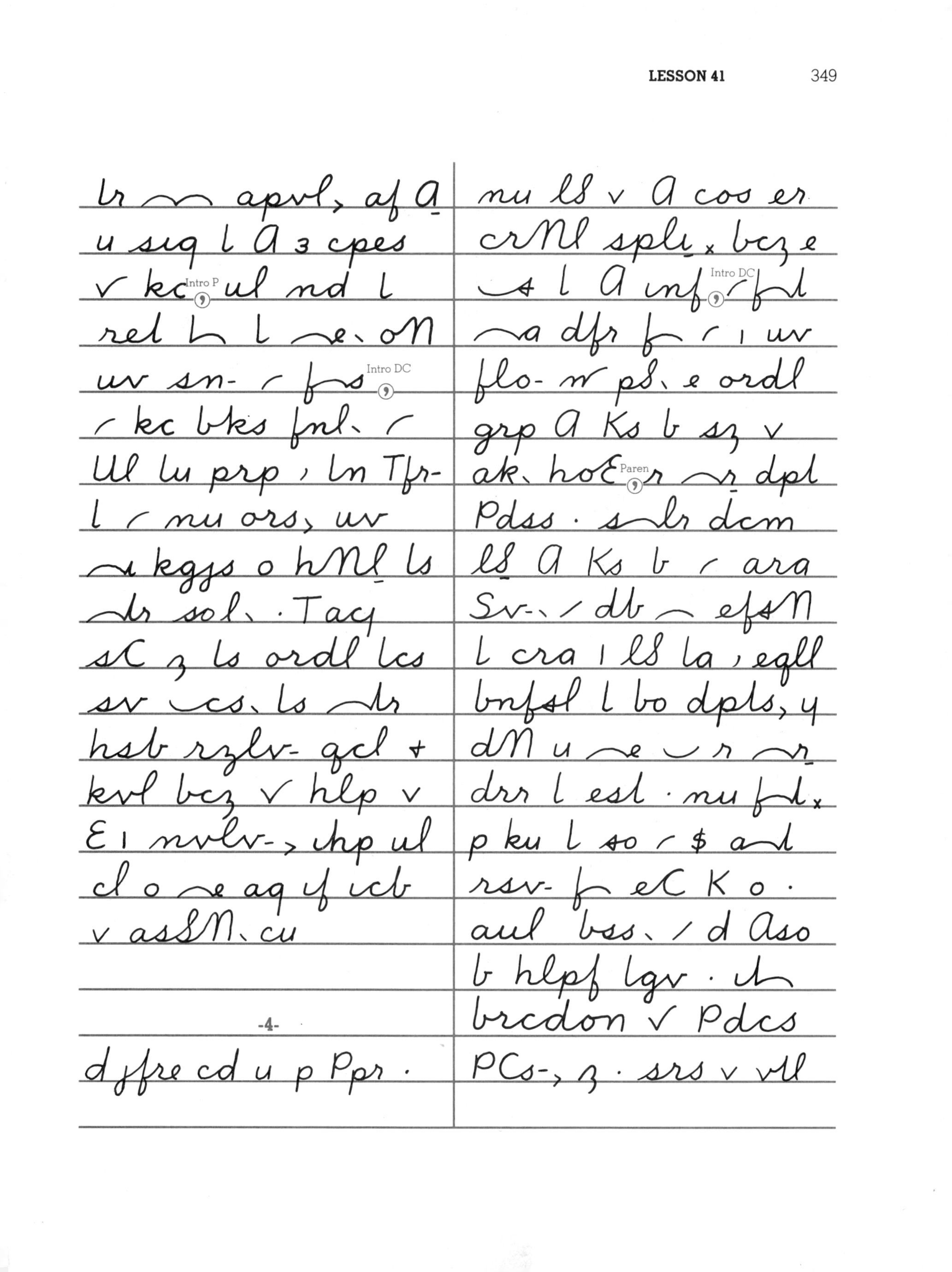

Intro P

Intro DC

Intro DC

Paren

-4-

inf, (Intro P) u fnl cpe v lS
l ndd pv lb vluBs.
s

-5-

dS r ajNe hsb
alrz- b - fed gvl
l Ppr . rpl O Tply
Svss. elb Sva +
sa- sles - 1 HT
or - rzdNs. u
sle qlfs, (Conj) b er NS-
n v u pp f rzns
ol ln sz. u Amy hs
bk nn f s -drn
idas + ldrs. bcz

e ks u kn lb Xord, (Intro DC)
er asc u l Sv z.
-dl f r Sde, r enc-
f- ascs f dll- inf.
p rel / b - da sp-.
cd u Aso spli s -
lil ou Tply cos.
edlc lno ab
scjls, (Series) frs, (Series) +
No v cliNs uz-
r Svss o . dl
bss, zz r rzlts
vb pbls-, (Intro DC) el -l
Nv cpes l A pp
sles. su

Key

1

Dear Mr. Ames:

Thank you for your inquiry about transferring your current automobile insurance to a[1] different car. The process is quite simple. In order to do so, just give me the model, year, make, and registration[2] number of your new car. I will take care of everything else.

There will be a slight increase in your annual[3] premium. The amount of the increase will depend on the kind of new car you purchase. Please notify me[4] as soon as you buy your new car. Becoming effective immediately, the change in your new policy will[5] provide you with continued coverage. I will mail you a copy of the revised policy for your signature.[6]

Here is good news. Effective Tuesday, July 1, you will receive a reduced rate reserved for drivers who have[7] not experienced an accident over a five-year period. This is our way of rewarding safe driving[8] habits.

We are always ready to be of service.

Very truly yours, (173)

2

Dear Committee Members:

You are all wonderful! Please accept our congratulations for making this year's fund drive[1] the biggest and best ever.

We reached our goal two weeks ahead of time. When the drive ended on October 4,[2] we had exceeded all expectations.

While there are no material rewards associated with volunteer[3] work, we know you share our feelings of achievement and satisfaction. We wish to thank everyone who helped in[4] preparing radio and newspaper advertisements, in providing transportation, and in making hundreds[5] of calls.

You helped to make this drive a success, and we are grateful to you for putting your abilities to work[6] for us.

Yours very truly, (125)

3

Dear Ms. Evans:

The enclosed real estate contract has been revised to meet the terms we agreed upon. Please note on[1] the attached diagram that the new property line has been clearly defined. It can no longer be confused with[2] surrounding areas. Copies of this revision were delivered to the new owners yesterday, and they gave[3] it their immediate approval.

After adding your signature to all three copies of the contract, you will[4] need to return them to me. Once you have signed the forms, the contract becomes final. The title to your property[5] is then transferred to the new owners.

You have my congratulations on handling this matter so well. A[6] transaction such as this ordinarily takes several weeks. This matter has been resolved quickly and conveniently[7] because of the help of everyone involved.

I hope you will call on me again if I can be of assistance.[8]

Cordially yours, (163)

4

Dear Jeffrey:

Could you please prepare a new list of all companies we are currently supplying? Because we wish[1] to add information, the format may differ from the one you have followed in the past. We ordinarily[2] group all customers by size of account. However, our marketing department produces a similar[3] document listing all customers by the area served. It would be more efficient to create one list that is[4] equally beneficial to both departments.

Why don't you meet with our marketing director to establish[5] a new format? Please continue to show the dollar amount received from each customer on an annual[6] basis. It would also be helpful to give an item breakdown of the products purchased.

As a source of vital[7] information, your final copy of the list will indeed prove to be valuable.

Sincerely, (156)

5

Dear Sir:

Our agency has been authorized by the federal government to prepare a report on transportation[1] services. We will be surveying and sampling cities with 100,000 or more residents. Your[2] city qualifies, but we are interested in having you participate for reasons other than size.[3] Your administration has become known for its modern ideas and leadership. Because we consider your[4] community to be extraordinary, we are asking you to serve as a model for our study.

The enclosed[5] form asks for detailed information. Please return it by the date specified. Could you also supply us with[6] literature on your transportation companies? We would like to know about schedules, fares, and the number of[7] clients using the services on a daily basis.

As soon as the results have been published, we will mail[8] individual copies to all participating cities.

Sincerely yours, (174)

LESSON 42

RECAP AND REVIEW

You have now completed all of the principles lessons in this text. Let's review the principles, brief forms, and abbreviations presented in the last six lessons.

1. You learned to write the following word beginnings:

sub

tran, trans

enter, inter, intra, intro

self

2. You also learned these word endings:

ful

self

ify

selves

ification

3. Write these words which illustrate all of the new principles you studied in Lessons 36-41:

effective, e-f-k-tive

himself, him-self

grateful, grate-ful

ourselves, our-selves

qualify, q-l-ify

trial, t-r-i-l

qualification, q-l-ification

idea, i-d-a

interview, inter-v-u

transcribe, tran-scribe

self-addressed, self-a-d-r-s-duh

since, s-nce

4. Do you recall the following abbreviations?

5. How quickly can you write these brief forms?

usual	once	work
circumstance	manufacture	administrate
world	significance	signature
significant	particular	sample
control		

Reading and Writing Exercises

-1-

Intro P

Paren

Intro DC

-2-

. grN hsb aw-f ls
Pjc, grN sf, gi
. akm, kgjs q lu +
ol Nvs hu s-l-
Ppzl, idb hpe l
Sv ou brd v drrs Conj
b icn ac pzf v
P, Amv dles d
rq ln P
Sks alo, hoE Paren ic
lq v sv ppl hu v
d siq kbjs n
vlntr o, d u
lc e l rcm loz
hu b NS- n bk
Px, ifl p- Lb ks- f
ls pzf, lqf vo v
kfdN, cu

-3-

d ble . fu cs aq

u prs- NS n o
f r co, / la eh
no opn lofr u,
sN Sks v Cnj- Intro DC ic
no rf u l . pzf
C bk avlS ol
ySrd, enc . jb
dS f ofs v Amv
sec, A aplcNs
S v Pves p n
ofs o + scl n
srlhN l glf f ls
pzf, zi rcl Intro DC uv
Ar esl- . prsv
bcgroN C ds
ri + TS srlhN
PfsNl, if u sl
apli Intro DC p cl ofs
b Fr afnn, ec ln
ar . Nvu l Dcs
pzf frlr, uvl

-4-

Paren

Conj

Intro DC

Paren Paren

-5-

Intro DC

Conj

Intro P

Conj

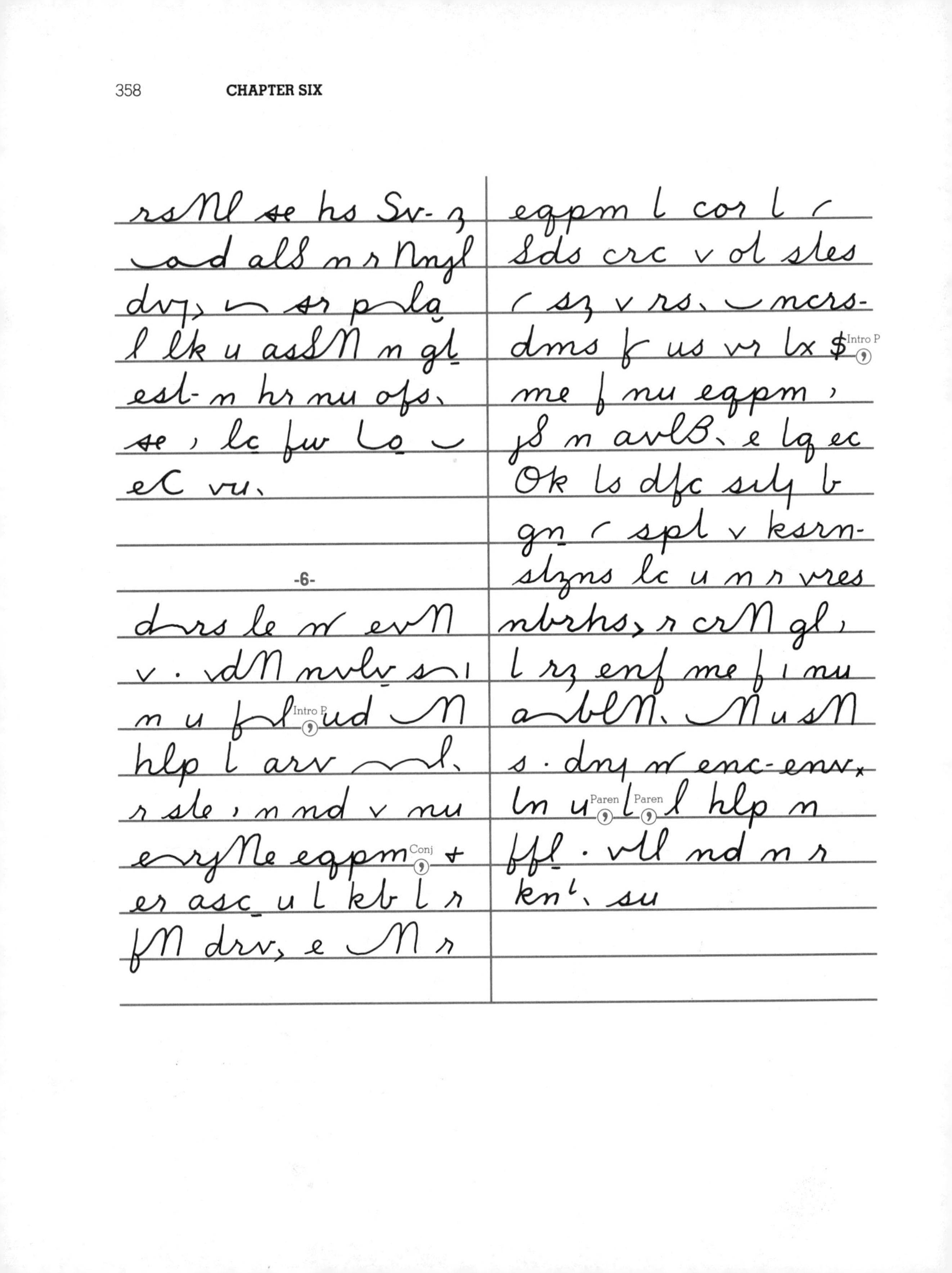

-6-

Intro P

Conj

Intro P

Paren Paren

Key

Abbreviations

establish superintendent

Brief Forms

1

Dear Ms. Jackson:

Our request for funds has been approved. To serve our city and surrounding area, we can now[1] establish our proposed leadership program. I am sure you understand the social significance of this program.[2] Clients chosen to participate will be trained in leadership methods. Once the clients have completed our course,[3] they will be encouraged to direct other similar programs in our community.

Our objective now is[4] to locate an experienced person to lead our training sessions. We believe you to be the most qualified[5] person because of your achievements in volunteer work. Would you be willing to serve as president?

Of course, you[6] will wish to give this matter careful consideration. Please allow me to answer any questions you may have[7] at this time.

Sincerely, (145)

2

Dear Mr. Wilson:

Your announcement came as wonderful news. Such a program is certain to be successful in[1] this community. Did I understand correctly that a grant has been awarded for this project? The grant itself[2] is quite an accomplishment. Congratulations go to you and the other individuals who submitted[3] the proposal.

I would be happy to serve on your board of directors, but I cannot accept the position[4] of president. The administrative duties would require more time than my present circumstances allow.[5] However, I can think of several people who have made significant contributions in volunteer work.[6] Would you like me to recommend those who might be interested in becoming president?

I feel pleased to be[7] considered for this position. Thank you for your vote of confidence.

Cordially yours, (156)

3

Dear Betty:

A few weeks ago you expressed interest in working for our company. At that time we had no[1] openings to offer you. Since circumstances have changed, I can now refer you to a position which became[2] available only yesterday.

I am enclosing a job description for the office of administrative[3] secretary. All applicants must have previous experience in office work and skill in shorthand[4] to qualify for this position. As I recall, you have already established an impressive background which[5] includes writing and transcribing shorthand proficiently.

If you wish to apply, please call my office by Friday[6] afternoon. We can then arrange an interview to discuss the position further.

Yours very truly, (139)

4

Dear Mr. Roberts:

I have a question regarding our usual procedure for paying insurance claims for[1] medical visits.

We ordinarily advise the employee to present the form for the doctor's signature[2] during the visit. In some cases, the doctor requests additional time for entering information[3] relative to that visit. The form is then mailed to the employee, and the employee submits it to our office.[4]

This procedure adds several days between the time the employee pays for the visit and the date the form[5] arrives in our office. Once the forms come in, we process them immediately and issue a check to the[6] employee. By that time, however, the total transaction has taken up to three weeks.

There must be a way to save[7] processing time. I would be grateful for your ideas on this subject.

Yours truly, (155)

5

MEMO TO: All Employees

Pamela Carlson will become general manager of our manufacturing[1] division as of July 1.

When the change becomes effective, the manufacturing division will be[2] expanded to include two new departments. The office of industrial research will be responsible for[3] long-range planning, and a systems control department will ensure continued excellence for our product. You will be[4] hearing more about both of these developments in the near future.

Having joined our staff as an engineer,[5] Pamela brought many fine ideas to our operation. She has acted as superintendent for special[6] projects, and most recently she has served as worldwide analyst in our international division.

I am[7] sure Pamela will welcome your assistance in getting established in her new office. She is looking forward[8] to working with each of you. (165)

6

Dear Mrs. Lee:

In the event of an accident involving someone in your family, you would want help to[1] arrive immediately. Our city is in need of new emergency equipment, and we are asking you[2] to contribute to our fund drive.

We want our equipment to correspond to the standards characteristic of[3] other cities the size of ours. With increased demands for the use of our tax dollars, money for new equipment[4] is just not available. We think we can overcome this difficult situation by gaining the support[5] of concerned citizens like you in our various neighborhoods.

Our current goal is to raise enough money for[6] one new ambulance. Won't you send us a donation in the enclosed envelope? Then you, too, will help in fulfilling[7] a vital need in our community.

Sincerely yours, (151)

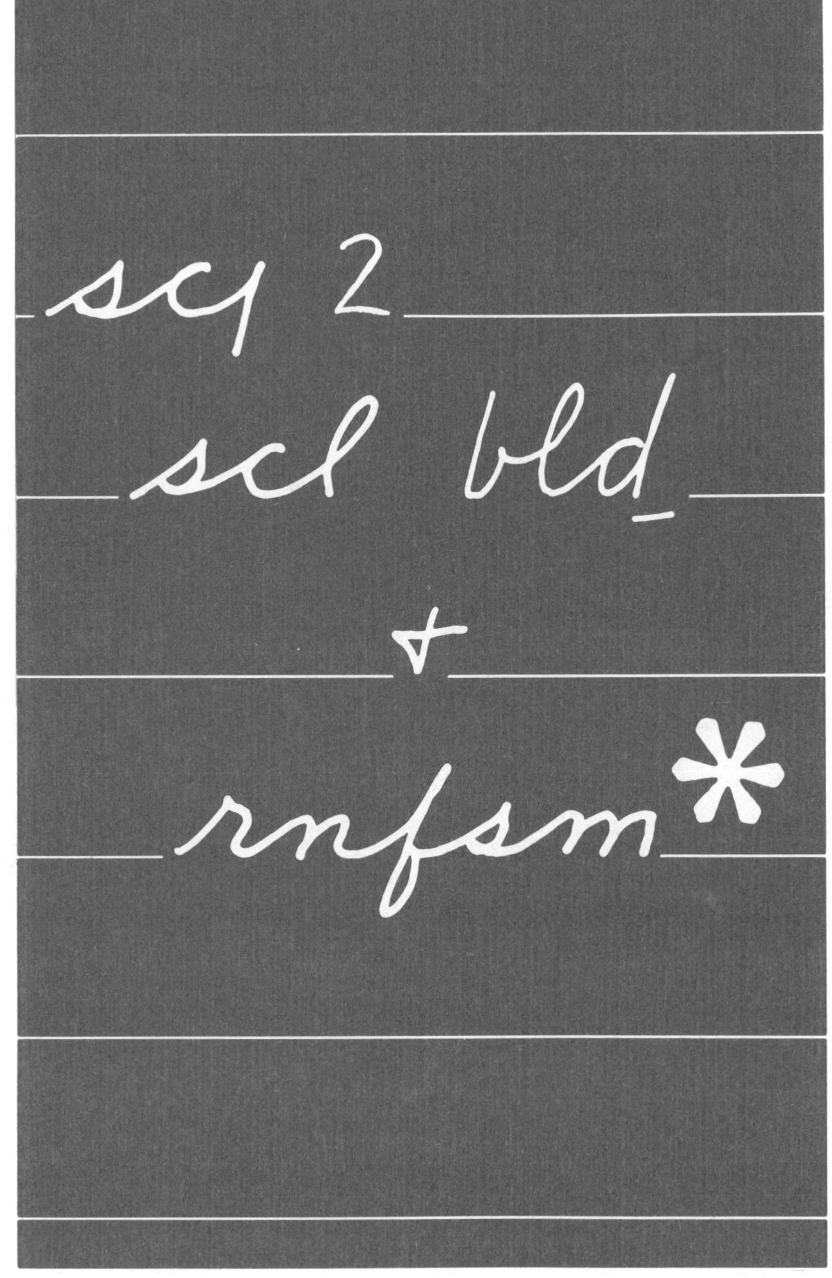

*SECTION TWO
SKILL BUILDING
AND
REINFORCEMENT

WHAT MAKES AN EMPLOYMENT INTERVIEW SUCCESSFUL?

Employment interviews have two main purposes: to exchange information and to make a favorable impression. The information you give and receive will help you and the employer decide if you and the job are right for each other.

Before the Interview

Know your facts. Learn about the company in advance—its size, products, and locations. Know the position title for which you are interviewing and the salary range for that position. (School counselors and the classified pages are excellent sources for obtaining such information.)

Anticipate questions. Be ready to answer routine interview questions: What

***Chapter Seven**

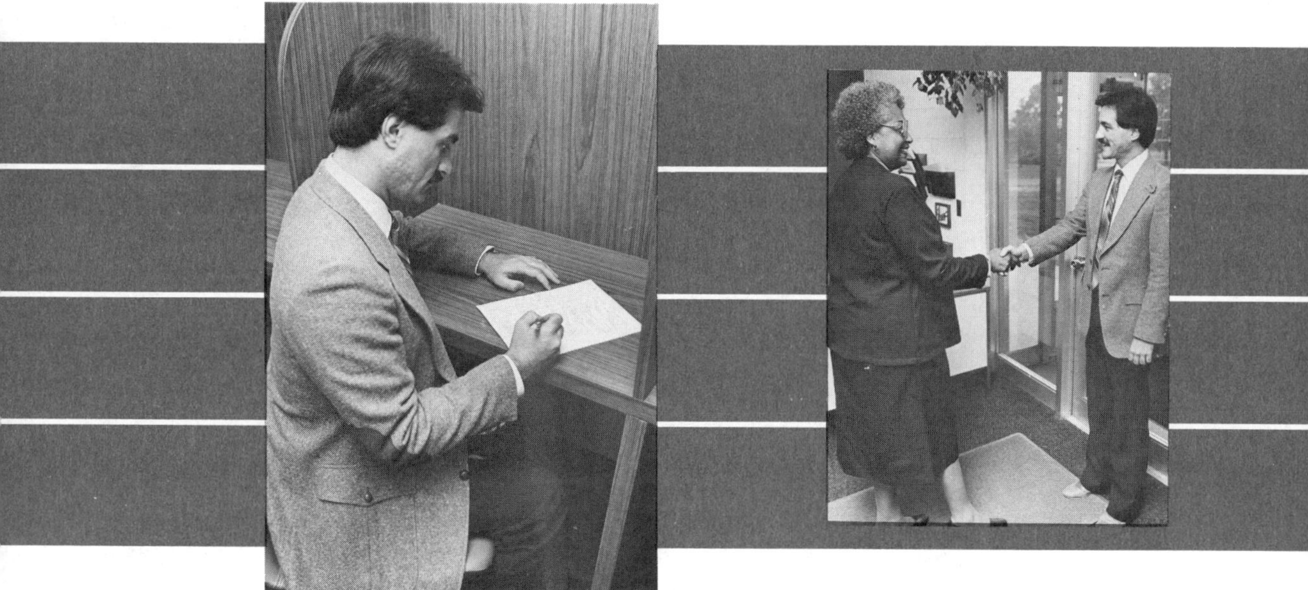

attracted you to this position? What do you know about the company? What are your career goals and salary expectations for this job?

Have questions ready. Be prepared to ask specific questions related to the job: What are the primary duties? What performance evaluation procedures are utilized? What are the advancement opportunities? What are the insurance and vacation benefits? What is the salary range for the position being discussed?

Dress appropriately. Your attire and personal grooming reflect your attitude, judgment, and personality. For a polished and professional image, dress conservatively and neatly.

Psych yourself up. Enthusiasm is infectious. Allow yourself to enjoy the pride and excitement that comes from entering the work force. You are a trained individual with marketable skills and talents—a trait to be proud of! The enthusiasm you feel for yourself and your future will have a positive impact on the interviewer. People who feel good about themselves and their company are usually happy and well-liked employees.

Take what you'll need for the interview. Have these aids easily accessible: two reliable pens, a note pad (with possible notes or questions for the interview), a pocket-size dictionary, and an extra copy of your resumé.

Leave home in time to arrive early. Before announcing yourself to the receptionist, visit a nearby lounge or dressing room to be certain you are well groomed. Knowing you look your very best will give you confidence during the interview. Announce yourself to the receptionist ten to fifteen minutes before the interview. You may be given application forms to complete during this time.

During the Interview

Once inside the interviewer's office, try to relax. While this interview is important, it should also be enjoyable. Remember, you are a skilled individual about to exchange information with another professional. Also expect the interviewer to be friendly and professional. Also expect the interviewer to look for an employee with those same qualities—friendliness and professionalism.

Be professional. Greet your interviewer with a smile and a firm handshake.

Be poised but comfortable. Arrange your body comfortably on the chair to avoid stiffness, fidgeting, fatigue, and awkwardness. Avoid nervous habits. Never chew gum, tap your fingers, or smoke during an interview.

Listen carefully. Listen attentively to the interviewer's description of the company, job, and related information. Save your questions until the interviewer has completed his or her initial explanation.

Answer questions. Always answer questions directly, honestly, politely, and briefly. Phrase statements positively—"I enjoy working in a small office," rather than "I don't like large offices." Be courteous—respect and friendliness are always admired traits. Be honest—don't try to flatter or mislead the interviewer. Be specific—give the interviewer the information he or she wants, but do not overwhelm the interviewer with long, complicated explanations.

Ask intelligent questions. When the interviewer asks for questions, ask anything not covered in his or her initial explanation: When will the decision for hiring be made; what kind of training or orientation program is planned for the job, for example.

Be positive. Even if you are not impressed by what you learn during the interview, maintain a polite and positive attitude throughout the meeting.

After the Interview

Thank the interviewer warmly and exit as soon as he or she signals that the interview has come to a close. If additional information is expected of you (skill tests, academic information, or a follow-up call), be certain you understand when and how you are to proceed.

Once away from the office, mentally evaluate the interview. Were there questions you didn't anticipate? What areas would you improve upon for future interviews?

What were your impressions of the company, the interviewer, and the position described? If you were strongly attracted to the job, write a follow-up letter thanking the interviewer and stating that you would enjoy working for the company in that capacity.

While you're waiting for the job offer, send other applications and schedule other interviews. Expect to interview several times—as many times as necessary—before acquiring that special first job. The job search is often just that—a search. Through repeat performances, you will not only sharpen your interviewing skills, but you will also increase your knowledge about different working environments, thereby giving you a greater basis for comparing jobs and companies.

Of course, when you do accept a job, notify those companies to whom you made application that you have accepted employment elsewhere. Tell them where you will be working and what you will be doing. They may want to keep this information with your original application for future reference.

LESSON 43

Brief Form Review

appropriate	accept
necessary	during
determine	other
perhaps	after
include	part
market	full
manage	very
letter	why

Abbreviation Review

attention	north
Christmas	south
enclose	east
second	west
junior	senior

Commonly Misspelled Words

schedule

receiving

Reading and Writing Exercises

-1-

mo l a secl +
clrcl Sf me vu v
vprs-NS n lrn sjs
no b scyl-. Pps v
lz sjs, l Nds a
Sf mbrs l Cnys
-d nes b adjs l
r ofs inf sS-, lz
-o+ps l bgn n
erl pl v Jl. sycs
lb cvr- d nu Psyrs
n -y -oflo, [Series] D inf, [Series]
+ ce + cd cpe. el
aso Dcs avN-
-lds f D ofs rpls
+ f T-d ol fs v
Nofs -l, enc-
ppr Pvds. lS v
das + Ls f sp -o
sjs. p nl la er asc
u l Cz u Pfr- Ls.
af uv dl- u frS +
sec Cyss, [Intro DC] p fl n
apo inf + rel f
l s, l kp r scyl o
L, [Intro P] el nd a rsps
b N v ls -c. u
-m all db ap-.

-2-

dr crsn ls L,
n rsp lu rsN
artcl o crprt grl
+ pln, v aso dn
rSC n la ara, [Intro P]
idlc l py ol flo
idas fu ksy. -l grl
-a v lvl- of n E
f L b, [Intro DC] me bs exs
vpc ls kdj l lS. v

srl h, e se me
nu frs b bll w
S, (Conj) b esd Aso lc (
rzns y n od l vu
ls rzll — apo
fss, f me yrs sC
grl z PvN- b . srly
v Sln nes rsrss.
— (dvm v Ns uz
hi lcnlje, (Intro P) hoE, (Paren) bo
(Wrn + Srn pls
v cNre v njy- .
pw s q n lr ecos.
ls sfl n rs ns
. blr Dj f nj z .
hl, i njy- u ri +
s u ku- suc. s

-3-

drs hSr af rd u

rpl o dv . ri lb
f us n r hi scl, (Intro P) i
S A i kgjs l (
me ols ur rsv, (
Ppz- lb ofrs me
Nrf adjs l r ri
Pq hr. du i USN
crcl la (lb lb
opn l SdNs w
jr cls zlz loz w sr
cls, uv asc- f sugjs
o ho l fN ls pl
pln. ic Slnl Avz
u o grNs la i b
avlB. (enc- lS
gvs (ns v kb
ogjs + f dlls o ho
l klc h, lr lb
C ldu n s l .
fnl Ppzl. p ac i

snsr ofr l hlp
~c ls dr~ . rel.
ul

-4-

mo l j~s olsn Ap , 4
dpl ~yr lqf nqe
re r scjl f 4 +
rsv du / hlds. /
asr lu q, ys=el
cp s~ 1 o dle lruol
/ hlds ~ / pj v
X~s d, / rzn8 l
as~ la 4ms lb
m~l du ls pred.
lrf Paren , a uuz- 4 pllf~s
lb clz- ~ / pj v
1. / N pllf~ 4db
~mln- / a l~s f
ld + rsv gs, ~8
dpls lb clz-or op

o . pl= l~ bss du /
l8 ~c v Dc. Ph
u4d lc drl ~ /
dla Pss dpl l~o
ol . pln f ~ rec
+ Pss v invs.

-5-

dk mbr / rzlls
vr fN drv r n Conj , +
ev gn O r orjnl
gl. lrf Paren , a v Pjcs
Czn ls yr cb fN-
z pln-, ~n u alN
nx ~os ~e Intro DC , p brq
/ Pjc Ppzls ~ u.
l v . f rpl o fN
drv + ho / me, lb
spN, n adj Paren , w hrd
me ns kNs o s~r
Pq er ofr l SdNs

n grds , bru 6 ,
scl ofsls — alspa
. Srg rsp Conj , b evn
ly — Sprz- lse la
me clss — f af ,
frS hr v rjSry , ,

lp + kpur clss fl-
frS Conj , b NS z aso
Srg n arl + dra,
M , rw l pla .
pl n pl ls fn Pq
lglr x ul

1

MEMO TO: All Secretarial and Clerical Staff

Many of you have expressed interest in the training[1] sessions now being scheduled. The purpose of these sessions is to introduce all staff members to the changes made[2] necessary by additions to our office information system.

These workshops will begin in the early[3] part of July. The subjects to be covered include new procedures in managing workflow, distributing[4] information, and keying and coding copy. We will also discuss advanced methods for distributing office[5] reports and for transmitting other forms of interoffice mail.

The enclosed paper provides a list of dates and[6] times for specific work sessions. Please note that we are asking you to choose your preferred times. After you have determined[7] your first and second choices, please fill in the appropriate information and return the form to us.

To[8] complete our schedule on time, we will need all responses by the end of this week. Your immediate attention[9] would be appreciated. (185)

2

Dear Mr. Carson:

This letter is in response to your recent article on corporate growth and planning.

Having[1] also done research in that area, I would like to point out the following ideas for your consideration.[2] While growth may have leveled off in the East for the time being, many business executives expect this[3] condition to last a very short time. We see many new firms being built in the South, but we should also look[4] at the reasons why in order to view this result with appropriate emphasis.

For many years such growth was[5] prevented by a shortage of certain necessary resources. With the development of industries[6] using high technology, however, both the western and southern parts of the country have enjoyed an upward[7] swing in their economies. This shift in markets means a better distribution for the nation as a whole.

I[8] enjoyed your writing and wish you continued success.

Sincerely, (171)

3

Dear Mrs. Hester:

After reading your report on developing a writing lab for use in our high school, I[1] must add my congratulations to the many others you are receiving.

The proposed lab offers many[2] wonderful additions to our writing program here. Do I understand correctly that the lab will be open to[3] students in the junior class as well as those in the senior class?

You have asked for suggestions on how to fund this[4] important plan. I can certainly advise you on grants that might be available. The enclosed listing gives the[5] names of contributing organizations and full details on how to contact them.

There will be much to do in[6] submitting a final proposal. Please accept my sincere offer to help make this dream a reality.

Yours[7] truly, (141)

4

MEMO TO: James Olson, Shipping Department Manager

Thank you for your inquiry regarding our schedule for[1] shipping and receiving during the holidays. The answer to your question is yes—we will keep someone on[2] duty throughout the holidays with the exception of Christmas Day.

It is reasonable to assume that shipments[3] will be minimal during this period. Therefore, all unused shipping platforms will be closed with the exception[4] of one. The north platform should be maintained at all times for loading and receiving goods.

Most departments will be closed[5] or operating on a part-time basis during the last week of December. Perhaps you should talk directly[6] with the data processing department to work out a plan for the immediate recording and processing[7] of invoices. (143)

5

Dear Committee Member:

The results of our fund drive are in, and we have gone over our original goal.[1] Therefore, all of the projects chosen this year can be funded as planned.

When you attend next month's meeting, please bring the[2] project proposals with you. I will have a full report on the fund drive and how the money is to be spent.

In[3] addition, I have heard many nice comments on the summer program we are offering to students in grades one through[4] six. School officials were anticipating a strong response, but even they were surprised to see that many classes[5] were full after the first hour of registration. The typing and computer classes filled first, but interest[6] was also strong in art and drama.

Isn't it rewarding to play a part in putting this fine program together?[7] Yours truly, (143)

LESSON 44

Brief Form Review

manufacture
appreciate
individual
complete
standard
industry
develop
present

employ
world
would
point
about
work
both
am

Abbreviation Review

merchandise
information
department
economic
question

example
catalog
America
credit
Ms.

Commonly Misspelled Words

efficiency
identifying

Reading and Writing Exercises

-1-

ddr dvdsn — ri
o bhf vr ecos cls
l lqf fn P, o nCrl
rsrss aroN r —o,
u —d . lN py ab
r grl v N la hlp-
s se ho r nrje
Pbl— dv-. Wrn
cMres no dpN po
yl + nCrl gs f —S
v ls nrje nds. n
a— [Paren] f ex [Paren] lz Pdcs
spli O hf v nrje
ks—-. z dv cMres
bgn l rli — poN [Intro DC]
ls nds l gro. el
ln fs evn grs srlys
v gs + yl, ll s
rmbr aso la r
srss v ls dzrv
eql cr + Plc. lz
r gflt v lN. esd
a lrn l ap — z pl
v —os ll. ul

-2-

mo l a dpl hds
es Nds . nu —d
f us n —c Pf—N
evlys, p nl la r
alC- f— dz n Cn
r Sds f —zr —o
efsNe [Conj] b / dz asc
f — inf f— r —pe.
ls inf l Sv me
Ppss n r ogs, r rzlls
lb hlpf n idNf-
aras v —pvm o.
Nv lvl + aso o.
dpl lvl. r Sva

lb uz-z . bss f dl
… ncrss + P-ys. /
l aso ll s ab / crr
gls + lvl v jb saly
vp-b …pes, p P / qr
… bgn v eC Nvu
l alo aql … f Dcy
v kp-f…, elb hpe
l asr ne qs u …a
v.

-3-

dS … ru l rqS
inf ou kp ln v
c…p eqpm, lS …c
i alN-. lrvl so
…r i sa u Pdcs o
Dpla. uz …prs-bo
… / ql vu cos …o
+ … / ecol prss v
…dse. sN … pln

. s…r c…p f by
scols, (Intro DC) i …a pls sv
ods, … plcl NS- n
bcpcs + cc eqpm.
cd u aso …l cS
fgrs f UNs lry enf
l akda 4 ppl. uf
u co …fs …s f
…lr spls, (Intro DC) p so …e
…l uv avlB, idlc
/ cal …l- l …h
adrs sn abv. bcz
cS, . …pl fcr, (Intro DC) p py
ol ne Dk u ofr l
scol grps. ul

-4-

d…s jsn cd i suq
l … lpc f r aul
pln …e x, ublv

ed a bnfl f . Dq
v ho Nvs + grps
mc dsjs + arv /
jjms, dsj=mc / .
acv n inf Pss. eC
v s mcs dsjs E d
vr lvs. c SdN
dsds po . crr. . jb
aplcN Czs f avlB
opn. . mpe dls ho
mC o l Pds U
. nu sS , r Dq
cdb bs- o lz qs: l
inf dz . Nv uz n
mc . dsj, l , c
lvl v mpl pls- 6
inf, ho dz c Psn
uz la inf n arv
/ . Cys, , if u lc ls
Intro DC
ida, il gldl hlp dv

c mlrel f sC . Dq. su

-5-

drs mrfe er dli-
l lk u z . G K.
edlc l lc . mm
l U u ab c me
bnfls n Sr fu, u
G crd l opn c
dr l opls C r
n avlB l rglr
Paren
Ks. f ex, oN . mo
e hld . sl rzrv- f
cr=crd PCss. ul
rsv . blln prir
Series
l lz evNs lS ths,
Series
prss, + dpls. l cd
mc sp ezer or m
ecol, ul Aso rsv
AvN nls v a ol

sls n adj l . hld
cal P gfl idas f E
Paren
mbr v fl. hoE, r
Dir Ad
bl bns ev lofr, rs
Dir Ad
rfe, , r prl Svs

e pln lgv u, las
r a v sa er hpe
l l u n r spsl
fl v G Ks. cu

1

Dear Dr. Davidson:

I am writing on behalf of our economics class to thank you for your fine presentation[1] on natural resources around the world.

You made an excellent point about the growth of industry[2] that helped us see how the energy problem developed. Western countries now depend upon oil and natural[3] gas for most of their energy needs. In America, for example, these products supply over half of the[4] energy consumed. As developing countries begin to rely more upon industry, their needs will grow.[5] We will then face even greater shortages of gas and oil.

Let us remember also that our sources of water[6] deserve equal care and protection. These are gifts of the land. We should all learn to appreciate them as part of[7] the world's wealth.

Yours truly, (144)

2

MEMO TO: All Department Heads

We are introducing a new method for use in making performance[1] evaluations.

Please note that the attached form does not change our standards for measuring work efficiency, but it[2] does ask for more information from the employee. This information will serve many purposes in our[3] organization.

The results will be helpful in identifying areas of improvement on an[4] individual level and also on a departmental level. The survey will be used as a basis for[5] determining wage increases and promotions. It will also tell us about the career goals and level of job[6] satisfaction experienced by employees.

Please present the questionnaire at the beginning of each interview[7] to allow adequate time for discussion of the completed form.

We will be happy to answer any[8] questions you may have. (163)

3

Dear Sir:

I am writing to request information on your complete line of camping equipment.

Last week I[1] attended a travel show where I saw your products on display. I was impressed both with the quality of your[2] company's work and with the economical prices of the merchandise. Since I am planning a summer camp for[3] Boy Scouts, I may place several orders.

I am particularly interested in backpacks and cooking equipment.[4] Could you also include cost figures for tents large enough to accommodate four people? If your company[5] manufactures items for water sports, please show me what you have available.

I would like the catalog[6] mailed to my home address shown above. Because cost is an important factor, please point out any discount you[7] offer to scout groups.

Yours truly, (145)

4

Dear Ms. Jason:

Could I suggest one more topic for our annual planning meeting?

I believe we would all[1] benefit from a discussion of how individuals and groups make decisions and arrive at judgments.[2]

Decision-making is an activity in information processing. Each of us makes decisions every day[3] of our lives. The student decides upon a career. A job applicant chooses from available openings.[4] An employee determines how much work to produce under a new system.

Our discussion could be based on these[5] questions: What information does an individual use in making a decision? What is the level[6] of importance placed on the information? How does the person use that information in arriving at a[7] choice?

If you like this idea, I will gladly help develop the material for such a discussion.[8]

Sincerely yours, (163)

5

Dear Mrs. Murphy:

We are delighted to welcome you as a charge customer. We would like to take a moment[1] to tell you about the many benefits in store for you.

Your charge card will open the door to opportunities[2] which are not available to regular customers. For example, once a month we hold a sale reserved[3] for credit-card purchases. You will receive a bulletin prior to these events listing items, prices, and[4] departments. What could make shopping easier or more economical?

You will also receive advance notice[5] of all other sales in addition to a holiday catalog presenting gift ideas for every member[6] of the family. However, the best bonus we have to offer, Mrs. Murphy, is the expert service we[7] plan to give you.

That's our way of saying we are happy to include you in our special family of charge[8] customers.

Cordially yours, (165)

LESSON 45

Brief Form Review

administrate	am	please	p
correspondence	cor	between	btn
opportunity	opt	next	nx
signature	sig	over	O
participate	pp	business	bs
approximate	apx	already	Ar
contribute	kb	able	B
opinion	opn	as	z

Abbreviation Review

corporation	corp	amount	amt
executive	ex	volume	vol
secretary	sec	total	tot
establish	est	Miss	M
number	No	day	d

Commonly Misspelled Words

exceeded xd-

procedures Psjrs

Reading and Writing Exercises

-1-

ds rnze eC sr
r kn' Ps . fSvl f
arls, z pl v Pg, (Intro P) e
nvi l=nn ppl
lvzl r sle + pp
n Pdcjs, Pf Ms
r hld E Fr evn
du r o v Jl 6
frN ln vr crlhos.
r gSs apr bf . grp
v apxl 5H ppl. r
evn Pg ls r gS
Pfr + , flo- b .
nfl rspj, er
cryll nvi u clN, (Ap)
rc lgn, (Ap) l pp n
ls yrs evN. h hs
est- . lq + sucf
hSre n fl N + ,
l rcgnz- f , spl
v Pf arls, z r
ofsl rep v r lgn, (Intro P)
d u ks r enc- das
+ gv s u rsp n
30 ds. vlu

-2-

dM lr lqf nqe
ab drn ofs Psyrs,
r S sres Pbl
yrs fs , r srly v
l. if dsjs r d l
gcl or ol Aql
ksl v A r fcs nvlv-, (Intro DC)
MUSN a dv, l
srly , cz- b . Pbl
e rf l z Old. Svzrs
kpln v b brdn-
ppr o. ly r uS lgv
r Ppr al v U nd-

Lc / bS Cyss + Sl
mln . efsN flo
v o, sN / vol v
kncjs , ncrs rls
ln dcrs (Intro DC) ofss S
uz atlc ms v
Pss inf. elnc eqpm
ofrs . fSr (Series) ecol (Series) +
acrl al kl
Sd rpls + cor, hp
brf kNs v hlp-.
p klc e uf uc kb
frlr. s

-3-

mo l drs v av r
nx asnm f NWrn
corp , l dv . gr
lb uz- n lr r rSC,
p oqu dla so la /
asrs a b grp- n

kv clgres + Pss-
r uz kpur Pq, a
dB = Cc / klN vu
Sva. , eC q nes.
, / sig l / Pps v
Sde. dz / Dlg
bln fc + opn. rmbr (Paren)
aso (Paren) la fnl suc dpNs
po K rsp. p dzn /
dcm so la ppl nd
n b . dfc lsc, oq .
efcv gr , . gr akm
n sf. pS ps v Nca-
la / S sucf Pjcs
loz la cdb kp- n
. fu mls . rznB
dgre v ez.

-4-

dfrN / da f r fl'
fSvl , dra nr. /

-5-

evNs pln-f Sl l
. 2= ~l jq + . crs=
cNre rn. / ajNa
f Sn lb b-l- l r
lrdjl bscl rs, / lol
No v Nres rsv- so
fr hs Ar vd- / fgrs
f lS yr. fCnll, [Paren] me
ppl v Ar klc- r pln
k ab hlp. hoE, [Paren] ~
vlntrs r nd- l nsr
la / evNs r ~q- l.
e nd hlp n rjSr
ppNs, [Series] jj-, [Series] b-, [Series] + mln
recs. lr l Aso b opls
f hlp n jn Amj v
evN, lu b avlB l
asS n ls cz. if uc pp, [Intro DC]
p Ufn ~e / b ne
b af 5 p or klc
r sec, [Ap] ~re nlsn. su

d bs grjul r u egr
lgl ahd n bs ~o.
ln und . pbj la Us
u vcl l , q o n bss
aroN / ~o E d v
~c, und lno / laS
n nz + dvms, [Conj] + u
~N la inf z / hpns
= n af / evN hsb
Cnj, [Series] edl-, [Series] + A S
fgln. ri., las y exs
Er r sS l r dl
blln, [Ap] A ld. o loz
pjs ly rd ab ~yr
isus fs ~ym / A
lvls, hrs ho uc
f u o opn. A u
siq l / enc-f
+ rsv . sa sS,
kpl fre v G, dN
jS lq / O = lc / O.

u Pd l rsp l nB u	u cN afd l M. cu
l lc Avq v. bs opl	

1

Dear Ms. Ramsey:

Each summer our community presents a festival for the arts. As part of the program, we[1] invite well-known people to visit our city and participate in the productions.

Performances are held[2] every Friday evening during the month of July on the front lawn of our courthouse. Our guests appear before a[3] group of approximately 500 people. The evening program includes our guest performer and is followed[4] by an informal reception.

We are cordially inviting your client, Mark Logan, to participate in[5] this year's event. He has established a long and successful history in the film industry and is well[6] recognized for his support of the performing arts.

As the official representative of Mr. Logan, would[7] you consider the enclosed dates and give us your response within 30 days?

Very truly yours, (157)

2

Dear Miss Miller:

Thank you for your inquiry about modern office procedures.

The most serious problem[1] managers face is the shortage of time. If decisions are made too quickly or without adequate consideration[2] of all the facts involved, misunderstandings may develop.

Time shortage is caused by a problem we refer[3] to as overload. Supervisors complain of being burdened with paperwork. They are unable to give the[4] proper amount of thought needed to make the best choices and still maintain an efficient flow of work.

Since[5] the volume of communications is increasing rather than decreasing, offices must use automatic means of[6] processing information. Electronic equipment offers a faster, more economical, and more[7] accurate way to control standard reports and correspondence.

I hope my brief comments have helped. Please contact me if[8] I can contribute further.

Sincerely, (167)

3

MEMO TO: Director of Advertising

Our next assignment for Northwestern Corporation is to develop[1] a questionnaire to be used in their market research.

Please organize your data so that the answers may be[2] grouped in convenient categories and processed with our usual computer program.

Always double-check the[3] content of your survey. Is each question necessary? Is it significant to the purpose of the study?[4] Does it distinguish between fact and opinion? Remember, also, that final success depends upon customer[5] response. Please design the document so that participation need not be a difficult task.

Organizing[6] an effective questionnaire is a great accomplishment in itself. Past experiences have indicated[7] that the most successful projects were those that could be completed in a few minutes with a reasonable[8] degree of ease. (163)

4

Dear Friend:

The date for our fitness festival is drawing near. The events planned for Saturday include a two-mile[1] jog and a cross-country run. The agenda for Sunday will be limited to our traditional bicycle[2] race.

The total number of entries received so far has already exceeded the figures from last year. Fortunately,[3] many people have already contacted our planning committee about helping. However, more volunteers[4] are needed to ensure that the events are managed well. We need help in registering participants,[5] judging, timing, and maintaining records. There will also be opportunities for helping in the general[6] administration of the event.

Will you be available to assist in this cause? If you can participate,[7] please telephone me at home any time after 5 p.m. or contact our secretary, Mary Nelson.[8]

Sincerely yours, (163)

5

Dear Business Graduate:

Are you eager to get ahead in the business world? Then you need a publication that[1] tells you exactly what is going on in businesses around the world every day of the week.

You need to know[2] the latest in news and developments, and you want that information as it happens—not after the event[3] has been changed, edited, and almost forgotten. Right?

That's why executives everywhere are subscribing to our[4] daily bulletin, *America Today*. On those pages they read about major issues facing management[5] at all levels.

Here's how you can form your own opinion. Add your signature to the enclosed form and receive[6] a sample subscription completely free of charge.

Don't just think it over—look it over. Your prompt response will[7] enable you to take advantage of a business opportunity you can't afford to miss.

Cordially yours,[8] (160)

LESSON 46

Brief Form Review

circumstance	contract
experience	customer
advantage	suggest
immediate	success
difficult	specify
property	public
against	once
sample	buy

Abbreviation Review

representative	advertise
government	American
literature	federal
especially	million
represent	okay

Commonly Misspelled Words

believe

among

Reading and Writing Exercises

-1-

d hnre idlc l suq
. Cny n u nvSm
pln f k yr, nu
Sks v cz- e l rvz
i vus o PCs pb Sc.
ls no s Ub sv
avjs f ppl hu b
srs n pb ull ls. hr
r r rzns y, r fed
gvl hs lcn Sps l
hlp por cos gl
cpll +, Pvd jnrs
lx bnfls f Schldrs.
n u b srs n lry
elc ull ls [Intro DC], uc apli
u dvdNs lw adyl
PCss v Sc / . szB
Dk, z adyl ncrym
l nvS rvnu [Intro P], r gvl
alos u l ddc C
v loz dvdNs ag u
lxB nk. f u hld u
Scs f . pred v 5 yrs [Intro DC],
u ern r lx- / . ra
ksB ls ln r Sd %,
Ph esd e ag lq
O lz nu dvms. S
ds nx c r ok
e. ul

-2-

d h or f u nyy u
h [Intro DC], u PbB v no
plns l w + vn
blr-l fN ol scrN
rl. hoE [Paren], du u
relz lau hos cb.
vluB srs v nk evn
l u lv n / x, las
ri. u dN v l sl u

h n od l c+ n o
s vlu, oN uv apli-
f . eqle ln, [Intro DC] u prp,
aprz-b r rep. e ln
slrc / upd blN
vu rgs f s crN
r vlu. uc ln bro
pl / f a d vu eqle,
Ms v a s r lc
avj v ls nu srs v
cr. s uz / X me
f nvSms, [Series] f spsl PCss, [Series]
or evn f ol nk, .
s pl Ufn cl l gv
u a / dlls und. zu
sv + ln co, [Intro P] e lc prd
n P lz opls. su

-3-

dr rgn i S
lqu aq fu psN. ch

P s- l rpl lu n 3
cs, [Conj] b u bc Ppzl z
v dll- + rq- h
ln ch U / d, idb
gld l rep u o +
ar v s pblsrs n
m. i foN u nS
Ub NS, [Series] l rln, [Series] + esp
rC n orjnl drel.
bs- o pS sls v slr
cNs v lil, [Intro P] lr, E rzn
l blv la ls bc l v q
r apl, alo u sa
Cplrs gi rep vu
ri Sl, [Intro DC] uz Psjr
, l P/ nlr nS n
od l scr / bS psB
kc. c u ll e no
n u pc lv / drel
kp-x, lc fw Uhr f
u + Sv zu ajN. vlu

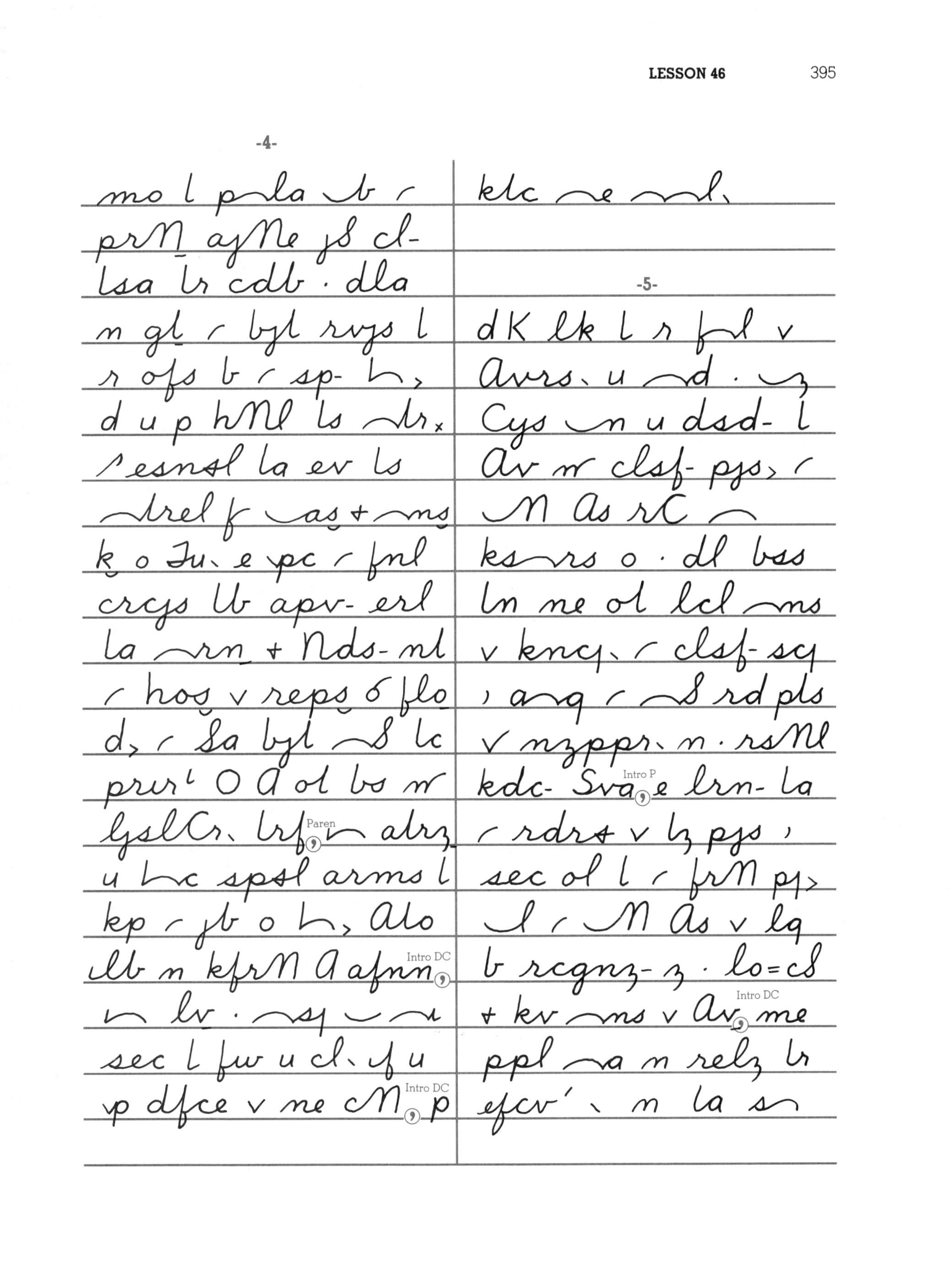

-4-

Paren

Intro DC

Intro DC

-5-

Intro P

Intro DC

Sva e lrn- la
. lpcl a v 3 lns
rsvs . avrj rsp v
23 cls + Pdss . sl
b r flo d, ⌣ sal

rzlts lc lz Intro P ; r eze
lse y Ks ku l lc
avj vr Svss, e ⌣
u r s⌢ suc, cu

1

Dear Henry:

I would like to suggest a change in your investment plan for the coming year.

New circumstances have[1] caused me to revise my views on purchasing public stock. There now seem to be several advantages for[2] people who buy shares in public utilities. Here are the reasons why.

The federal government has taken steps[3] to help power companies get more capital and is providing generous tax benefits for stockholders.[4] When you buy shares in large electric utilities, you can apply your dividends toward additional[5] purchases of stock at a sizable discount.

As additional encouragement to invest revenue, the[6] government allows you to deduct much of those dividends against your taxable income. If you hold your stocks for[7] a period of five years, your earnings are taxed at a rate considerably less than the standard percentage.[8]

Perhaps we should meet again to go over these new developments. Most days next week are okay with me.

Yours[9] truly, (181)

2

Dear Homeowner:

If you enjoy your home, you probably have no plans to move and have not bothered to find out its[1] current worth. However, do you realize that your house can be a valuable source of income even while you[2] live in it?

That's right. You don't have to sell your home in order to cash in on its value.

Once you have applied for[3] an equity loan, your property is appraised by our respresentative. We then subtract the unpaid balance[4] of your mortgage from its current market value. You can then borrow up to the full amount of your equity.[5]

Millions of Americans are taking advantage of this new source of credit. Some use the extra money for investments, for[6] special purchases, or even for monthly income.

A[7] simple telephone call will give you all the details you need. As your savings and loan company, we take pride in[8] presenting these opportunities.

Sincerely yours, (169)

3

Dear Mr. Morgan:

I must thank you again for your patience. I had promised to report to you in three weeks, but[1] your book proposal was very detailed and required more time than I had thought it would.

I would be glad to represent[2] your work and already have some publishers in mind. I found your manuscript to be interesting, well written,[3] and especially rich in original material. Based on the past sales of similar kinds of[4] literature, there is every reason to believe that this book will have good market appeal.

Although your sample[5] chapters were quite representative of your writing style, my usual procedure is to present the entire[6] manuscript in order to secure the best possible contract. Can you let me know when you expect to have the[7] material completed?

I look forward to hearing from you and serving as your agent.

Very truly yours,[8] (160)

4

MEMO TO: Pamela Webb

The printing agency just called to say there could be a delay in getting the[1] budget revisions to our office by the specified time.

Would you please handle this matter? It is essential that[2] we have this material for the Ways and Means Committee on Tuesday. We expect the final corrections to[3] be approved early that morning and introduced into the House of Representatives on the following day.[4]

The state budget must take priority over all other business in the legislature. Therefore, I am[5] authorizing you to make special arrangements to complete the job on time.

Although I will be in conference all[6] afternoon, I am leaving a message with my secretary to forward your call. If you experience[7] difficulty of any kind, please contact me immediately. (151)

5

Dear Customer:

Welcome to our family of advertisers. You made a wise choice when you decided to[1] advertise in the classified pages.

The want ads reach more consumers on a daily basis than any other[2] local means of communication. The classified section is among the most read parts of the newspaper. In[3] a recently conducted survey, we learned that the readership of these pages is second only to the front[4] page.

While the want ads have long been recognized as a low-cost and convenient means of advertising, many[5] people may not realize their effectiveness. In that same survey we learned that a typical ad of three lines[6] receives an average response of 23 calls and produces a sale by the following day.

With satisfying[7] results like these, it is easy to see why customers continue to take advantage of our services.[8] We wish you the same success.

Cordially yours, (168)

LESSON 47

Brief Form Review

characteristic	crc	hospital	hsp
significance	siq	response	rsp
convenience	kv	operate	op
acknowledge	acq	satisfy	sat
particular	ptc	doctor	dr
accomplish	ak	they	ty
associate	aso	come	k
specific	sp	too	t

Abbreviation Review

incorporate	inc	record	rec
insurance	ins	avenue	ave
president	P	month	
thousand	T	Mrs.	
et cetera	etc	Mr.	

Commonly Misspelled Words

receipt	rse
experiencing	xp

Reading and Writing Exercises

-1-

d-rs prcr ls L , l
acj u pam v Ja 8.
ev cr- u ak — r
a-l s-l- [Conj] + er enc
. rse fu recs, lqf
rc l pln y uv fln
bhN n -rc u -ol
nSlms. e grl ap u
lc r b l ll s no
r rzn fu dla, e
USN lau + u f-l
r vp . dfc sily + r
dy u bS l rzlv r
Pbl. bcz v lz plc
Sks [Intro P] r mm pam u
sug- lb sal ull r
blN hsb pd n f,
hlp Ks hs a b .
crc lae prodl aso
— r fr. p k l s aq
-n ur n nd v spsl
arms. vlu

-2-

d-r + -rs hNrsn
er esp p- l lk u z.
nu plsehldrs. no la
u'v dsd- l trS u hll
bnfls l s [Intro DC] ehp ul
vp r scr + ps v m
la v k l Ts v ol
cliNs hu njy r f
Plcy vr ins, r enc-
crd nllls u l -yr
-dcl cvry / ne
hsp n a-. r crd
klns u ch- No [Series]
ak No [Series] + ssl scr
No. l fl . ch- f
hsp pNs or f drs

fes, [Intro P] p b Ppr-l Pds
a 3 Nos, r enc-
p~fll Pvds jn inf.
chp ul alo ~e l
asr sp qs z ly k
p. if f s~ rzn
ucn rC ~e, [Intro DC] ~i
asos r rde + egr
l hlp. ly r qlf-Nvs
hu lc lr rspBls
sresl. cu

-3-

dr jcsn ~n r
Tply kp ~d l ls
evn, [Intro DC] sv lgs k l
~i all, r arpl
prp ds sv bld o
arln ave ~C r
rN-l Nvs. n od
l sal fed rqms, [Intro P]

e ~S Nds nu
lr~s efcv ls yr.
~i avzrs sa / l
n b dfc l inc r
nu lr~s nl r S
kcs, alo / hs nvr
b r objcv l ern
Pfls f~ ls prp, [Intro DC] ~
l ar v rz cSs
rq- l op vpNv
eqpm, [Series] l ~p Sf, [Series]
l hoz arcrft, [Series] elc.
ne X rvnu lb uz-
l cvr ol nes amv
vpNs, bcz ls , .
~dr v sSnsl siq
l r sle bjl, [Intro DC] ~
apy. sk ldl ~l
r rN ncrss sdb.
uvl

-4-

ddr rCrds i +
l kq u ou apym
l c rq v Pfsr, u
asos n dpl U e
la ls, . P C,
l dzrv- + l pv Ub
. v dvm f U zlz
fu, v NS- n
plc rSC n C
ur no nvlv-, du
i USN crcl la uv
kp- . nu Tlj v erl
Ern ru, if ls, c
cs, Intro DC idb grf f opl
l Dcs u fN frlr,
i, Paren l, Paren v lq b NS- n
ns erlS ru, af i
hrd . dll- dSj vu
fN, Intro DC i U e u b B
l hlp eC ol, cd
e ar . h l e /

u kv x su

-5-

d jy l alN . nyl
kfrN lS c, Intro P i
rsv- . ns kplm
lai + l ps o lu,
i vr lrjS Ks sd
Nrf lgs ab c
Cnjs uv ak- sN
as u nu rspBls,
h py- ol sv aras
la v Ugn gr pvm
n fu os sN u
Tfr l c rjnl ofs,
i, Paren l, Paren prs-
u akms, l ev
vp- . sig ncrs n
sls, Intro DC ev Aso sn.
yr rdcj n vpNs,
n u erl yrs

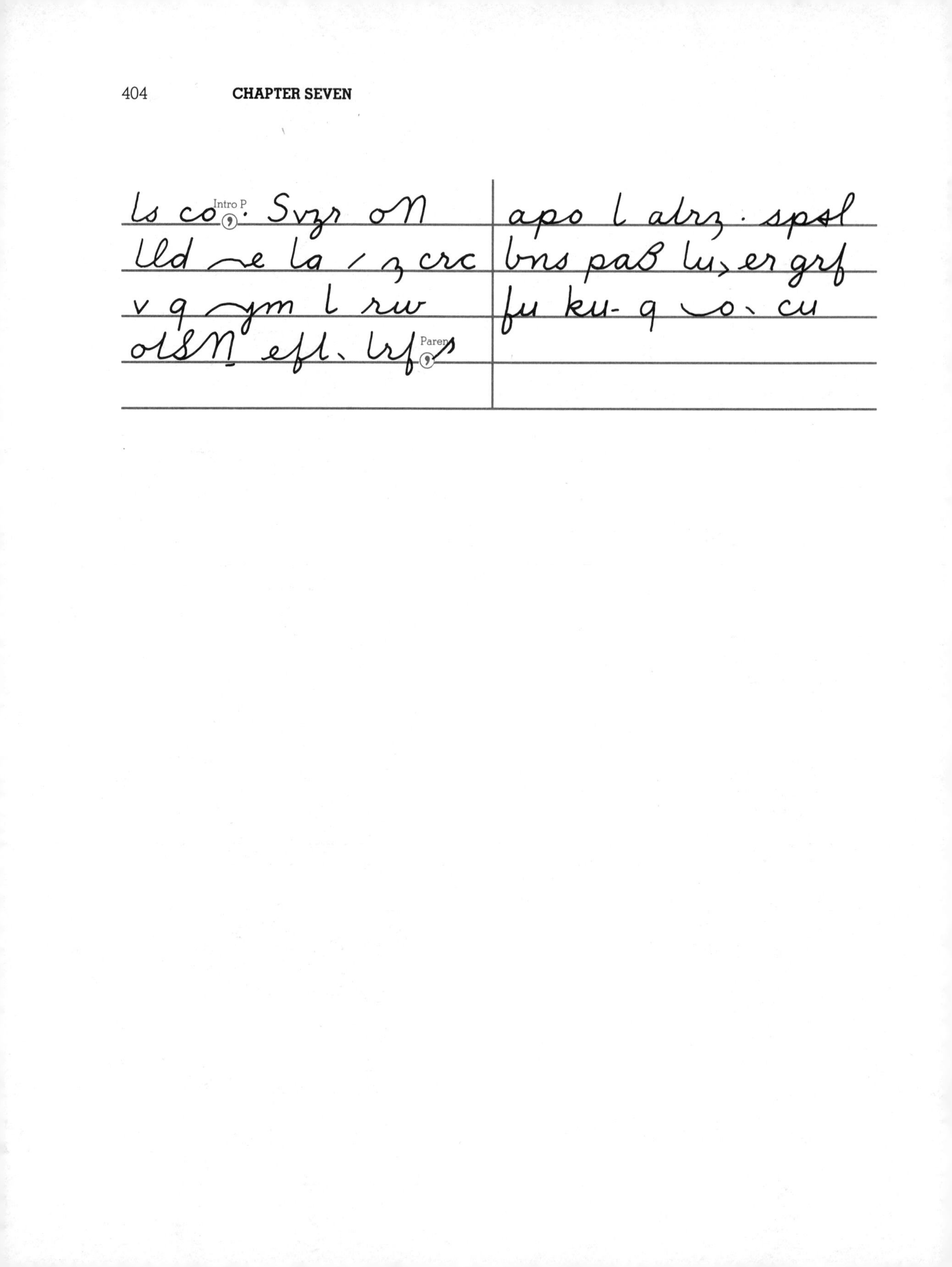

Intro P

Paren

1

Dear Mrs. Parker:

This letter is to acknowledge your payment of January 8. We have credited your[1] account with the amount submitted, and we are enclosing a receipt for your records.

Thank you for writing to[2] explain why you have fallen behind in making your monthly installments. We greatly appreciate your taking[3] the time to let us know the reason for your delay.

We understand that you and your family are experiencing[4] a difficult situation and are doing your best to resolve the problem. Because of these particular[5] circumstances, the minimum payment you suggested will be satisfactory until the balance[6] has been paid in full.

Helping customers has always been a characteristic that we proudly associate[7] with our firm. Please come to us again when you are in need of special arrangements.

Very truly yours, (158)

2

Dear Mr. and Mrs. Henderson:

We are especially pleased to welcome you as a new policyholder.[1] Now that you've decided to trust your health benefits to us, we hope you will experience the security[2] and peace of mind that have come to thousands of other clients who enjoy the full protection of our insurance.[3]

The enclosed card entitles you to major medical coverage at any hospital in America.[4] The card contains your claim number, account number, and social security number. To file a claim for hospital[5] expenses or for doctors' fees, please be prepared to produce all three numbers.

The enclosed pamphlet provides general[6] information. I hope you will allow me to answer specific questions as they come up. If for some reason[7] you cannot reach me, my associates are ready and eager to help. They are qualified individuals[8] who take their responsibilities seriously.

Cordially yours, (174)

3

Dear Mr. Jackson:

When the Transportation Commission met last evening, several things came to my attention.[1]

Our airport property includes several buildings on Airline Avenue which are rented to individuals.[2] In order to satisfy federal requirements, we must introduce new terms effective this year. My advisers[3] say it will not be difficult to incorporate the new terms into the existing contracts.

Although it[4] has never been our objective to earn profits from this property, I am well aware of the rising costs[5] required to operate expensive equipment, to employ staff, to house aircraft, etc. Any extra[6] revenue will be used to cover other necessary administrative expenses.

Because this is a[7] matter of substantial significance to our city budget, I am appointing a subcommittee to[8] determine what the rent increases should be.

Yours very truly, (171)

4

Dear Dr. Richards:

I wish to congratulate you on your appointment to the rank of professor. Your associates[1] in the department tell me that this is a promotion which is well deserved and will prove to be an exciting[2] development for the university as well as for you.

I am very interested in the[3] particular research in which you are now involved. Do I understand correctly that you have completed a[4] new translation of early Eastern writings?

If this is the case, I would be grateful for the opportunity[5] to discuss your findings further. I, too, have long been interested in man's earliest writings.

After I heard[6] a detailed description of your findings, I thought we might be able to help each other. Could we arrange a time[7] to meet at your convenience?

Sincerely yours, (148)

5

Dear Joy:

While attending a national conference last week, I received a nice compliment that I wish to pass[1] on to you.

One of our largest customers said wonderful things about the changes you have accomplished since[2] assuming your new responsibilities. He pointed out several areas that have undergone great[3] improvement in the few months since your transfer to the regional office. I, too, am impressed with your accomplishments.[4] While we have experienced a significant increase in sales, we have also seen a major reduction in[5] expenses.

In my early years with this company, a supervisor once told me that it was characteristic[6] of good management to reward outstanding effort. Therefore, it is appropriate to authorize a special[7] bonus payable to you.

We are grateful for your continued good work.

Cordially yours, (156)

LESSON 48

Brief Form Review

distribute	D	every	E
character	crc	again	ag
consider	ks	those	loz
continue	ku	ever	E
ordinary	ord	note	nl
situate	sil	from	f
deliver	dl	own	o
control	kl	was	z

Abbreviation Review

university	U	hundred	H
envelope	env	billion	B
company	co	regard	re
invoice	inv	cents	¢
return	rel	hour	hr

Commonly Misspelled Words

immediately ml

neighborhood nbrh

Reading and Writing Exercises

-1-

q ls L, l acq u od
v Aq 7, n acrdN
⌣ u rqS, Intro P er prN
6H cpes v Lhd +
X envs l aco /
Sjre. loz ch-s lb
prN- / u rglr kc
ra + dl- lu ofs /
no adjl C, aq, Paren i
⌣4 l pln y u lS
4m arv- la. z
4n ou cpe v inv, Intro P
e 4- E o scjl.
ufCnlL, Paren a v NSa
hi as ⌣ lar clz-
du l ualspa- bd
ch. i aplyz f ne
nkv u ⌒a v vp-, Conj
b / sily z cz- b
Sks beN r kl, r
4 Svzr, edw bron.
y und Psnl Svs, Intro DC
klc h ⌒l. h hs
. Xord scl f slv
Pbl-s o . ⌒ms
nls. su

-2-

d-rs ⌣bSr lqf L
v nge re r aplms.
r pln- knt ofrs me
Avjs l yq f-ls, er
lca- nx l . rlvl
nu sdv7. r aplms
r sil- o . blef si
SoN- b lry lres.
er ⌣n ⌣c DlN
v . ⌒yr 4p sNr, Series
. hll clb, Series + . glf
crs. / scls n r

nbrh r aq (
bS n ls sle, Tply
arms r eze bc.
bss lv E hr f
donlon, (Conj) + lrn S,
, ol . fu mls aa
b aloB. NSa
h as c / kv
l drv ne r W sle,
rzdNs sa la r
aplms Pvd . Xordl
nyyB p. lu alo s
l pv h ru dl
aplms r opn E
d. p Ufn r ofs l
ar . apym n AvN.
s

-3-

dr flds sN

ls nl z . rmr lau
Svs kc, du l pr
S N v ls o, lc
me ol fn nvSms, (Intro P)
ls kc bks vluB
aj. Alo u apluN
, Sl n lN kdj +
sd yld me yrs
v q Svs, (Intro DC) (CNs v
/ nd rprs ncrs
E yr la gs b.
evn n u o (bS
v eqpm, (Intro DC) lr, A (
psBl la, Svs cl l
cS z C z . nlr
yr v Plcj Ur agrem,
r pln Plcs u ag la
psBl. fu kv ev Ppr-
. nu kc fu siq. p
sn + rel bo cpes

b r da sp- so lau
cvrj l ku ol
Npj. ul

-4-

dS O 2H yrs
aq sv uhpe slzns
d hSre b lro.
Sprz ple n bSn, f
ppl hu lv q le, Intro P l
. sd d la S vb!
vprls sa r Dagrem
h ldu lxs + n
r gl v le. e Slnl
hp so. z Drs v fn
le, Intro P ev lrn- la srl
Ks cb v plc + M
sll f ne ls ln r
dlcl flvr e ofr, v
crs, Paren r ord Pdc flo
aroN bSn z n r
brN. l edu n
ch lno C ab
lxs + repj, Intro DC edu
no r le. r spsl
drs Pss ylds sC.
lN flvr la nobde
d E dp r Obrd=
n evn lc. bq
pllcl spls, ou nx
vzl lu nbrh r, Intro P
pv r l usf. lc.
lp f bSn + lro
u old brN Obrd.
r fu X ¢ u a
pa l dfnll b rl
. gr lS n le. cu

-5-

dM gra i rd
NS u nzppr arlcl
asc f nmjs f aul

kn^l Svs aw. af ks
Intro P
a v aras v Svs dS-,
i [illegible] l rcm [illegible]
byd f ls aw, , crs
r me. h oN Sv- б
fclle v . [illegible] U +
rsNl z . mbr v
k rspB f rvz + pda
r Sa las. [illegible] n . adj
Intro DC
z suq- f hsp, h z
frS l oq + D inf f

fN drv, du , rzdNe
Intro P
n ls sle, h hs [illegible]
[illegible] rs siq kbjs. h
kus l Sv r kn^l [illegible]
nd dvs, lr , . old
vpry uz- l dS olSN
crc. id [illegible] . sli
Cny [illegible] py ab
[illegible]: n ls lon e ks
h Ub i n . B. cu

1

Gentlemen:

This letter is to acknowledge your order of August 7.

In accordance with your request, we[1] are printing 600 copies of the letterhead and extra envelopes to accompany the stationery.[2] Those items will be printed at your regular contract rate and delivered to your office at no additional[3] charge.

Again, I wish to explain why your last shipment arrived late. As shown on your copy of the invoice, we[4] shipped everything on schedule. Unfortunately, all of the interstate highways were later closed due to[5] unanticipated bad weather. I apologize for any inconvenience you may have experienced,[6] but the situation was caused by circumstances beyond our control.

Our shipping supervisor is Edward Brown.[7] If you need personal service, contact him immediately. He has an extraordinary skill for solving[8] problems on a moment's notice.

Sincerely yours, (169)

2

Dear Mrs. Webster:

Thank you for your letter of inquiry regarding our apartments. Our planned community[1] offers many advantages to young families.

We are located next to a relatively new subdivision.[2] Our apartments are situated on a beautiful site surrounded by large trees. We are within walking[3] distance of a major shopping center, a health club, and a golf course. The schools in our neighborhood are among[4] the best in this city.

Transportation arrangements are easy to make. Buses leave every hour for downtown, and[5] the train station is only a few minutes away by automobile. Interstate highways make it convenient[6] to drive anywhere in the city.

Residents say that our apartments provide an extraordinarily[7] enjoyable experience. Will you allow us to prove them right? Model apartments are open every day. Please[8] telephone our office to arrange an appointment in advance.

Sincerely, (174)

3

Dear Mr. Fields:

I am sending this note as a reminder that your service contract is due to expire at the[1] end of this month.

Like many other fine investments, this contract becomes more valuable with age. Although your[2] appliance is still in excellent condition and should yield many more years of good service, the chances of it[3] needing repairs increase with every year that goes by. Even when you own the best of equipment, there is always the[4] possibility that one service call will cost as much as an entire year of protection under our agreement.[5]

Our plan protects you against that possibility. For your convenience we have prepared a new contract for[6] your signature. Please sign and return both copies by the date specified so that your coverage will continue[7] without interruption.

Yours truly, (146)

4

Dear Sir or Madam:

Over 200 years ago several unhappy citizens made history by throwing[1] a surprise party in Boston. For people who love good tea, what a sad day that must have been!

Experts say the[2] disagreement had to do with taxes and not with the quality of the tea. We certainly hope so. As[3] distributors of fine tea, we have learned that smart customers can be very particular and won't settle for[4] anything less than the delicate flavor we offer.

Of course, the ordinary product floating around Boston[5] was not our brand. While we do not claim to know much about taxes and representation, we do know our tea. Our[6] special drying process yields such an excellent flavor that nobody would ever dump it overboard—not[7] even to make a big political splash.

On your next visit to your neighborhood market, prove it to yourself.[8] Take a tip from Boston and throw your old brand overboard. The few extra cents you may pay will definitely be[9] worth a great taste in tea.

Cordially yours, (187)

5

Dear Miss Gray:

I read with interest your newspaper article asking for nominations for the annual[1] community service award. After considering all of the areas of service described, I wish to[2] recommend Michael Boyd for this award.

His credits are many. He once served on the faculty of a major[3] university and recently was a member of the committee responsible for revising and[4] updating our state laws. When an addition was suggested for the hospital, he was the first to organize[5] and distribute information for the fund drive.

During his residency in this city, he has made numerous[6] significant contributions. He continues to serve our community whenever the need develops.

There[7] is an old expression used to describe outstanding character. I would make a slight change to make my point about[8] Michael: In this town we consider him to be one in a billion.

Cordially yours, (176)

LESSON 49

Brief Form Review

importance	usual
correspond	prove
convenient	order
committee	under
organize	ship
arrange	port
several	came
charge	up

Abbreviation Review

superintendent	dollars
incorporated	street
agriculture	inch
economy	yard
percent	and

Commonly Misspelled Words

annually

achievement

Reading and Writing Exercises

-1-

dS (nys lrjS fr v kpurs, elncs inc, , Nds . sS la , ab l Cnj (N, ev cra- . S nu plB kpur. (Nprz , kvl sl enf l pls nsd . alsa cs, yl s Xord n s Bls, s gcl bk . fvrl f us n ejcyl clsrs, bss, + Pfyl ofss, no ol co ks cls l C r gc + prl Svs. e op rpr sNrs a O (o + p apxl 30T ppl, if ur lg v PCs . nu kpur, dN M ls 1. / a b (kpur uvb a f. uvl

-2-

ds rln lgf ar l dl (rt sm e rqS- b llfn, p nf u dle Psn la s lb hr lrsv (gs (l v arvl. r bld S l c Sln la s , P (W hcre S NrN du (24=hr pred u sp- bgn (12 nn o Mn, Nv 9, e op U . Sd Psys v Cc eC crln. ls Pss lcs ol . fu mls + uzl elmas MUSN la cd dv. if ne ls r n n agrem r cpe v od, . sp nl lb d o inv, er

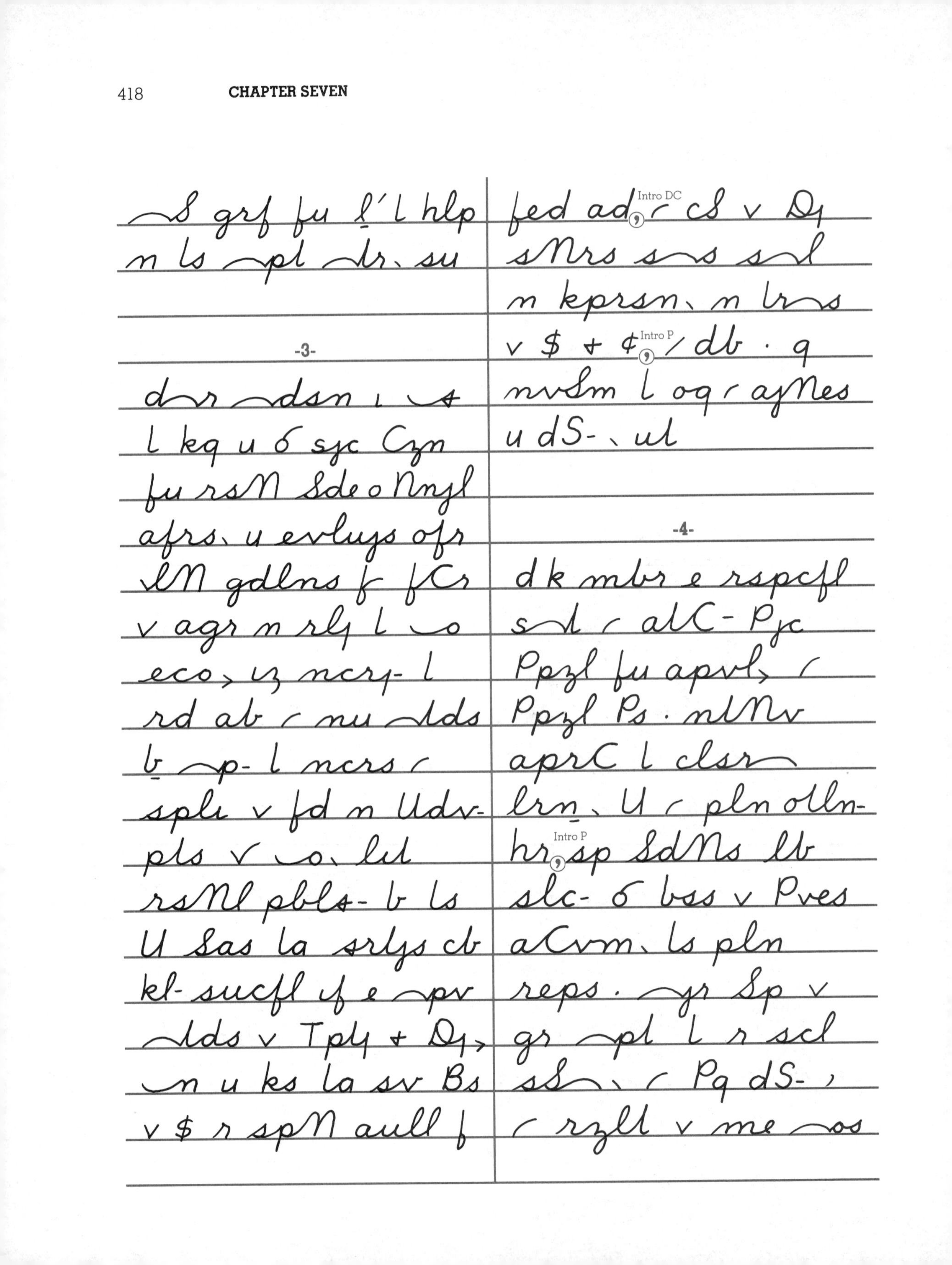

Intro DC

-3-

Intro P

-4-

Intro P

v Sde + , bs-po
rcmjs b (S vr
scl Dlrc, sC .
Pq l kb ⌒C l (
lN ar n SN (
ls jr hi scl. er
grf la ls kn' kus
l dmSra NS n
⌒mln r hi gl' v
ejcj , (Conj) + eap (opl l
s⌒l ls f⌒l rqS. cu

-5-

d⌒rs evns ⌒ p-
l nf⌒ u la (fbrc
Czn fu Cr cvz hsb
od- (20% Dk e
Dcs- + lb G- lu
ak. u od , scjl- l
arv (frS ⌒c v

ap. sN (lbr l
rq apxl 2 ⌒cs , (Intro DC) l
lq ec v (Crs
rcvr- + rde f dle
b Ma 1, r ⌒zrms
Nca la el nd . lol
v 8 yds v 60 = ⌒n
⌒lrel. acrd l ⌒u
rvz- eS⌒l , (Intro P) la l lv
1 adjl yd f ⌒C
plos, . nu sm v
⌒lrels ⌒C db
apo fu nu drps
k n ySrd. lr r sv
clrs + plrns la d
cor l ⌒ u OA dzn
cd u Sp b (Sr
s⌒l ls ⌒c lc
. slcj . su

1

Dear Sir or Madam:

The nation's largest manufacturer of computers, Electronics Incorporated,[1] is introducing a system that is about to change the industry.

We have created a super new[2] portable computer. The ENTERPRISE is conveniently small enough to place inside an attaché case, yet[3] it is extraordinary in its abilities. It is quickly becoming a favorite for use in[4] educational classrooms, businesses, and professional offices.

No other company comes close to matching[5] our quick and expert service. We operate repair centers all over the world and employ approximately[6] 30,000 people.

If you are thinking of purchasing a new computer, don't miss this one. It may be the[7] computer you have been waiting for.

Yours very truly, (149)

2

Dear Ms. Martin:

Thank you for arranging to deliver the rush shipment we requested by telephone.

Please inform[1] your delivery person that someone will be here to receive the goods at the time of arrival. Our building[2] superintendent will make certain that someone is present at the West Hickory Street entrance during the[3] 24-hour period you specified beginning at 12 noon on Monday, November 9.

We operate[4] under a standard procedure of checking each carton. This process takes only a few minutes and usually[5] eliminates misunderstandings that could develop. If any items are not in agreement with our[6] copy of the order, a specific notation will be made on the invoice.

We are most grateful for your[7] willingness to help in this important matter.

Sincerely yours, (151)

3

Dear Mr. Madison:

I wish to congratulate you on the subject chosen for your recent study on[1] international affairs. Your evaluations offer excellent guidelines for the future of agriculture[2] in relation to world economy.

I was encouraged to read about the new methods being employed to[3] increase the supply of food in underdeveloped parts of the world. Literature recently published by this[4] university states that shortages can be controlled successfully if we improve methods of transportation[5] and distribution.

When you consider that several billions of dollars are spent annually for federal[6] aid, the cost of distribution centers seems small in comparison. In terms of dollars and cents, it would be[7] a good investment to organize the agencies you described.

Yours truly, (154)

4

Dear Committee Member:

We respectfully submit the attached project proposal for your approval.

The[1] proposal presents an intensive approach to classroom learning. Under the plan outlined here, specific students[2] will be selected on the basis of previous achievement. This plan represents a major step of great[3] importance to our school system. The program described is the result of many months of study and is based upon[4] recommendations by the superintendent of our school district.

Such a program will contribute much to the[5] excellence already in existence at this junior high school. We are grateful that this community continues[6] to demonstrate interest in maintaining our high quality of education, and we appeciate the[7] opportunity to submit this formal request.

Cordially yours, (152)

5

Dear Mrs. Evans:

I am pleased to inform you that the fabric chosen for your chair covering has been ordered[1] at the 20 percent discount we discussed and will be charged to your account. Your order is scheduled to arrive[2] the first week of April. Since the labor will require approximately two weeks, I think we can have the chairs[3] recovered and ready for delivery by May 1.

Our measurements indicate that we will need a total of[4] eight yards of the 60-inch material. According to my revised estimate, that will leave one additional[5] yard for the matching pillows.

A new shipment of materials which would be appropriate for your new drapes[6] came in yesterday. There are several colors and patterns that would correspond well with your overall design.[7] Could you stop by the store sometime this week to make a selection?

Sincerely yours, (154)

LESSON 50

Brief Form Review

congratulate	kq	refer	rf
satisfactory	sat	great	gr
significant	sig	firm	fr
important	mpt	good	g
general	jn	more	m
respond	rsp	that	ta
always	a	has	hs
direct	dr	go	g

Abbreviation Review

vice president	VP	ounce	oz
boulevard	blvd	pound	lb
enclosure	enc	quart	qt
dollar	$	square	sq
cent	¢	feet	ft

Commonly Misspelled Words

privilege prvlj

assistance asSN

Reading and Writing Exercises

-1-

mo l —Mr crsn
sn r Av dpl l
anoN r nu Pdc
l r jn pb, bcz dr
—l —a ofr grr
Avjs n P— (Intro DC) ers ks
. rcmj lae D fre
sa—s n adj l
spNz . lMr Av
c—pn, pcjs db dl-
l E h— n —yr
rzdnsl nbrhs,
eC pcj d —l . 8=oz
sa— + . cvr L
Nds r Pdc, r d
Aso —l . cpn ofr
50¢ of r rll prs
v 2=lb bx + . 1$
cpn f 4=lb sz,
r Dj db h-
so la r sa—s d
arv o 5l d flo r
insl Avm, d u p
rd + rsp l r alC-
sa— L.

-2-

d rzdN nsd ls
pcj ulfN . Sprz
enc, er —l . fre
sa— v . u nu
lNre sp, y r
Pdc Sprz. bcz v
. sig Dcvre (Intro P) ev
dv- . nu Pss +
cra- . nu f—la
—C rzll- n X
cln B', r sp ofrs
— cln por ln ne
ol Pdc o —r, Ks

sa / acCull
aprs l rSr nCrl
clr l old fbrcs,
l pv r py Intro P , e nvi
u l kpr gl^l, (enc-
cpns nUl u l . 50¢
Dk ou nx PCs v
2=lb bx + . 1$
Dk 6 4=lb bx,
ln kpr prss, n
/ ks l cln por Intro DC ,
r 2=lb eco sz l
olLS , gl v ld
lgd, yl / cSs 60¢
ls, / cs q sN
l b . gl^l Pdc +
sv me s
, ul

-3-

d mbr v brd /
hsb brl l
all la (P v brd
v drrs lb ol v
lon nx c, bcz
ls e l v . sug
pc o fCr acj Intro DC ,
sug lae dla
(e ull (flo
Wd, z , evdN 6
enc- ajNa Intro DC , r n
sjc v Dcj lb (
Ppz- PCs v prp o
lr a blvd,
l . cpe vr pln-
adj l (Sry bld
C Ss o la prp,
if (nu fsl^l, bll
acrd l lz spjs Intro DC , el
v . lol v 25T sq
fl n rhos sps,
s X l pl lae

k l . dfnl dsj o
ls ⌒lr + kfr arms
du r nx ⌒e, lc
fw lse u ln. ru

-4-

j lgf dmSra u
kfdN n r ⌒nlnN
Svss. s . prvlj lvu
z . nu kc K, z Pfjls
n ls bs (Intro P), e A Srv
f hu Sds. n O 40
yrs v bs (Intro P), ev nvr
lS . K bcz v pr
Svs. e lg s fr lcl
la gi . akm, I rzn
fr suc , c frNl
rljs e nzy ⌒ eC
cliN. if usd E fN
la ne jb , ls ln
sal (Intro DC), i ⌒N u l
klc ⌒e Psnll. il
se la c slj , crc-
⌒l, z sr VP v
ls co (Intro P), ic asr u la
er s⌒l enf l dl
Psnl Svs b lrj
enf lgl c jb dn
lu salj. su

-5-

d brbra kgjs! i
rmbr c d ⌒n u
nrl- w frS grd.
no ⌒ p- l lrn
laul rsv u dgre
f clj n ls ln .
⌒o. ⌒r dd c h
gx, u flr lls ⌒e
lau pln l bgn .
crr n Psnl ⌒m.
ndls lsa (Paren), uv ⌒d

. ⌣z Cys. lr r me
fn opls avlB, [Conj] + .
Psn ⌣ u B', Sln
ldu l, if ucb v
asSN n u jbSC, [Intro DC]
chp ul ll ⌣e no.
ur a U hel vu.

ur . fn ex v . frN
+ . ddca- SdN.
udb ⌣S hpe l Sv
z . rfN fu, ul
a v ⌣u bS ⌣ss
f E suc. cu

1

MEMO TO: Walter Carson

Soon our advertising department will announce our new product to the general[1] public. Because direct mail may offer greater advantages in promotion, we are considering a[2] recommendation that we distribute free samples in addition to sponsoring an extensive advertising[3] campaign.

Packages would be delivered to every home in major residential neighborhoods. Each package would[4] include an 8-ounce sample and a cover letter introducing the product. It would also include a coupon[5] offering 50¢ off the retail price of the 2-pound box and a $1 coupon for the 4-pound[6] size.

The distribution would be timed so that the samples would arrive on the fifth day following our initial[7] advertisement.

Would you please read and respond to the attached sample letter? (154)

2

Dear Resident:

Inside this package you will find a surprising enclosure. We are including a free sample[1] of an exciting new laundry soap.

Why is our product surprising? Because of a significant discovery,[2] we have developed a new process and created a new formula which resulted in extra cleaning[3] ability. Our soap offers more cleaning power than any other product on the market. Customers say[4] it actually appears to restore natural color to old fabrics.

To prove our point, we invite you to[5] compare quality. The enclosed coupons entitle you to a 50¢ discount on your next purchase of the[6] 2-pound box and a $1 discount on the 4-pound box.

Then compare prices. When it comes to cleaning power,[7] our 2-pound economy size will outlast one quart of the leading liquid. Yet it costs 60¢ less.

It makes[8] good sense to buy a quality product and save money at the same time.

Yours truly, (175)

3

Dear Member of the Board:

It has been brought to my attention that the president of the Board of Directors will[1] be out of town next week. Because this meeting will have a significant impact on future action, I am[2] suggesting that we delay the meeting until the following Wednesday.

As is evident on the enclosed agenda,[3] our main subject of discussion will be the proposed purchase of property on Waterway Boulevard. I am[4] including a copy of our planned addition to the storage building which exists on that property. If the[5] new facility is built according to these specifications, we will have a total of 25,000 square[6] feet in warehouse space.

It is extremely important that we come to a definite decision on this[7] matter and confirm arrangements during our next meeting.

I look forward to seeing you then.

Respectfully[8] yours, (161)

4

Gentlemen:

Thank you for demonstrating your confidence in our maintenance services. It is a privilege to[1] have you as a new contract customer.

As professionals in this business, we always strive for high standards.[2] In over 40 years of business, we have never lost a customer because of poor service. We think it is[3] fair to call that quite an accomplishment.

One reason for our success is the friendly relationship we enjoy[4] with each client. If you should ever find that any job is less than satisfactory, I want you to contact[5] me personally. I will see that the situation is corrected immediately.

As senior vice[6] president of this company, I can assure you that we are small enough to deliver personal service but[7] large enough to get the job done to your satisfaction.

Sincerely yours, (152)

5

Dear Barbara:

Congratulations! I remember the day when you enrolled in the first grade. Now I am pleased to learn[1] that you will receive your degree from college in less than a month. Where did the time go?

Your father tells me that you[2] plan to begin a career in personnel management. Needless to say, you have made a wise choice. There are many[3] fine opportunities available, and a person with your ability is certain to do well.

If I[4] can be of assistance in your job search, I hope you will let me know. I have always thought highly of you. You are[5] a fine example of a friend and a dedicated student. I would be most happy to serve as a reference[6] for you.

You will always have my best wishes for every success.

Cordially yours, (135)

PREPARING TO GIVE DICTATION

Administrative assistants and secretaries may frequently have occasion, themselves, to dictate material to others. Whether a person dictates "live" to another individual or to a machine for transcription at a later time, proper dictation techniques can enhance the quality of the transcription.

In planning for dictation, the material to be transcribed immediately should be designated top priority. Material which could be transcribed at any time within the next few days should be designated low priority.

Prior to responding to correspondence, organize your thoughts by underlining and making marginal notations on the original correspondence regarding the most important points of each letter or memorandum being answered. Also, attach other material to the correspondence being answered when such attachments would help in preparing the response.

Immediately before the actual dictation of each piece of correspondence begins, indicate any special instructions. If there is a special letter style to be used or if more than one file copy is needed, make such notations at this time.

When dictation begins, speak distinctly in a relaxed, natural manner. Give instructions for special capitalization and punctuation such as hyphens, dashes, colons, apostrophes, and paragraph endings. Material to be typed in all capitals or material to be underscored should be designated. Difficult words and "sound-alike" words should be spelled in order to avoid confusion. Unusual spellings should also be dictated; i.e., the name Smythe might be spelled—s-m-y as in yesterday-t-h-e.

At the completion of the dictation, indicate any special mailing instructions; and if other individuals are to receive a copy of the correspondence, give their names and addresses.

Effective dictation and transcription skills are indeed complementary abilities. The ability to dictate competently and transcribe accurately can do much to increase the productivity of any office.

INDEX OF BRIEF FORMS

ALPHABETICAL LISTING

a (an)	.
able	B
about	ab
accept	ac
accomplish	ak
acknowledge	acj
administrate	Am
advantage	Avj
after	af
again (against)	ag
against (again)	ag
already	Ar
always	a
am (more)	⌢
an (a)	.
appreciate	ap
appropriate	apo
approximate	apx
are (our)	r
arrange	ar
as (was)	z
associate	aso
at (it)	/
be (been, but, buy, by)	b
been (be, but, buy, by)	b
between	btn
both	bo
business	bs
but (be, been, buy, by)	b
buy (be, been, but, by)	b
by (be, been, but, buy)	b
came (come, committee)	k
can	c
character (characteristic)	crc
characteristic (character)	crc
charge	Cj
circumstance	Sk
come (came, committee)	k
committee (came, come)	k
complete	kp

congratulate	kg	firm	fr
consider	ks	for (full)	f
continue	ku	from	f
contract	kc	full (for)	f
contribute	kb	general	jn
control	kl	go (good)	g
convenience (convenient)	kv	good (go)	g
convenient (convenience)	kv	grate (great)	gr
correspond (correspondence)	cor	great (grate)	gr
correspondence (correspond)	cor	had (he, him)	h
customer	K	has	hs
deliver	dl	have (of, very)	v
determine	dl	he (had, him)	h
develop	dv	him (had, he)	h
difficult	dfc	his (is)	)
direct (doctor)	dr	hospital	hsp
distribute	D	immediate	⌒
doctor (direct)	dr	importance (important)	⌒pl
during	du̲	important (importance)	⌒pl
employ	⌒p	in (not)	n
ever (every)	E	include	⌣l
every (ever)	E	individual	Nv
experience	vp	industry	N

is (his)
it (at)
letter
manage
manufacture
market
more (am)
necessary
next
not (in)
note
of (have, very)
on (own)
once
operate
opinion
opportunity
order
ordinary
organize
other
our (are)
over

own (on)
part (port)
participate
particular
perhaps
please (up)
point
port (part)
present
property
prove
public
refer
respond (response)
response (respond)
sample
satisfactory (satisfy)
satisfy (satisfactory)
several
ship
signature (significance, significant)

significance (signature, significant)

significant (signature, significance)

situate

specific (specify)

specify (specific)

standard

success

suggest

that

the

they

those

to (too)

too (to)

under

up (please)

us

usual

very (have, of)

was (as)

we

well (will)

were (with)

why

will (well)

with (were)

work (world)

world (work)

would

your

INDEX OF BRIEF FORMS

LISTED BY ORDER OF PRESENTATION

Lesson 1

a
an
at
his
in
is
it
not
the
to
too
we
well
will

Lesson 2

are
can
for
full
have
of
our
us
very

Lesson 4

firm
from
letter
manage
market
on
own
part
perhaps
port
would
your

Lesson 6

accept

after	af
appropriate	apo
be	b
been	b
but	b
buy	b
by	b
determine	dl
during	du
necessary	nes
why	y

Lesson 9

arrange	ar
as	z
general	jn
grate	gr
great	gr
hospital	hsp
that	la
was	z
were	⌣
with	⌣

Lesson 11

between	bln
operate	op
participate	pp
point	py
property	prp
refer	rf
respond	rsp
response	rsp
ship	s
situate	sil
suggest	sug
those	loz

Lesson 13

am	⌢
charge	C
direct	dr
doctor	dr
go	g
good	g
had	h
he	h

him
more
they

Lesson 16

appreciate
correspond
correspondence
distribute
please
present
specific
specify
up

Lesson 18

about
customer
has
include
order
over
under

Lesson 20

advantage
again
against
business
several

Lesson 22

character
characteristic
ever
every
industry
other
satisfactory
satisfy

Lesson 24

accomplish
came
come
committee
complete
continue

contribute

convenience

convenient

deliver

opportunity

Lesson 26

both

importance

important

individual

public

Lesson 27

always

consider

note

ordinary

prove

Lesson 30

already

approximate

experience

immediate

next

Lesson 32

able

contract

difficult

employ

opinion

Lesson 34

acknowledge

associate

congratulate

develop

organize

standard

success

Lesson 37

manufacture

signature

significance

significant

usual

work

world

Lesson 39

administrate

circumstance

control

once

particular

sample

INDEX OF ABBREVIATIONS

ALPHABETICAL LISTING

advertise	av	dollars (dollar)	$
agriculture	agr	east	E
America (American)	Am	economic (economy)	eco
American (America)	Am	economy (economic)	eco
amount	amt	enclose (enclosure)	enc
and	+	enclosure (enclose)	enc
attention	att	envelope	env
avenue	ave	especially	esp
billion	B	establish	est
boulevard	blvd	et cetera	etc
catalog	cat	example (executive)	ex
cent (cents)	¢	executive (example)	ex
cents (cent)	¢	federal	fed
Christmas	Xms	feet	ft
company	co	government	gvt
corporation	corp	hour	hr
credit	cr	hundred	H
day	d	inch	in
department	dpt	incorporate (incorporated)	inc
dollar (dollars)	$	incorporated (incorporate)	inc

information	inf
insurance	ins
invoice	inv
junior	jr
literature	lit
merchandise	mdse
million	M
Miss	M
month	mo
Mr.	mr
Mrs.	mrs
Ms.	ms
north	N
number	No
okay	ok
ounce	oz
percent	%
pound	lb
president	P
quart	qt
question	q
record	rec
regard	re
represent (representative)	rep
representative (represent)	rep
return	ret
second (secretary)	sec
secretary (second)	sec
senior	sr
south	S
square	sq
street	st
superintendent	S
thousand	T
total	tot
university	U
vice president	VP
volume	vol
west	W
yard	yd

INDEX OF ABBREVIATIONS

LISTED BY ORDER OF PRESENTATION

Lesson 2

and	&
catalog	cat
company	co
information	inf
president	p
return	ret
vice president	VP

Lesson 4

Miss	M
Mr.	mr
Mrs.	mrs
Ms.	ms

Lesson 6

corporation	corp
east	E
enclose	enc
enclosure	enc
north	N
south	S
west	W

Lesson 9

amount	amt
attention	att
credit	cr
number	No
percent	%
total	tot

Lesson 11

department	dpt
envelope	env
insurance	ins
invoice	inv
regard	re

Lesson 13

junior	jr
second	sec
secretary	sec
senior	sr

Lesson 16

avenue	ave
boulevard	blvd
day	d
example	ex
executive	ex
hour	hr
month	mo
record	rec

Lesson 18

billion	B
cent	¢
cents	¢
dollar	$
dollars	$
hundred	H
inch	in
million	M
ounce	oz
pound	lb
thousand	T

Lesson 20

agriculture	agr
economic	eco
economy	eco
feet	ft
square	sq
yard	yd

Lesson 22

especially	esp
et cetera	etc
merchandise	mdse
quart	qt
question	q
university	U

Lesson 24

federal	fed
government	gvt
incorporate	inc

incorporated	inc
okay	ok
represent	rep
representative	rep
street	S

Lesson 27

advertise	av
Christmas	Xs

Lesson 34

America	a
American	a
literature	lit
volume	vol

Lesson 39

establish	est
superintendent	S

INDEX OF PHRASES

The following phrases are presented in alphabetical segments beginning with the pronouns I, we, and you plus a verb, followed by infinitive phrases (to plus a verb), high-frequency word combinations, and word combinations with words omitted.

The phrase list presents the 147 phrases in alphabetical segments.

Type	Number
"I" + a verb	25
"We" + a verb	26
"You" + a verb	20
"To" + a verb (infinitive phrase)	24
High-Frequency Word Combinations	44
Words Omitted and Word Compounds with a Word Omitted	8
Total	147

Phrase	Shorthand	Phrase	Shorthand
I am	im	I know	ino
I appreciate	iap	I look	ilc
I believe	iblv	I shall	isl
I can	ic	I should	isd
I can be	icb	I was	iz
I cannot	icn	I will	il
I could	icd	I will be	ilb
I do	idu	I would	id
I feel	ifl	I would appreciate	idap
I had	ih	I would be	idb
I have	iv	I would like	idlc
I have been	ivb	we appreciate	eap
I have had	ivh	we are	er
I hope	ihp	we are not	ern

we are pleased	erp-	you are	ur
we believe	eblv	you can	uc
we can	ec	you cannot	ucn
we can be	ecb	you can be	ucb
we cannot	ecn	you could	ucd
we could	ecd	you do	udu
we do	edu	you had	uh
we feel	efl	you have	uv
we had	eh	you have been	uvb
we have	ev	you have had	uvh
we have been	evb	you know	uno
we have had	evh	you need	und
we hope	ehp	you should	usd
we know	eno	you were	u—
we shall	esl	you will	ul
we should	esd	you will be	ulb
we were	e—	you will find	ulfN
we will	el	you would	ud
we will be	elb	you would be	udb
we would	ed	you would like	udlc
we would appreciate	edap	to be	Lb
we would be	edb	to call	Lcl
we would like	edlc	to come	Lk

of your	vu
on the	σ
on you	ou
on your	ou
should be	sdb
thank you	lqu
that I	lai
that we	lae
that you	lau
that you are	laur
that you will	laul
that your	lau
to you	lu
to your	lu
will be	lb
will you	lu
will your	lu
would be	db
would like	dlc
as soon as	zz
nevertheless	nvrls
nonetheless	nnls
thank you for	lqf
thank you for your	lqf
thank you for your letter	lqfL
time to time	l-l
up to date	pda

IDENTIFICATION INITIALS FOR UNITED STATES AND TERRITORIES

Alabama (AL)	AL
Alaska (AK)	AK
Arizona (AZ)	AZ
Arkansas (AR)	AR
California (CA)	CA
Colorado (CO)	CO
Connecticut (CT)	CT
Delaware (DE)	DE
District of Columbia (DC)	DC
Florida (FL)	FL
Georgia (GA)	GA
Hawaii (HI)	HI
Idaho (ID)	ID
Illinois (IL)	IL
Indiana (IN)	IN
Iowa (IA)	IA
Kansas (KS)	KS
Kentucky (KY)	KY
Louisiana (LA)	LA
Maine (ME)	ME
Maryland (MD)	MD
Massachusetts (MA)	MA
Michigan (MI)	MI
Minnesota (MN)	MN
Mississippi (MS)	MS
Missouri (MO)	MO
Montana (MT)	MT
Nebraska (NE)	NE
Nevada (NV)	NV
New Hampshire (NH)	NH
New Jersey (NJ)	NJ
New Mexico (NM)	NM
New York (NY)	NY
North Carolina (NC)	NC
North Dakota (ND)	ND
Ohio (OH)	OH
Oklahoma (OK)	OK
Oregon (OR)	OR
Pennsylvania (PA)	PA
Rhode Island (RI)	RI

South Carolina (SC)	SC	West Virginia (WV)	WV
South Dakota (SD)	SD	Wisconsin (WI)	WI
Tennessee (TN)	TN	Wyoming (WY)	WY
Texas (TX)	TX		
Utah (UT)	UT	Canal Zone (CZ)	CZ
Vermont (VT)	VT	Guam (GU)	GU
Virginia (VA)	VA	Puerto Rico (PR)	PR
Washington (WA)	WA	Virgin Islands (VI)	VI

CANADIAN PROVINCES AND TERRITORIES

Alberta (AB)	AB	Nova Scotia (NS)	NS
British Columbia (BC)	BC	Ontario (ON)	ON
Labrador (LB)	LB	Prince Edward Island (PE)	PE
Manitoba (MB)	MB	Quebec (PQ)	PQ
New Brunswick (NB)	NB	Saskatchewan (SK)	SK
Newfoundland (NF)	NF	Yukon Territory (YT)	YT
Northwest Territories (NT)	NT		

METRIC TERMS

	(length) meter m	(capacity) liter l	(weight) gram g
kilo	km	kl	kg
hecto	hm	hl	hg
deca	dam	dal	dag
deci	dm	dl	dg
centi	cm	cl	cg
milli	mm	ml	mg
micro	vcrm	vcrl	vcrg
nano	nm	nl	ng

SUMMARY OF SPEEDWRITING SHORTHAND PRINCIPLES

BY ORDER OF PRESENTATION

Principle	Word	Outline	Word	Outline
1. Write what you hear	high	hi		
2. Drop medial vowels	build	bld		
3. Write initial and final vowels	office	ofs	fee	fe
4. Write c for the sound of *k*	copy	cpe		
5. Write a capital C for the sound of *ch*	check	Cc		
6. Write ⌒ for the sound of *m*	may	⌒a		
7. Write ‿ for the sound of *w* and *wh*	way	‿a	when	‿n
8. Underscore the last letter of any outline to add *ing* or *thing* as a word ending	billing	bl̲	something	s⌒̲
9. To form the plural of any outline ending in a mark of punctuation, double the last mark of punctuation	savings	sv̲̲		
10. Write s to form the plural of any outline, to show possession, or to add s to a verb	books	bcs	runs	rns
11. Write m for the sounds of *mem* and *mum*	memo	mo		
12. Write m for the sounds of *men*, *mon*, *mun*	menu	mu	money	me

Rule	Word	Outline	Word	Outline
13. Write m for the word endings *mand, mend, mind, ment*	demand	dm	amend	am
	remind	rm	payment	pam
14. Write a capital N for the sound of *nt*	sent	sN		
15. Write ꜱ for the sound of *ish* or *sh*	finish	fnꜱ		
16. Write a capital A for the word beginnings *ad, all, al*	admit	Ad	also	Aso
17. Write n for the initial sound of *in* or *en*	indent	ndN		
18. Write o for the sound of *ow*	allow	alo		
19. Write a printed capital S (joined) for the word beginnings *cer, cir, ser, sur*	certain	Stn	survey	Sva
20. To form the past tense of a regular verb, write a hyphen after the outline	used	uz-		
21. Write L for the sound of *ith* or *th*	them	Lm		
22. Write l for the word ending *ly* or *ily*	family	fl		
23. Write a capital D for the word beginning *dis*	discuss	Dcs		
24. Write a capital M for the word beginning *mis*	misplace	Mpls		
25. Retain beginning or ending vowels when building compound words	payroll	parl	headache	hdac
26. Retain root-word vowels when adding prefixes and suffixes	disappear	Dapr	payment	pam

Principle	Word	Shorthand	Word	Shorthand
27. Write a capital P (disjoined) for the word beginnings *per, pur, pre, pro, pro* (prah)	person	Psn	prepare	Ppr
	provide	Pvd	problem	Pbl
28. Write g for the word ending *gram*	telegram	tlg		
29. Write y for the sound of *oi*	boy	by		
30. For words ending in a long vowel + *t*, omit the *t* and write the vowel	rate	ra	meet	me
31. Write a for the word beginning *an*	answer	asr		
32. Write q for the medial or final sound of any vowel + *nk*	bank	bq	link	lq
33. Write a capital S (disjoined) for the word beginning *super* and for the word endings *scribe* and *script*	supervise	Svz	describe	dS
	manuscript	mnS		
34. Write el for the word beginning *electr*	electronic	elnc		
35. Write w for the word ending *ward*	backward	bcw		
36. Write h for the word ending *hood*	boyhood	byh		
37. Write ㇋ for the word ending *tion* or *sion*	vacation	v㇋		
38. Write a for the initial and final sound of *aw*	law	la	audit	adt
39. Write q for the sound of *kw*	quick	qc		
40. Write a capital N for the sound of *nd*	friend	frN		
41. Write ⌒ for the initial sound of *em* or *im*	emphasize	⌒fsz	impress	⌒prs

42. Omit *p* in the sound of *mpt*	prompt	P⌣l		
43. Write k for the sounds of *com, con, coun, count*	common	kn	convey	kva
	counsel	ksl	account	ak
44. Write S for the sound of *st*	rest	rS		
45. Write g for the word ending *quire*	require	rg		
46. Write z for the sound of *zh*	pleasure	plzr		
47. Write ′ for the word ending *ness*	kindness	cN′		
48. Write \ for words beginning with the sound of any vowel + *x*	explain	\pln	accident	\dN
49. Write x for the medial and final sound of *x*	boxes	bxs	relax	rlx
50. Write X for the word beginnings *extr* and *extra*	extreme	X⌣		
	extraordinary	Xord		
51. Write q for the medial or final sound of any vowel + *ng*	rang	rq	single	sgl
52. Write B for the word endings *bil, ble, bly*	possible	psB	probably	PbB
53. Omit the final *t* of a root word after the sound of *k*	act	ac		
54. Write a slightly raised and disjoined l for the word ending *ity*	quality	ql^l		
55. Write u for the word beginning *un*	until	ull		
56. Write ɬl for the sound of *shul* and for the word ending *chul*	financial	fnnɬl		

57. Write M for the sounds of *ance, ence, nce, nse* — expense vpN

58. Write s for the word beginning *sub* — submit s-t

59. Write v for the medial and final sound of *tive* — effective efcv

60. Write f for the word endings *ful* and *ify* — careful crf, justify jSf

61. Write fy for the word ending *ification* — qualifications qlfys

62. Write a capital N for the word beginnings *enter, inter, intra, intro* — enterprise Nprz, introduce Nds, interest NS

63. Write sf for the word beginning and ending *self* — self-made sf-d, myself -sf

64. Write svs for the word ending *selves* — ourselves rsvs

65. When a word contains two medial, consecutively pronounced vowels, write the first vowel — trial tril

66. When a word ends in two consecutively pronounced vowels, write only the last vowel — idea ida

67. Write T for the word beginnings *tran* and *trans* — transfer Tfr

SUMMARY OF SPEEDWRITING SHORTHAND PRINCIPLES

BY SYSTEM CATEGORY

Simple Sounds

Principle	Word	Outline	Lesson
1. Write what you hear	high	hi	1
2. Write c for the sound of *k*	copy	cpe	2
3. Write ⌒ for the sound of *m*	may	⌒a	2
4. Write ‿ for the sound of *w*	way	‿a	2
5. Write s to form the plural of any outline, to show possession, or to add s to a verb	books	bcs	
	runs	rns	2
6. Omit *p* in the sound of *mpt*	empty	⌒le	22
7. Write x for the medial and final sound of *x*	boxes	bxs	
	tax	tx	29
8. Omit the final *t* of a root word after the sound of *k*	act	ac	31

Vowels

Principle	Word	Outline	Lesson
1. Drop medial vowels	build	bld	1
2. Write initial and final vowels	office	ofs	
	fee	fe	1
3. Retain beginning or ending vowels when building compound words	payroll	parl	
	headache	hdac	9

4. Retain root-word vowels when adding prefixes and suffixes	disappear	Dapr	
	payment	pam	9
5. For words ending in a long vowel + *t*, omit the *t* and write the vowel	rate	ra	
	meet	me	12
6. When a word contains two medial, consecutively pronounced vowels, write the first vowel	trial	tril	40
7. When a word ends in two consecutively pronounced vowels, write only the last vowel	idea	ida	40

Vowel Blends

1. Write o for the sound of *ow*	allow	alo	5
2. Write y for the sound of *oi*	boy	by	11
3. Write a for the initial and final sound of *aw*	law	la	
	audit	adl	19

Consonant Blends

1. Write a capital C for the sound of *ch*	check	Cc	2
2. Write ⌣ for the sound of *wh*	when	wn	2
3. Write a capital N for the sound of *nt*	sent	sN	3
4. Write s for the sound of *ish* or *sh*	finish	fns	4
5. Write l for the sound of *ith* or *th*	them	lm	8

Rule	Word	Outline	Page
6. Write *q* for the medial or final sound of any vowel + *nk*	bank	bq	
	link	lq	13
7. Write *q* for the sound of *kw*	quick	qc	19
8. Write a capital *N* for the sound of *nd*	friend	frN	20
9. Write *S* for the sound of *st*	rest	rS	23
10. Write *z* for the sound of *zh*	pleasure	plzr	25
11. Write *q* for the medial or final sound of any vowel plus *ng*	rang	rq	
	single	sgl	30
12. Write *M* for the sounds of *ance, ence, nce, nse*	balance	blM	36

Compound Sounds

Rule	Word	Outline	Page
1. Write *m* for the sounds of *mem* and *mum*	memo	mo	3
2. Write *m* for the sounds of *men, mon, mun*	menu	mu	
	money	me	3
3. Write *k* for the sounds of *com, con, coun, count*	common	kn	
	convey	kva	
	counsel	ksl	
	account	ak	23

Word Beginnings

1. Write a capital A for the word beginnings *ad, all,* and *al*

admit

also 4

2. Write n for the initial sound of *in* and *en*

indent 4

3. Write a printed capital S (joined) for the word beginnings *cer, cir, ser, sur*

certain

survey 5

4. Write a capital D for the word beginning *dis*

discuss 8

5. Write a capital M for the word beginning *mis*

misplace 8

6. Write a capital P (disjoined) for the word beginnings *per, pur, pre, pro, pro* (prah)

person

prepare

provide

problem 10

7. Write a for the word beginning *an*

answer 13

8. Write a capital S (disjoined) for the word beginning *super*

supervise 15

9. Write el for the word beginning *electr*

electronic 15

10. Write ⌒ for the initial sound of *em* or *im*

emphasize

impress 22

11. Write \ for words beginning with the sound of any vowel + *x*

explain

accident 29

Rule	Word	Outline	Lesson
12. Write X for the word beginnings *extr* and *extra*	extreme	Xm	
	extraordinary	Xord	29
13. Write u for the word beginning *un*	until	ull	33
14. Write s for the word beginning *sub*	submit	smt	36
15. Write a capital N for the word beginnings *enter, inter, intra, intro*	enterprise	Nprz	
	interest	Ns	
	introduce	Nds	39
16. Write sf for the word beginning *self*	self-made	sfmd	39
17. Write T for the word beginnings *tran* and *trans*	transfer	Tfr	41

Word Endings

Rule	Word	Outline	Lesson
1. Underscore the last letter of the outline to add *ing* or *thing* as a word ending	billing	bl̲	
	something	sm̲	2
2. To form the plural of any outline ending in a mark of punctuation, double the last mark of punctuation	savings	sv̳	2
3. To form the past tense of a regular verb, write a hyphen after the outline	used	uz-	6
4. Write m for the word endings *mand, mend, mind, ment*	demand	dm	
	amend	am	
	remind	rm	
	payment	pam	3

Principle	Word	Shorthand	Lesson
5. Write l for the word ending *ly* or *ily*	family	fml	8
6. Write g for the word ending *gram*	telegram	tlg	10
7. Write a capital S (disjoined) for the word endings *scribe* and *script*	describe	dS	
	manuscript	mnS	15
8. Write w for the word ending *ward*	backward	bcw	16
9. Write h for the word ending *hood*	boyhood	byh	16
10. Write / for the word ending *tion* or *sion*	vacation	vc/	17
11. Write q for the word ending *quire*	require	rq	25
12. Write ' for the word ending *ness*	kindness	kN'	26
13. Write B for the word endings *bil, ble, bly*	possible	psB	
	probably	PbB	31
14. Write a slightly raised and disjoined l for the word ending *ity*	quality	ql l	32
15. Write sl for the sound of *shul* and the word ending *chul*	financial	fnnsl	34
16. Write v for the medial and final sound of *tive*	effective	efcv	37
17. Write f for the word endings *ful* and *ify*	careful	crf	
	justify	jsf	38
18. Write fy for the word ending *ification*	qualifications	qlfys	38

19. Write sf for the word ending *self* myself msf 39

20. Write svs for the word ending *selves* ourselves rsvs 39

Marks of Punctuation

1. Underscore the last letter of the outline to add *ing* or *thing* as a word ending billing bl
something s 2

2. To form the plural of any outline ending in a mark of punctuation, double the last mark of punctuation savings sv 2

3. To form the past tense of a regular verb, write a hyphen after the outline used uz- 6

4. Write / for the word ending *ness* kindness kn' 26

5. To show capitalization, draw a small curved line under the last letter of the outline Bill bl 1

6. Write \ to indicate a period at the end of a sentence 1

7. Write x to indicate a question mark 1

8. Write > to indicate the end of a paragraph 1

9. Write ! to indicate an exclamation mark 5

10. Write = to indicate a dash 5

11. Write = to indicate a hyphen 5

12. To indicate solid capitalization, double the curved line underneath the last letter of the outline 5

13. To indicate an underlined title, draw a solid line under the outline — 5

14. Write [shorthand symbols] to indicate parentheses — 32

Miscellaneous

1. Cardinal numbers — 6
2. Ordinal numbers — 9
3. Months of the year — 11
4. Days of the week — 24
5. Amounts of money — 18
6. Indicating time — 31
7. Cities and states — 25
8. State initials — Appendix
9. Phrasing — 13
10. Phrasing list — Appendix